HEIDELBERG STUDIES
IN PACIFIC ANTHROPOLOGY
Volume 6

Edited by
JÜRG WASSMANN

ALEXIS TH. VON POSER
ANITA VON POSER (Eds.)

Facets of Fieldwork

Essays in Honor of
Jürg Wassmann

Universitätsverlag
WINTER
Heidelberg

Bibliografische Information der Deutschen Nationalbibliothek
Die Deutsche Nationalbibliothek verzeichnet diese Publikation
in der Deutschen Nationalbibliografie;
detaillierte bibliografische Daten sind im Internet
über *http://dnb.d-nb.de* abrufbar.

UMSCHLAGBILD:
Jürg Wassmann during fieldwork in Gua,
Finisterre Range, Papua New Guinea
© Verena Keck, 2000

ISBN 978-3-8253-6624-7

Dieses Werk einschließlich aller seiner Teile ist urheberrechtlich geschützt.
Jede Verwertung außerhalb der engen Grenzen des Urheberrechtsgesetzes
ist ohne Zustimmung des Verlages unzulässig und strafbar. Das gilt ins-
besondere für Vervielfältigungen, Übersetzungen, Mikroverfilmungen und
die Einspeicherung und Verarbeitung in elektronischen Systemen.

© 2017 Universitätsverlag Winter GmbH Heidelberg
Imprimé en Allemagne · Printed in Germany
Umschlaggestaltung: Klaus Brecht GmbH, Heidelberg
Druck: Memminger MedienCentrum, 87700 Memmingen

Gedruckt auf umweltfreundlichem, chlorfrei gebleichtem
und alterungsbeständigem Papier

Den Verlag erreichen Sie im Internet unter:
www.winter-verlag.de

Contents

List of Illustrations ix

Foreword
MEINHARD SCHUSTER xi

1 Introduction
ANITA VON POSER AND ALEXIS TH. VON POSER 1

2 *Taim Bipo*.
The Quest for the Past by the Members of the
Basel Sepik Expedition 1972–74
MARKUS SCHINDLBECK 19

3 Thinking Along the Same Lines.
Varieties of Initiation and Varieties of Fieldwork in Sepik and
Madang
PATRICK F. GESCH 41

4 The Coral Gardens are Losing Their Magic.
The Social and Cultural Impact of Climate Change
and Overpopulation for the Trobriand Islanders
GUNTER SENFT 57

5 Group Dialogues, Videos and Multilocality
in Researching Rituals
ANTJE DENNER 69

6 "I didn't know that there were other worlds out there".
   Inside a Multi-Sited Ethnography
   STEPHANIE WALDA-MANDEL 85

7 "Houses Jumbled Everywhere"?
   Visions of a "Village" in Papua New Guinea
   ANITA VON POSER 101

8 The Chase for Archival Material and Biographical Information
   in the "Field" of Archives. Remarks about a Research Project,
   carried out in Chile, Rapanui and Other Places
   HERMANN MÜCKLER 123

9 References to Time and Space in Melanesian Music
   RAYMOND AMMANN 139

10 The Early Field and Commercial Recordings of Kuman Music.
   Research Using Repatriated Music in Papua New Guinea,
   and Recent Threats to Cultural Diversity
   DON NILES AND EDWARD GENDE 147

11 Foreign Confidants. A Field Diary Narrative
   ANGELLA MEINERZAG 173

12 Endangered Fields.
   Experiencing Anthropological Research in Iran
   SHAHNAZ R. NADJMABADI 185

13 Exchanging Anthropological Knowledge.
   A University Partnership Program
   between Madang and Heidelberg
   VERENA KECK 197

Contents

14 The Restitution of a Carving Pattern to Kayan,
   Papua New Guinea
   ALEXIS TH. VON POSER 223

15 Challenges and Profits of Interdisciplinary Fieldwork in
   Linguistic and Cognitive Anthropology
   SVENJA VÖLKEL 235

16 The Trouble of Having a Psychologist Sharing Fieldwork
   PIERRE R. DASEN 255

17 "Just Plain Folks". Anthropology Meets Psychology
   JOACHIM FUNKE 273

Notes on Contributors 281

Index 289

List of Illustrations and Figures

Copyright of illustrations and figures, which appear in this volume, is held by the respective authors unless stated otherwise.

Illustrations

1.1:	Oceania workgroup meeting at Jürg's flat (2001, photo by V. Keck)	6
5.1:	*Am furis* performance at the funeral of Paul Munbal	74
5.2:	Ceremonial greeting between two leaders	77
6.1:	Women from the Southwest Islands celebrating the new year in Echang together	92
10.1:	Ray Sheridan discussing his activities concerning Papua New Guinea music (2003, photo by Don Niles)	152
10.2:	*Music of New Guinea*, Ray Sheridan's LP released in 1958	153
13.1:	Entrance gate of the Divine Word University (2008)	201
13.2:	Divine Word University students (2008)	202
13.3:	Cultural Day at the Divine Word University, a student in her traditional *bilas* (decoration) (2009)	207
13.4:	Reading Malinowski's Argonauts with students at Divine Word University (2008)	211
13.5:	"Interpreting Cultures"-course, Divine Word University (2008) (with P. Gesch as guest auditor)	212
13.6:	Staff meeting, Divine Word University (2008)	213
14.1:	The slit drum from Mannheim (copyright: Reiss-Engelhorn-Museums Mannheim)	224
14.2:	Blasius Jong identifies the *yor mbermber* pattern	230
14.3:	Finally: the *yor mbermber* pattern appears on a new drum (photo by A. Yambisang)	231
17.1:	Jürg Wassmann with the author (July 2013)	274
17.2:	Jürg Wassmann (August 2015) in his Feldberg office, writing his next book	277

Figures

4.1:	Papua New Guinea	58
4.2:	The Trobriand Islands	59

MEINHARD SCHUSTER

Foreword

Fieldwork in cultural anthropology – understood here in the traditional sense of the longer-term, onsite primary research of a non-European culture by researchers coming from the background of the European scientific traditions – is the soul of cultural anthropology. This work process is marked externally by the circumstance of a thoroughly organized, indigenous society, mostly of the size of a village, with a fully developed cultural life being confronted by one or two foreign visitors who have no knowledge of the local world and therefore are not able to classify their experiences; they must first gain the knowledge necessary for this understanding step by step as observant and enquiring attendees. In doing so the tendency is, at least initially, to focus their search for answers on issues inherent to the researchers, i.e. that come from outside the research locality. However, in the daily contact with the life of the local inhabitants, these issues are corrected and extended through unexpected, new issues which often transcend the local setting and are thereby able to lead to new, more general insights and perspectives. Fieldwork is therefore, more so than a further intellectual consolidation of what is already known, also the fountain of youth of cultural anthropology.

Against this background, it becomes understandable that conducting your first own field research is awarded the rank of an actual initiation into cultural anthropology as a field of study. Jürg Wassmann, too, took this path and also in his later research work at new locations and in other thematic contexts, he always placed particular importance upon fieldwork.

Basel, 2017

ANITA VON POSER AND ALEXIS TH. VON POSER

1 Introduction

This compilation of essays, which tackles some of the facets of fieldwork which anthropologists are usually faced with before, during or after research in a particular "field," is a *Festschrift* in honor of Jürg Wassmann who celebrated his 70th birthday in 2016. As former students of Jürg's, first as his undergraduate students and later as his doctoral candidates, we decided to invite those anthropological scholars, (interdisciplinary) colleagues, and/or academic friends whom we ourselves encountered as we grew as anthropologists at Heidelberg University where Jürg was head of the Institute of Anthropology in the years 1995 to 2007.[1]

We are pleased that Meinhard Schuster, Jürg's first academic mentor and former professor of the Basel Institute of Anthropology (1970 to 2000), agreed to write the foreword to this *Festschrift*. The foreword certainly bears witness to the anthropological *Zeitgeist* into which Jürg was born as a young academic and from which he embarked on his own professional journey. Much, of course, has changed since Jürg's entry into the discipline: bounded notions of culture and of tradition have vanished, dichotomies between the "West" / "European" and the "Rest" / "Non-European" have been forcefully deconstructed, anthropologists have been moving more frequently between field sites as their interlocutors do, and field sites per se need not necessarily be as far away as "traditional anthropology" requested. Jürg himself was open to utilizing new approaches during his entire academic life-course but was always certain to maintain one premise: he has always been in favor of the empiricist tradition within anthropology. This was very probably fully instilled at the time when he started conducting fieldwork as part of Meinhard Schuster's anthropological research team in the Sepik River area of Papua New Guinea in the first half of the 1970s (after his first research experiences with the Sami people in Sweden) and extended through his whole scientific career.

Because of what we knew about Jürg's passion for fieldwork we decided to ask each contributor to our volume to arrange his or her essay around a particular facet of fieldwork. This volume does not provide an overview of what has been said about fieldwork in our discipline. There is, in fact, a considerable amount of literature dealing with the topic of fieldwork (just to name a few more recent publications: Faubion and Marcus 2009; Spencer and Davies 2010; Robben and Sluka 2012; MacClancy and Fuentes 2013; Orne and Mayerfeld Bell 2015). Rather, we decided to strongly tie the *Festschrift* to Jürg's own academic as well as personal life-course by inviting those contributors whom we ourselves were able to meet as they either came to visit Heidelberg over the years in order to give academic lectures and/or worked there as staff, or as we ourselves traveled to academic and ethnographic places and made contacts with them through Jürg.

In the first part of our introduction, we look at Jürg's life-course as a fieldworker. The life-course perspective is a common approach in studies on aging and has been applied by several disciplines such as demography, psychology, sociology, social history, and anthropology (A. von Poser, forthcoming). Following the anthropologists Danely and Lynch,

> [a] life-course approach to aging recognizes that as individuals age, their lives unfold in conjunction with those of people of different ages, and that all of these actors, who occupy different and changing positions and multiple cultural and physical environments over a period of historical time, are shaping and influencing each other in important ways (...). A focus on the life course, therefore, helps us to see not only the possibilities for individual development and maturity, but also how intergenerational conflict, cooperation, and contact can reconfigure values and redistribute roles and resources (2013: 3).

The way we reconstructed Jürg's life-course is based on our knowledge of his work through his publications, and through talking to him academically and personally over the years.

In the second part, we introduce our contributors as well as the facets they address in relation to the issue of fieldwork. As our contributors belong to different generations of researchers, we do not only hope to make a plea for the continued importance of fieldwork, but we also aim at drawing attention to the very nature of fieldwork: It is an ongoing creative and adaptive process with changing aspects which unfold in relation to certain research traditions, on the one hand, and within certain times and spaces, on the other.

The life-course of a fieldworker

Jürg was born on 16th of March 1946 in Lugano, which is located in the Italian part of Switzerland. He took his final exams at the Liceo cantonale in 1966 and in the following year he started his studies of anthropology, sociology, music and psychology at the University of Basel. In his introduction to *Pacific Answers to Western Hegemony* (1998a), a compilation of essays dealing with cultural practices of identity construction, Jürg offers a personal glimpse into his own life-course and the way it shaped his identity:

> Having grown up in Southern Switzerland, I therefore spoke Italian with my friends and at school; at home, however, I spoke a Swiss German dialect – not becoming fluent in High German until much later, while studying in Basel […]. I remember well how I had no school on Wednesday and Saturday afternoons and set out, first on foot, later with a small moped, to explore the surroundings: a rural area outside the city of Lugano […], with chestnut woods, open streams, clearly separated villages with old stone houses; the local dialect was spoken, there was no television. When I go back nowadays, I can see how my parental home has been swallowed up by suburbia, there are new buildings everywhere whose inhabitants for the most part did not grow up there (although my parents, after all, had also been newcomers), the streams are now running underground in pipes, there is a bus connection to the centre of town, a bank and two shopping centres; the language predominantly spoken now is a kind of "television Italian." And I myself am playing around with my identity: in Germany, where I now live, I present myself as an affable Southern Swiss; when I am visiting my family, however, I pretend to be more of a down-to-earth Northern Swiss (while strongly doubting that anybody believes this) – but, in every instance, I am trying to be "different" (Wassmann 1998a: 1).

Jürg gathered his first fieldwork experience in Northern Sweden, where he worked among the Sami people for five months in 1969. This region, however, did not last as a focus of Jürg's research interests. In 1972, the foundation was laid for an ongoing relationship with the field, when Jürg became part of the Basel research project on the Sepik River. His professor Meinhard Schuster went, together with a group of his students, to Papua New Guinea and installed them in different places along the middle Sepik (see Schindlbeck, this volume). This first encounter with Papua New Guinea lasted twelve months and established in Jürg a lasting love for and commitment to the Iatmul people of the place Kandingei, and he kept returning to this country for the following forty-something years.

Jürg went back for re-studies to Kandingei in 1983, 1984 and 2000, and the dense material he collected on mythological and genealogical history resulted in two voluminous monographs comprising more than 1,000 pages (Wassmann 1982, 1988, see also Wassmann 1987, 2001). He also published articles on time and space perceptions (Wassmann 1984, 1990), so his interest in indigenous cosmologies became as manifest as his focus on cognition. Despite favoring ethnographies based on local empirical research, he nevertheless engaged broader views and comparative perspectives, thus also dealing with aspects of globalization (Wassmann 1998b; Keck and Wassmann 2007). Another important theme of his understanding of fieldwork became apparent as well: he considers it important for both the ethnographer and the results of his or her work to return to the field. An edited and abridged version of his first monograph on Kandingei was later published in Papua New Guinea (Wassmann 1991). Currently, he is working on another revised version (Wassmann n.d.), which includes unpublished material as well as several chapters by colleagues from anthropology as well as neuropsychology.

A short anecdote comes to our mind with regard to the long-lasting relationship between ethnographers and their interlocutors. In 2004, when Jürg and his colleague/wife Verena Keck went with us to Papua New Guinea to introduce us to our own respective field sites in the Lower Ramu River area, we were able to meet one of his interlocutors and friends in the field, a middle-aged Kandingei man. He had come to Madang to spend a few weeks with Jürg. Everyone who has been to Madang knows that every evening the sky is full of flying foxes on their way to feed. On one such evening, the man pointed towards the sky, telling us that these were his ancestors and that if we wanted to know more about it we should read Jürg's book *The Song to the Flying Fox*, as everything important to know about it was in the book. Indeed, the man continued telling us that Jürg had spent many years sitting with the man's antecedents, gathering information. Moreover, he was still in contact with a number of contemporary Kandingei. As fieldwork was still ahead of us, we were deeply impressed, as talking to this consociate of Jürg's gave us an idea of the possibilities of long-term involvement and of obligation within the ethnographic encounter.

During the second half of the 1980s, Jürg moved to another field site in Papua New Guinea. Together with Verena Keck, he decided for the mountainous region of the Finisterre Range where he went to the Yupno valley for twenty months of in-depth research on cognitive phenomena, with a main focus on spatial orientation. He was not only accompanied and supported by fellow anthropologists for this task, but also by a trained psychologist (see Dasen, this volume), to gain an interdisciplinary approach. The research project on "everyday cognition" resulted in a large number of publications in both disciplines, and was later also undertaken in Bali, Indonesia (Wassmann 1992b, 1993a, 1993b, 1993c, 1994, 1995, 1997; Wassmann and Dasen 1993, 1994a, 1994b, 1998, 2006; Dasen and Wassmann 2008). Several follow-up projects eventually manifested Jürg's role as a leading figure in cognitive anthropology (Nunez, Cooperrider and Wassmann 2012; Nunez, Cooperrider, Doan and Wassmann 2012; Ammann, Keck and Wassmann 2013; Wassmann and Bender 2015; see also Wassmann 2003a, 2003b).

After his working period at the Max Planck Institute for Psycholinguistics in Nijmegen from 1991 to 1993, where he belonged to the research team of Stephen Levinson, Jürg went to Heidelberg to become the first director of the newly established Institute of Anthropology in 1995. Whereby interdisciplinary work remained at the core of his research agenda, much collaboration with scientists from other fields such as human geography or neuroscience followed (Wassmann 2011; Wassmann, Kluge and Albrecht 2011). From 1997 to 1999, when he was chairperson of the German Anthropological Association (GAA)[2], he also organized the GAA's biannual congress, together with colleagues and student assistants from the Heidelberg Institute of Anthropology, on the subject of "Interdisciplinarity: Social Anthropology and Its Relations to Neighboring Disciplines." As a member of the interdisciplinary Marsilius-Kolleg from 2006 onwards, he represented Anthropology in a circle of excellent scientists from many disciplines (von Poser, Fuchs and Wassmann 2012). He also pushed his students towards interdisciplinary work by introducing shared seminars with psychology, for example, and by securing funding for corresponding tandem-research projects. From this, a compilation of interdisciplinary contributions evolved on the

Theory of Mind in the Pacific (Wassmann, Träuble and Funke 2013, Wassmann and Funke 2013, see also Funke, this volume).

To prepare his students for fieldwork, Jürg used a very special method: from virtually all over the world he invited guest lecturers to the Oceania workgroup who gave seminars at the institute but who were also asked to talk to the students about their fieldwork experiences in personal meetings at Jürg's flat. Every one of these meetings was packed, with staff and students from different levels all listening to the individual stories from the fields in the Asia-Pacific region (Illustration 1.1).

Illustration 1.1: Oceania workgroup meeting at Jürg's flat (2001, photo by Verena Keck)

This way, the students learned in a very personal and direct way from those with first-hand experience what could happen in the field and what would be suitable solutions for problems which occur. Among the contributors to this volume are some of his former students (Meinerzag, A. von Poser, A. Th. von Poser, Walda-Mandel). The rather informal setting of these gatherings formed the ground from which several doctoral theses finally grew (e.g. A. von Poser 2013; A. Th. von Poser 2014; Meinerzag 2015; Walda-Mandel 2016; Herbst 2016). In addition, preparatory seminars were held in which basic questions about topics such as choice of equipment and malaria prophylaxis, note-keeping and emergency procedures as well as ethical concerns during fieldwork were discussed. So, when it came to the actual fieldwork, his former students were well equipped with a sense of the light and shadow of their task. Also, Jürg more than once motivated his undergraduate students to travel to conferences, such as the European Society for Oceanists (ESfO), which he founded in Nijmegen in 1992 together with other anthropologists working in Oceania. Thus, he helped his students in establishing important contacts with well-known researchers.

The network of cooperation with other institutions expanded continuously. No less than 13 memoranda of cooperation were signed with research centers on Oceania in Australia, Papua New Guinea and Guam, among others. As founding member of the ESfO, a society with a healthy number of members, he contributed largely to connecting European – and to a growing number outer-European – scientists of the Pacific. From 2008 on, he established an Anthropology strand for Bachelor students together with colleagues from the Papua New Guinea Studies Department at Papua New Guinea's Divine Word University (DWU) in Madang (see Keck, this volume).

Since 2009, Jürg has remained a very active emeritus. One of his more recent research interests is the anthropology of aging (Keck and Wassmann 2010). Two book series are currently running under his editorship: "Person, Space and Memory in the Contemporary Pacific" (five volumes so far) and "Heidelberg Studies in Pacific Anthropology" (five volumes so far). For the revision of his habilitation, he added several new chapters that arose from collaborative research with colleagues from anthropology and beyond (Wassmann 2016).

Facets of fieldwork

Our volume starts with a contribution by Markus Schindlbeck, a fellow student of Jürg's, who describes the genesis of the "Basel Sepik Expedition," which marks Jürg's entry into anthropological research in Papua New Guinea. The "Basel Sepik Expedition" took place in the years 1972 to 1974 and was headed by Meinhard Schuster. Both being his students, Markus Schindlbeck and Jürg became part of Meinhard

Schuster's research team. Markus Schindlbeck not only highlights the tradition of fieldwork in which the undertaking was situated, he also puts the project into a larger picture by hinting, in a more general way, at the academic genealogy which stands behind any research project, and by shedding light on personal fieldwork experiences, including competitive relations between members of a research team.

The contribution by Patrick F. Gesch, another contemporary of Jürg's early research in Papua New Guinea as well as co-founder of the Anthropology program at DWU, provides insights from the perspective of a priest as well as an academic of religious studies, thus complementing the results from the "Basel Sepik expedition" with a longer-term experience and immersion that exceeds the presence of the anthropological team by far. Patrick F. Gesch arrived in the Sepik area shortly after Meinhard Schuster's team but has stayed in the country ever since. In his double role, he faced the dilemma of being interested in the very cultural world which he was, through his profession as a priest, instrumental in changing. The method of extended fieldwork may have made his work with the people questionable in the eyes of his church superiors. He maintains, however, that "it is the only way to get to understand another community of persons when the books and road signs are missing."

Another representative of long-term fieldwork experience is linguistic and cognitive anthropologist Gunter Senft, a colleague from Jürg's time at the Max Planck Institute for Psycholinguistics in Nijmegen. His repeated visits to the field in the Trobriand Islands of Papua New Guinea granted him a long-time perspective that encompasses the phenomenon of social and cultural change to a large extent. Starting in the early 1980s, for over 30 years Gunter Senft has become witness to the natural and demographic changes over that time span. In the ethnographic region which influenced Bronislaw Malinowski (1922) to postulate his famous fieldwork premises, Gunter Senft shows how his initial romantic expectations, as he openly describes his first perceptions, soon gave way to the reality of the effects of climate change and overpopulation.

Antje Denner, a colleague of Jürg's when he was research assistant in Basel, throws a critical perspective on the reception by some colleagues of the notion of classic fieldwork in a supposedly "remote place." She presents fieldwork as the work with several interlocutors in different locations within one area, thus underlining the significance of multivocality and multilocality, which are by now standard features of contemporary fieldwork practice. Her use of video-media, in particular, was also added to the classic research toolbox. With regard to maintaining fieldwork as the major empirical road to gaining ethnographic knowledge, she states how crucial it is "to critically reflect on its conventional construction and the methodologies it involves."

In a similar way, Stephanie Walda-Mandel, who received her doctorate in anthropology from Jürg, addresses the truly classic method of anthropology – that of participant observation – in the context of changing and multiple research areas. Due to the multi-sitedness of the people she was working with, her research agenda necessarily had to include field sites in the Micronesian island of Sonsorol as well as in Portland, Oregon, in the USA. A supposedly "remote place" in the Pacific, in fact, turned out to be a connected locale within a wider globalized diasporic landscape scattered widely around the globe.

With the contributions by Anita von Poser and Hermann Mückler, yet two other facets of the field *site* become apparent. Anita von Poser, who also received her doctorate in anthropology under the guidance of Jürg, pays attention to the field as layered with different, that is, precolonial, colonial as well as postcolonial visions of a "village," thus revealing its fluid and ever-changing character. Being an anthropologist with a strong interest in history, a fellow Oceanist and early member of the ESfO, which Jürg helped to establish, Hermann Mückler asks whether the archive may equally be labeled a site of fieldwork, and eventually compares the fieldworker to a "profiler."

Raymond Ammann's contribution deals with concepts of time and space and its cultural configuration on Toman Island in Central Vanuatu. Concepts of time, space, and mythology, also in relation to local forms of knowledge transmission via song and music, always featured prominently in Jürg's curricula as they were of particular interest to his own research scope (Wassmann 1998c, 1998d). His own affinity to music might have equally contributed to the friendship with the ethnomusicologist Raymond Ammann, with whom he did research on *konggap*-melodies among the Yupno people in the Finisterre Range (Ammann, Keck, and Wassmann 2013). As with the *konggap*-melodies, Raymond Ammann explores in his contribution to this volume the connection to the ancestors that people establish through music.

The ethnomusicological bond also extends to Don Niles, head of the Institute of Papua New Guinea Studies, which is located in the country's capital Port Moresby and which has been a regular contact point whenever Jürg and his colleague/wife Verena Keck traveled the country. During an ethnomusicological survey in the Yupno/Nankina area in the 1980s, Don Niles collaborated with Jürg and Verena Keck while the two of them were conducting fieldwork in the Finisterre Range. It was also with the help of Don Niles that Jürg published his Sepik monograph, originally published in German, within the *Apwitihire* series of Papua New Guinea's National Research Institute. This made *The Song to the Flying Fox* (1991) available to a wider English-speaking readership, also in Papua New Guinea. In his contribution to this volume, Don Niles, together with Edward Gende, critically examines Papua New Guinea's current trend in moving towards a "mono-culture" by showing how the contemporary political leaders have been trying to unite the country by working against ancestral conventions, calling them demonic and ungodly. As Don Niles and Edward Gende critically reveal, the results of almost 150 years of ethnographic fieldwork[3] in Papua New Guinea, are currently being under threat.

Our contributors Angella Meinerzag and Shahnaz R. Nadjmabadi have decided to write about rather difficult personal moments during fieldwork, thus touching facets which have only rather recently been voiced in anthropological writings. Relating to the emerging *emotions in the field* (Davies and Spencer 2010) strand within psychological anthropology, Angella Meinerzag, another former doctoral candidate of Jürg's, gives a very personal insight into the way in which her own feelings were shaped and reshaped as her fieldwork proceeded in the Adelbert Range of Papua New Guinea. It becomes clear how her initial sense of feeling strange in an unfamiliar setting became intensified as she felt alone in the face of an "empty village." Only as fieldwork progressed was she able to realize that the "villagers" whom she had come to live with, turned out to be nomadic gardeners. Quite honestly and touchingly, she states in her field diary notes, parts of which are presented in this volume: "Slowly, I'm getting an idea of why there are so few reports about personal experiences during fieldwork. It's quite demanding and nobody gets to look good."

Not only does one not always look good during fieldwork. Sometimes, fieldwork also turns into a dangerous endeavor, creating yet another set of feelings, as the contribution by Shahnaz R. Nadjmabadi shows. A research associate at the Heidelberg Institute of Anthropology when we were still studying there under the guidance of Jürg, we were always highly appreciative of her Non-Pacific focus on things anthropological and how to relate more obviously universal issues of our discipline to our own regional prospects. Shahnaz R. Nadjmabadi talks in her contribution about difficult encounters during her first fieldwork in an endangered field of

Iran's border area and how she had to develop a heightened political sensitivity. Just as honestly as Angella Meinerzag, Shahnaz R. Nadjmabadi admits: "I felt threatened, helpless and in danger. In such a difficult situation, there are moments you lose – as an anthropologist – your illusions about text book methodologies in the field." Still, on the experiential level, it was these kinds of feelings that brought her – as a fieldworker – "closer to the people's lifeworld."

Another highly important facet of fieldwork is the reciprocity of knowledge transfer as touched on in the contributions by Verena Keck as well as Alexis Th. von Poser. Being Jürg's partner both in academic and private life, Verena Keck has chosen to write about an exchange project between the Heidelberg Institute of Anthropology and the Papua New Guinea Studies Department at DWU which she and Jürg were central in establishing. In this project, anthropological knowledge was taught to a young generation of students coming from different parts of Papua New Guinea, enabling them to prepare fieldwork in their own as well as in other locales. Thus, intangible goods were part of the exchange. Also, and highly importantly with regard to the overcoming of a "hegemonic" and "colonial attitude," Papua New Guinean lecturers from the Papua New Guinea Studies Department also came to teach students at Heidelberg University. We were lucky to be part of the project as well, lecturing at DWU, while at the same time moving between this inspiring academic place and our respective field sites in the country. Verena Keck's contribution, in fact, reads as an invitation to enabling more of these exchange projects between anthropologists and the people and places encountered on the way to or during fieldwork.

The contribution by Alexis Th. von Poser, also a former doctoral candidate of Jürg's and post-doc researcher in Jürg's project at the Marsilius-Kolleg of Heidelberg University, highlights the necessity as well as the possibilities of frequent visits to the field. Not only does he talk about how his research results were brought back to the field and how they were discussed and commented in situ, he also relates the return of a lost carving-pattern, which he had discovered in the storage of a museum, to Kayan, his field site at the North Coast of Papua New Guinea. This pattern, he writes, was immediately reintroduced into the local material culture, by using it on a newly carved slit drum. In this way, also tangible results of fieldwork exchange were produced.

The final contributions are dedicated to a subject always central to Jürg. He not only made attempts to convince his students of the empiricist necessity of long-term ethnographic fieldwork and personal life-long engagement with one's interlocutors in the field. He also convinced them that, in order to broaden one's understanding of the *conditio humana* as such, one should not hesitate to look into the work of colleagues from other disciplines and even to collaborate with them, in methodological terms, if they seek to answer similar questions.

Svenja Völkel, a linguist-anthropologist, whose ethnolinguistic work based on her research on the Polynesian Island of Tonga was co-supervised by Jürg, provides significant insights into the challenges as well as the profits of interdisciplinary fieldwork. She explains in detail the difficulties but also the potentials that arise when merging cultural, linguistic, and cognitive anthropology.

Pierre R. Dasen's contribution, which follows, is a very personal and detailed account of his interdisciplinary collaborations as a psychologist together with Jürg in two different field sites, one in Indonesia, the other in Papua New Guinea. What becomes apparent here is that, despite different research traditions and conceptions in the two disciplines, which sometimes would create "disturbances" while sharing the field, the joint efforts of both, Pierre R. Dasen and Jürg, have led to a very fruitful cooperation.

The *Festschrift* closes with Joachim Funke's equally personal memories of his relation to his interdisciplinary colleague Jürg. Coincidental parallels in his and Jürg's life-courses created the possibility of them meeting as students in Basel, where Joachim Funke was studying psychology while Jürg was studying anthropology. However, such a meeting never occurred. It was only many years later that they would meet as heads of their respective institutes at Heidelberg University, planning psychological-anthropological seminars together, thus preparing a new generation of students for the increasingly interdisciplinary world of present-day academia.

While compiling the contributions to this *Festschrift*, we eventually realized that we were not only putting academic texts together but texts that may give our readers an idea about the linkages between different academic life-courses as well as about friendships in academia. This is particularly relevant with the two last essays, but it also leads through the whole volume like a common thread. The contributors are situated at different points in Jürg's life-course, adding facets to the topic of fieldwork as they once added facets to Jürg's professional and private life.

Notes

1 We wish to thank each contributor to this volume for taking the time to share her or his perspective and for being patient with us. Our special thanks go to Verena Keck who, apart from contributing with a chapter, supported us in many ways in the making of this volume.
2 *Deutsche Gesellschaft für Völkerkunde e.V.* (DGV).
3 If one accepts pinpointing Nikolai Miklouho-Maclay's stay at the Rai Coast (Webster 1984) as the beginning of ethnographic fieldwork in Papua New Guinea.

References

Ammann, R., V. Keck, and J. Wassmann. 2013. The Sound of a Person. A Music-Cognitive Study in the Finisterre Range in Papua New Guinea. *Oceania* 83 (2): 63–87.
Danely, J., and C. Lynch. 2013. Introduction. Transitions and Transformations. Paradigms, Perspectives, and Possibilities. In *Transitions and Transformations. Cultural Perspectives on Aging and the Life Course*, eds. C. Lynch and J. Danely. New York and Oxford: Berghahn, pp. 3–20.
Dasen, P. R., and J. Wassmann. 2008. A Cross-cultural Comparison of Spatial Language and Encoding in Bali and Geneva. In *Advances in Cognitive Science*, eds. N. Srinivasan, A. K. Gupta and J. Pandey. New Delhi: Sage, pp. 264–276.
Davies, J., and D. Spencer. 2010. *Emotions in the Field. The Psychology and Anthropology of Fieldwork Experience*. Stanford: Stanford University Press.
Faubion, D., and G. E. Marcus. 2009. *Fieldwork Is Not What It Used to Be. Learning Anthropology's Method in a Time of Transition*. Ithaca: Cornell University Press.
Herbst, F. A. 2016. *Biomedical Entanglements. Conceptions of Personhood in a Papua New Guinea Society*. New York and Oxford: Berghahn. (Person, Space and Memory in the Contemporary Pacific, Vol. 5).
Keck, V. 2005. *Social Discord and Bodily Disorders. Healing among the Yupno of Papua New Guinea*. Durham: Carolina Academic Press.
Keck, V., and J. Wassmann. 2007. Introduction. In *Experiencing New Worlds*, eds. J. Wassmann and K. Stockhaus. New York and Oxford: Berghahn, pp. 1–20. (Person, Space and Memory in the Contemporary Pacific, Vol. 1).
— 2010. Das Älterwerden, der Tod und die Erinnerung – ein Beispiel aus Melanesien. In *Potenziale im Altern. Chancen und Aufgaben für Individuum und Gesellschaft*, ed. A. Kruse. Heidelberg: Akademische Verlagsgesellschaft, pp. 185–202.
MacClancy, J., and A. Fuentes (eds.) 2013. *Ethics in the Field. Contemporary Challenges*. New York and Oxford: Berghahn.

Malinowski, B. 1922. *Argonauts of the Western Pacific. An Account of Native Enterprise and Adventure in the Archipelagoes of Melanesian New Guinea.* London: Routledge and Kegan Paul.

Meinerzag, A. 2015. *Being "Mande." Person, Land and Names among the Hinihon in the Adelbert Range, Papua New Guinea.* Heidelberg: Universitätsverlag Winter. (Heidelberg Studies in Pacific Anthropology, Vol. 3).

Nunez, R., K. Cooperrider, and J. Wassmann. 2012. Number Concepts without Number Lines in an Indigenous Group of Papua New Guinea. P*LoS one* 7 (4): e35662.

Nunez, R., K. Cooperrider, D. Doan, and J. Wassmann. 2012. Contours of Time. Topographic Construals of Past, Present, and Future in the Yupno Valley of Papua New Guinea. *Cognition* 124 (1): 25–36.

Orne, J., and M. Mayerfeld Bell. 2015. *An Invitation to Qualitative Fieldwork. A Multilogical Approach.* New York: Routledge.

von Poser, A. 2013. *Foodways and Empathy. Relatedness in a Ramu River Society, Papua New Guinea.* New York and Oxford: Berghahn. (Person, Space and Memory in the Contemporary Pacific, Vol. 4).

— Forthcoming. Care as Process. A Life-Course Perspective on the Remaking of Ethics and Values of Care in Daiden, Papua New Guinea. *Journal of Ethics and Social Welfare.* doi:10.1080/17496535.2017.1300303.

von Poser, A. Th. 2014. *The Accounts of Jong. A Discussion of Time, Space, and Person in Kayan, Papua New Guinea.* Heidelberg: Universitätsverlag Winter. (Heidelberg Studies in Pacific Anthropology, Vol. 2).

von Poser, A. Th., T. Fuchs, and J. Wassmann (eds.) 2012. *Formen menschlicher Personalität. Eine interdisziplinäre Gegenüberstellung* Heidelberg: Universitätsverlag Winter. (Schriften des Marsilius-Kollegs, Vol. 9).

Robben, A. C. G. M., and J. A. Sluka (eds.) 2012. *Ethnographic Fieldwork. An Anthropological Reader.* 2nd edition. Chichester: Wiley-Blackwell.

Spencer, D., and J. Davies (eds.) 2010. *Anthropological Fieldwork. A Relational Process.* Newcastle: Cambridge Scholars Publishing.

Walda-Mandel, S. 2016. *"There is no place like home". Migration and Cultural Identity of the Sonsorolese, Micronesia.* Heidelberg: Universitätsverlag Winter. (Heidelberg Studies in Pacific Anthropology, Vol. 5).

Wassmann, J. 1982. *Der Gesang an den Fliegenden Hund. Untersuchungen zu den totemistischen Gesängen und geheimen Namen des Dorfes Kandingei am Mittelsepik (Papua New Guinea) anhand der kirugu-Knotenschnüre.* Basel: Ethnologisches Seminar der Universität und Museum für Völkerkunde. (Basler Beiträge zur Ethnologie Bd. 22).

— 1984. Die Vergangenheits-Konzeption der Nyaura (Papua-Neuguinea). *Diachronica, Ethnologica Helvetica* 8: 117–138.

1 Introduction   15

— 1987. Der Biss des Krokodils. Die ordnungsstiftende Funktion der Namen in der Beziehung zwischen Mensch und Umwelt am Beispiel der Initiation, Nyaura, Mittel-Sepik. In *Neuguinea. Nutzung und Deutung der Umwelt Band 2*, ed. M. Münzel. Frankfurt/Main: Museum für Völkerkunde, pp. 511–557.
— 1988. Der Gesang an das Krokodil. *Die rituellen Gesänge des Dorfes Kandingei an Land und Meer, Pflanzen und Tiere (Mittelsepik, Papua New Guinea)*. Basel: Ethnologisches Seminar der Universität und Museum für Völkerkunde. (Basler Beiträge zur Ethnologie Bd. 28).
— 1990. The Nyaura Concepts of Space and Time. In *Sepik Heritage. Tradition and Change in Papua New Guinea*, ed. N. Lutkehaus *et al*. Durham: Carolina Academic Press, pp. 23–35.
— 1991. *The Song to the Flying Fox. The Public and Esoteric Knowledge of the Important Men of Kandingei about Totemic Songs, Names, and Knotted Cords (Middle Sepik, Papua New Guinea)*. Port Moresby: The National Research Institute (Apwitihire: Studies in Papua New Guinea Music, vol. 2).
— (ed.) 1992a. *Abschied von der Vergangenheit. Ethnologische Berichte aus dem Finisterre-Gebirge in Papua New Guinea*. Berlin: Reimer.
— 1992b. "First Contact." Begegnungen im Yupnotal. In *Abschied von der Vergangenheit. Ethnologische Berichte aus dem Finisterre-Gebirge in Papua New Guinea*, ed. J. Wassmann. Berlin: Reimer, pp. 209–260.
— 1993a. *Das Ideal des leicht gebeugten Menschen. Eine ethno-kognitive Analyse der Yupno in Papua New Guinea*. Berlin: Reimer.
— 1993b. When Actions Speak Louder than Words. The Classification of Food among the Yupno of Papua New Guinea. *The Quarterly Newsletter of the Laboratory of Comparative Human Cognition* 15 (1): 30–40.
— 1993c. Worlds in Mind. The Experience of an Outside World in a Community of the Finisterre Range of Papua New Guinea. *Oceania* 64 (2): 117–145.
— 1994. The Yupno as Post-Newtonian Scientists. The Question of What is "Natural" in Spatial Descriptions. *Man* 29 (n.s.) (3): 645–66.
— 1995. The Final Requiem for the Omniscient Informant? An Interdisciplinary Approach to Everyday Cognition. *Culture and Psychology* 1 (2): 167–201.
— 1997. Finding the Right Path. The Route Knowledge of the Yupno of Papua New Guinea. In *Referring to Space. Studies in Austronesian and Papuan Languages*, ed. G. Senft. Oxford et al.: Oxford University Press, pp. 143–174.
— 1998a. Introduction. In *Pacific Answers to Western Hegemony. Cultural Practices of Identity Construction*, ed. J. Wassmann. Oxford and New York: Berg, pp. 1–34.
— (ed.) 1998b. *Pacific Answers to Western Hegemony. Cultural Practices of Identity Construction*. Oxford and New York: Berg.
— 1998c. The Music of the Yupno. In *The Garland Encyclopedia of World Music, Australia and the Pacific,* Volume 9, eds. A. L. Kaeppler and J. W. Love. Washington DC: Garland Publishing, pp. 303–304.

Wassmann, J. 1998d. The Music of the Iatmul. In *The Garland Encyclopedia of World Music, Australia and the Pacific*, Volume 9, eds. A. L. Kaeppler and J. W. Love, Washington DC: Garland Publishing, pp. 340–342.

— 2001. The Politics of Religious Secrecy. In *Emplaced Myth. Space, Narrative, and Knowledge in Aboriginal Australia and Papua New Guinea*, eds. A. Rumsey and J. F. Weiner. Honolulu: University of Hawai'i Press, pp. 43–72.

— 2003a. Kognitive Methoden. In *Methoden und Techniken der Feldforschung*, ed. B. Beer. Berlin: Reimer, pp. 161–182.

— 2003b. Kognitive Ethnologie. In *Ethnologie. Einführung und Überblick*, eds. H. Fischer and B. Beer. Berlin: Reimer, pp. 323–340.

— 2011. Person, Space, and Memory. Why Anthropology needs Cognitive Science and Human Geography. In *Cultural Memories. The Geographical Point of View*, eds. P. Meusburger, M. Heffernan and E. Wunder. Dordrecht and Heidelberg: Springer, pp. 347–360. (Knowledge and Space, Vol. 4).

— 2016. *The Gently Bowing Person. An Ideal among the Yupno in Papua New Guinea*. Heidelberg: Winter. (Heidelberg Studies in Pacific Anthropology, Vol. 4).

— (n.d.) *Journeys in a Mythological Topography. In the Swamps of the Sepik River in Papua New Guinea*. Manuscript.

Wassmann, J., and A. Bender. 2015. Cognitive Anthropology. In *International Encyclopedia of the Social and Behavioral Sciences* (2nd Ed., Vol. 4), ed. J. D. Wright. Oxford: Elsevier, pp. 16–22.

Wassmann, J., and P. R. Dasen (eds.) 1993. *Alltagswissen. Les Savoirs Quotidiens. Everyday Cognition*. Fribourg: Universitätsverlag.

— 1994a. Yupno Number System and Counting. *Journal of Cross-Cultural Psychology* 25 (1): 78–94.

— 1994b. Hot and Cold. Classification and Sorting among the Yupno of Papua New Guinea. *International Journal of Psychology* 29 (2): 19–38.

— 1998b. Balinese Spatial Orientation. Some Empirical Evidence of Moderate Linguistic Relativity. *The Journal of the Royal Anthropological Institute* 4 (4): 689–711.

— 2006. How to Orient Yourself in Balinese Space. Combining Ethnographic and Psychological Methods for the Study of Cognitive Processes. In *Pursuit of Meaning. Advances in Cultural and Cross-Cultural Psychology*, eds. J. Straub, D. Weidemann, C. Kölbl, and B. Zielke. Bielefeld: transcript, pp. 351–376.

Wassmann, J., and J. Funke. 2013. Epilogue. Reflections on Personhood and the Theory of Mind. In *Theory of Mind in the Pacific. Reasoning Across Cultures*, eds. J. Wassmann, B. Träuble and J. Funke. Heidelberg: Universitätsverlag Winter, pp. 233-256. (Heidelberg Studies in Pacific Anthropology, Vol. 1)

Wassmann, J., C. Kluge, and D. Albrecht. 2011. The Cognitive Context of Cognitive Anthropology. In *The Blackwell Companion to Cognitive Anthropology*, eds. D. Kronenfeld, G. Bennardo, V. C. de Munck and M. Fischer. Cambridge: Blackwell, pp. 47–60.

Wassmann, J., and K. Stockhaus (eds.) 2007. *Experiencing New Worlds*. New York and Oxford: Berghahn. (Person, Space and Memory in the Contemporary Pacific, Vol. 1).

Wassmann, J., B. Träuble, and J. Funke (eds.) 2013. *Theory of Mind in the Pacific. Reasoning Across Cultures.* Heidelberg: Universitätsverlag Winter. (Heidelberg Studies in Pacific Anthropology, Vol. 1).

Webster, E. M. 1984. *The Moon Man. A Biography of Nikolai Miklouhu-Maclay*. Berkeley, Los Angeles, and London: University of California Press.

MARKUS SCHINDLBECK

2 *Taim Bipo*.
The Quest for the Past by the Members of the Basel Sepik Expedition 1972–74

Introduction

The special feature of the Basel research in the area of the Sepik is the long research tradition that began a little over a hundred years ago when Felix Speiser studied anthropology in Berlin with Felix von Luschan. The Basel ethnographic collection had just been founded as an independent institution in 1893. The two cousins and zoologists Fritz Sarasin (1859-1942) and Paul Sarasin (1856-1929) appear in the background; they had worked on the commissions of the ethnographic and natural history museum from 1896 onwards and amassed ethnographic collections (Kaufmann 1998: 260). They are considered the founding fathers of the Basel Museum of Ethnology (Schuster 1998). Their interest in the area of Indonesia, the Austronesian-speaking countries and the Western Pacific would be decisive for subsequent research, collections and travel publications. However, neither Basel nor Switzerland had any colonial interests of their own. Thus Kaufmann recognizes at the start of the Basel Museum's interest in the Pacific "the scientific curiosity of evolutionist scientists and cultural historians" (1985a: 20). The Basel anthropological research in Oceania began first in New Caledonia and the Loyalty Islands (Fritz Sarasin 1911-12), and in the New Hebrides, now Vanuatu (Felix Speiser 1910-12) (see Bodenseh et al. 1993). The following remarks are intended to further an understanding of the formation and evolution of research that very often was based on personal networks, and which are rarely mentioned in the scientific publications.

The forerunners of the research

Felix Speiser, who spent a significant amount of time at the Berlin Museum of Ethnology during his anthropological training period, appears at the beginning of the involvement of Basel researchers with the Sepik. Felix Speiser (1880-1949) was engaged in the "African-Oceanic Department" of the Royal Museum of Ethnology from May 1908 until April 1909 and worked on the catalogue of objects. On April 11, 1909 he wrote to Felix von Luschan (1854-1924), head of the "African-Oceanic Department", and thanked him for the cooperation.[1] Speiser had been trained as a chemist, and after a stay in America and a short period of field research with the Hopi Indians, he studied physical anthropology and ethnography with Felix von Luschan: "Luschan's seminar was one of the academic centres of anthropological and ethnological studies in those days, and a large number of distinguished anthropologists were either trained there or were otherwise associated with the department," writes Leonhard Adam (1950: 66), who many years later had to leave Berlin because of the Nazis (Schindlbeck 2013: 375). In this way, Speiser forms a connecting link between the Berlin research, which was initiated by Felix von Luschan with the great Kaiserin-Augusta-Fluss Expedition (1912-13), and the later Basel Sepik research that began with Speiser's trip on the river in 1930. Why Felix von Luschan did not ask Felix Speiser to participate in the great Berlin Sepik expedition, but invited another chemist, Adolf Roesicke, remains an open question. When Speiser left Berlin, the plans for the Berlin expedition had not yet matured.

Felix Speiser did his first major fieldwork 1910-12 in the New Hebrides (now Vanuatu), one year after leaving Berlin. In the winter term of 1914/15 he held the first anthropological lecture at the University of Basel, when regular teaching in anthropology began (Schuster 1998: 247). During Speiser's time the settlement history of the Pacific was a main topic for Felix Speiser, but also physical anthropology interested him until the end of the twenties, when he shifted his research to religious studies and history of art (Kaufmann 1998: 260; 2000: 203). After the end of the German colonial era, the Australian colonial administration reopened the lower and middle Sepik region for explorers in the late twenties. When Speiser carried out his collecting trip to the Sepik in 1930, Gregory Bateson (1904-1980) had already begun his first field research on the middle Sepik in 1929. Speiser spent only a short

2 *Taim bipo*. The Basel Sepik Expedition 1972–74

time on the river because of financial problems. In November 1930 he stayed in the village of Kambrambo at the lower Sepik for a few days. On this occasion his companion Heini Hediger (1908-1992), a young zoologist, was able to take important film footage which documented for the first time an initiation ceremony. While the Basel Museum laid the foundation for its Sepik collection, the Berlin Museum of Ethnology sold, exchanged and gave away many parts of his extensive Sepik collection in the 1920s and 1930s, partly out of economic necessity, partly because of the incapacity of the curators and the relevant committees. The tradition of research highlighted by the Kaiserin-Augusta-Fluss Expedition could not be followed up after the departure of Felix von Luschan in 1911 and the premature death of Adolf Roesicke in 1919. While traveling to Dutch New Guinea Hans Nevermann, who had taken over the management of the collection after the departure of August Eichhorn in 1931, gave up a visit to the Sepik and delegated the inventory of the largely still-crated Sepik collections to the geologist Wilhelm Schmidt (1881-1945 ?) (Schindlbeck 2013: 380-381). Another important person who was associated at that time with Sepik research from Basel is Paul Wirz (1892-1955), son of a Moscow-based Swiss textile manufacturer. Paul Wirz studied with, among others, Otto Schlaginhaufen in Zürich. Schlaginhaufen had participated in the great Deutsche Marine-Expedition in New Ireland 1907-09, also initiated by Felix von Luschan in Berlin, and in Basel with Felix Speiser. He was a tireless traveler who was mainly known for his work on the Marind-anim. After the Second World War, he began his collecting activities in the Sepik region. "Wirz [was] a romantic; he loved indigenous people and nature wholeheartedly and was unhappy about the injustice that had befallen them by our civilization. On his travels he was hard on himself and tried to live together with the indigenous" (Hinderling 1956[2]). He died in an Abelam village to the north of the middle Sepik.

Almost simultaneously with the trip undertaken by Speiser to the Sepik, Alfred Bühler (1900-1981) started with his collection work and research in the South Pacific. Originally a geographer, but then as successor to Felix Speiser anthropologist at the museum and the university, he visited the Bismarck Archipelago first, in particular New Ireland in 1931/32, then later after World War II the Sepik (1955-56 and 1959)[3] twice. For the first trip on the Sepik his companion was the renowned photographer and filmmaker René Gardi (1909-2000) who later said in retrospect: "Almost none of my many trips has remained so vivid in my memory as the expedition to New Guinea" (Gardi in Baer 1982: 113). Especially through his popular books "Tambaran" and "Sepik" he made the Sepik area known to a vast audience. Alfred Bühler laid the foundation for a center of future research on Sepik cultures with his two collections at the Basel museum. On the one hand he bought the collections still located in New Guinea of Paul Wirz and Wirz's son,[4] on the other hand, he collected in the territory of Washkuk (Kwoma), on the middle Sepik and in the Maprik area. On their way downriver, Gardi and Bühler both visited the lagoon Kandingei which, seventeen years later, was to become the research field of Jürg Wassmann. Bühler wrote in his diary:

> Katangai and Yarangai still seem to be very original, they have beautiful men's houses and partially still good stuff. The best, however, broke down under the influence of the Catholic Mission. A particularly fanatical missionary rules in this area. In the men's houses an altar is erected everywhere. In two dwelling houses I saw magnificently overmodelled skulls, in one place one skull, in another three. Unfortunately, they were not prepared to sell them because they were the skulls of close relatives (Bühler 1955-56: 33).

By Europeans the lagoon was first discovered on 11th April 1913; Adolf Roesicke reported: "Above expectation large village, with three large mens houses, friendly reception, could even take pictures from women" (Schindlbeck 2015: 267). On April 24, 1913 Roesicke revisited Yaurangai and estimated, on the basis of the houses he counted, that this village was, after Tambunum, the largest settlement on the Sepik at his time. As the only European ever he was able to observe the return of the village's victorious group of headhunters.

On his second trip in 1959 Bühler was accompanied by Anthony Forge (1929-91), who had worked among the Abelam since 1958.[5] Again starting from the middle Sepik they visited the tributaries Korewori and Krosmeri and also upriver the village of Wagu and the Sawos area north of the Middle Sepik. It was here they assembled a first systematic collection of the Sawos. And they collected also at the May River, a southern tributary of the Sepik upper reaches, where they could only travel when accompanied by Australian colonial officials, and even continued up to the Yellow River. At the lower Sepik they visited the southern tributary Yuat.

Altogether the Basel museum and its personal network were able to establish a great base of knowledge of the Western Pacific, with a rapidly growing South Seas collection. Equally important were the numerous contacts with residents on the Sepik, colonial officials and missionaries. This enabled them to acquire the necessary infrastructure for the collection work, as well as for the acquisition of items, such as from the fathers and employees of the SVD-Order of the Catholic mission, which had been established for much longer in the territory of New Guinea. In the same period more intensive cooperation was set up with the Frobenius Institute in Frankfurt. In 1961 Eike Haberland (1924-1992) traveled with Meinhard Schuster (born in 1930) to the Sepik to create a large collection that was to have laid the foundation for the construction of a new building for the Frankfurt Museum of Ethnography together with the already existing objects.[6] This collection was later shown in a large exhibition in 1964 (Sepik 1964). Alfred Bühler had been in Frankfurt a.M. to give a lecture, and Meinhard Schuster had visited him in Basel in order to obtain detailed information before leaving for New Guinea. This trip from Frankfurt to the Sepik formed the basis for further research to supplement the expeditions of Bühler. Haberland, who after the trip would devote his attention exclusively to Africa, noted later that the years of the economic boom in Germany had provided the city of Frankfurt a.M. with "unique acquisitions means" (Haberland 1987: 31).

The expedition lasted from February to July 1961 and more than 4,000 ethnographic objects were acquired, almost half of them from the Middle Sepik. On this trip, Haberland also visited the Upper Korewori for two weeks. He returned there with Siegfried Seyfarth (1930-2014) from July to December 1963 for additional collections and to get more information (Haberland 1987: 34). The subsequent travels of Meinhard and Gisela Schuster (1935-2012), together with Christian Kaufmann, would be the spatially most extensive, as they led to the upper reaches, even up to the residents of the Sepik headwaters. The expedition departed from Basel and was initiated by Carl August Schmitz (1920-1966) as director of the Basel Museum of Ethnology. However, due to his unexpected departure to Frankfurt in 1965, he could no longer organize this expedition himself. For this reason Meinhard Schuster was asked to assume the management of this project. However, two local priorities existed during this trip: The pottery village Aibom visited earlier, and the area of the Kwoma, which was also a pottery center. Thus, the regional focus for the future research expedition of 1972/74 by the Ethnological Seminar of the University of Basel was established in the region of the Middle Sepik. Unlike the travels by Bühler in 1955/56 and 1959 and the one by Haberlandt/Schuster in 1961, the expedition of 1965/67 would primarily create scientific documentation for already existing collections as well as collect objects in relation to their technological research. Additional collections would be purchased at the headwaters of the Sepik. In the end 3,500 objects reached the museum of Basel (Schuster 1967: 273). For the documention of existing collections photographs were taken to the field. Particularly time-consuming was the production of films for the Institute of Scientific Film in Göttingen. Besides the collecting, an additional 11,000 photographs were taken. Schuster wrote down word lists from 25 different languages. Despite the long period of the expedition, the actual residence in a settlement was rather short: in the village Aibom three and a half months and in the village Meno among the Kwoma three months (ibid). Thus it made sense to organize another more detailed expedition and to expand its focus through a larger number of researchers; this was realized a few years later in 1972.[7]

The research on the Middle Sepik 1972-74

Meinhard Schuster placed the focus of the expedition of the Ethnological Seminar of the University of Basel on the Middle Sepik. Together with Christian Kaufmann he made the selection of the Iatmul villages to be visited. Decisive was the size of the village, the conditions of the men's houses and the location in the area of the Middle Sepik. Places should be investigated which had not previously been at the center of anthropological research (Schuster 1979, 1990). The prolonged field research which Gregory Bateson and Margaret Mead had already played a fundamental role, so that certain villages such as Kanganamun, Tambunum, Mindimbit or Chambri were not included.

The research topics were left to the participants of the expedition; however, they were to provide a total and comparable vision of Middle Sepik cultural life in 1972. The expedition of the university was done in close cooperation with the museum, a collaboration which was and still is rare in the German-speaking anthropological arena. Thus a number of village monographs were the result; these were, however, very different in their thematic orientation and therefore not always directly comparable. Nevertheless, Patricia K. Townsend noted in a review of the book by Hauser-Schäublin:

> Taken together with Schindlbeck's work on Gaikorobi (1980) it provides a unique account of traditional barter seen from both sides: Schindlbeck approaching the market with Gaikorobi women bringing sago and Hauser-Schäublin with Kararau women bringing fish. Each of the two monographs provides detailed data on the production leading up to the trade and on sharing and consumption back in the village after the exchange. Together these monographs make a significant contribution to economic anthropology as well as to women's studies (Townsend 1981: 409-410).

Townsend highlighted in the discussion of the book on Gaikorobi:

> This research must be something of a feminist landmark in the history of ethnology. We have indeed come a long way when a male ethnographer makes women's activities his central concern, overcoming obstacles to gain access to the female puberty rites at which women dance the *naven* (Townsend 1980: 548-549).

Townsend alludes here to a ritual which is restricted to women and which could only be observed after several attempts to participate. Generally speaking, one can detect in all the different monographs a rather strong emphasis on oral tradition. Middle Sepik men and women were eager and ready to transmit their knowledge during long hours of interviews and meetings with the anthropologists, a situation peculiar to this time of change when knowledge of the past was still present but at the same time awareness of the impending loss of this rich tradition was widespread among men and women. A study of the material culture and art was only partially possible, mainly because the once existing and so largely acclaimed diversity of objects was no longer present.

An important preparation for the fieldwork in 1972 was that the Swiss SVD Father J. Z'graggen (2011) recorded indigenous languages of the Madang district in Papua New Guinea in cooperation with the Institute of the Basel University, thus providing a corpus of Iatmul language material to be used in advance. The fieldwork projects by the many anthropologists from Basel were the culmination of a prolonged study of the area of the Sepik, but also a starting point for subsequent individual projects.

The participants

In what way and how were the participants of the Sepik expedition 1972/74 recruited? In the winter semester of 1970/71 there were 23 students majoring in anthropology, one year later 37 (Schuster 1973: 669). At that time only a limited number of students had chosen anthropology as a study and not all of them were willing to go to New Guinea. Some students insisted that such field research would only follow and prolong former colonial activities.[8] In 1971 a position for public relations was created at the museum and Brigitta Hauser-Schäublin was appointed. That was also the reason why she could stay only half a year on the Middle Sepik. The other participants were: Florence Weiss, Milan Stanek, Jürg Schmid, Jürg Wassmann and me.

The expedition lasted from early August 1972 to mid-March 1974, though the individual stays in the field by the participants differed during this period. The "[g]eneral theme was the common, approximately simultaneous, investigation into traditional and contemporary aspects of Iatmul culture taking place in different villages with different thematic focuses" (Schuster 1974: 13). While Meinhard and Gisela Schuster continued the research they had begun in 1965/67 working in the pottery village Aibom, Brigitta Hauser-Schäublin together with her husband Jörg were located in the lagoon of the Iatmul village of Kararau. The important village Palimbei, which was closely related to Kanganamun, where forty years earlier Gregory Bateson had made his enquiries, was to be examined by Florence Weiss and Milan Stanek. Jürg Wassmann and I went to the Western Iatmul, the group of Nyaura. Soon, however, it turned out that a stay of two male anthropologists in the highly competitive Iatmul society was extremely difficult. That was the reason why I preferred to leave the river and, due to numerous myths of origin assigned to the village of Ngaigoropi (Gaikorobi) north of the Sepik, I chose first the location Nangusap and then Gaikorobi for my own research. Another river village of the Central Iatmul was chosen as the home for Jürg Schmid.

Although the villages were far apart, monthly meetings took place with all participants in each one of the villages. Organizational but also research-oriented issues were discussed. Albeit the participants informed each other about their work, no substantial teamwork originated from these meetings. In fact, they were in strong competition with each other, which was emphasized by informants in the villages who tried to outdo the others in the very competitive arena of Sepik communities. Thus the competition of the villages was transferred to the researchers in the neighboring places.

Some of the areas of work were already fixed at the beginning of the study, others were changed during the stay. The following topics were covered: the role of women (Hauser-Schäublin), Sago complex (Schindlbeck), cultural change and initiation (Schmid), genealogical and spatial organization of the village (Schuster), language and culture (Stanek), the socialization process of the child (Weiss), and totemic chants (Wassmann) (Schuster 1974). The resulting monographs were later complemented and extended by various essays and contributions.[9]

Simultaneous to this expedition and partially as organizational preparation, the Head of the Oceania Department at the Museum of Ethnology Basel, Christian Kaufmann, together with his wife Annemarie Kaufmann-Heinimann, left in March 1972. The studies among the Kwoma in Meno from 1966 were to be followed up and comparisons made in adjacent groups. Above all, a detailed photographic and film documentation was to be prepared and thus the collecting work faded into the background. However, the film work was so complex that only the area of the Upper Korewori was additionally visited to document a collection of older wooden figures that had been at the museum since 1971 (Kaufmann 1974, Schuster 1973: 669).

The situation in the villages

Although each of the villages had very different sizes, and each had a singular history and had undergone various cultural changes, one could still find some common traits. In all of the villages there were usually several men's houses, the dwelling houses were still built in the traditional style, though often on a smaller scale and with a simpler construction of the walls, with upright palm leaf ribs and window openings.[10] The inventory of houses had also changed considerably; although the earthen stoves formed the fire places like in the past, numerous plastic containers and metal vessels were part of the equipment. Radio operation was sporadic but already existed. The largest change since the 1950s and 1960s had occurred with clothing; the fiber skirts of the women were only seen at festivals. Overall, there were still sporadic carvings, masks and other traditional objects, both in the dwellings as well as in the men's houses. Canoes were carved by the men; however, the carving of large slitgongs had disappeared completely. Thus, a study of the material culture and the traditional arts was possible only in a very restricted sense. The preparation and painting of palm leaf sheaths could still be observed, as well as the production of certain masks or flutes. The world of rituals had been limited compared with the time of Bateson, yet many initiations took place, as well as initiations of houses and canoes and mortuary ceremonies which could be observed in different villages. The famous *naven* ritual made known by Bateson was still part of the diverse ritual behavior. Nevertheless, it was soon realized that a strong migration had taken place, and that frequent migrations between the villages and the urban centers of Wewak or Lae, even of far-off places like Rabaul, occurred. This migration meant that some kinship groups or clans in the villages were little or poorly represented.

The area of the Middle Sepik was still under the influence of the Catholic Mission at that time. Only a few new fundamentalist evangelical missions were added. The mission station of Kapaimari formed the center of the Catholic Mission on the Middle Sepik. Historically seen it was the final stage of the Australian colonial administration in Papua New Guinea. The villages were visited by the Australian colonial officials, and the famous "kiap" system[11] was still vigorous. But the uncertainty was great when in 1973 the proclamation of "self-government" announced that Papua New Guinea would become independent in 1975. In general, the research in 1972/74 happened in a phase of a vanishing colonial era and the anthropological fieldwork took place "under the protection" of colonial structures.

The acceptance of the anthropologists

Although Schuster and Kaufmann had tested in advance the possible acceptance of anthropological fieldworkers in the mentioned Sepik villages with the exception of Gaikorobi, the resulting cooperation and integration in the villages had very different aspects. According to my own experience, the lowest degree of acceptance was to be encountered in the Nyaura village Kandingei, which was partly to be explained by the proximity to the place Pagwi, the end point of the Wewak Highway on to the Sepik, with all its consequences such as the permanent availability of all kinds of alcohol and beer.

The individual monographs contain very different or no information about the reception of the anthropologists in the villages. Today, however, it no longer has to be mentioned how important these data are for a consideration of the results. Hauser-Schäublin writes shortly after her return from New Guinea: "The social relations that the anthropologist builds and experiences with another population group in a reciprocal relationship, are not to be excluded and concealed in his published work" (1976: 9). Hauser-Schäublin remarks in a short contribution about the problem of a female researcher who initially worked mainly with men, but later mainly with women, with the result that men "no longer, or only reluctantly" (1976: 11) were available as informants and told almost no myths anymore. She also regretted the brevity of the stay and the situation of extreme floods, which made it impossible for their relocation to another village. Nevertheless, she was adopted. This very adoption in a particular kinship group clarified the expectation of the inhabitants of Kararau, "which was dominated by cargo thoughts" (1976: 11). Even though in 1972 no active cargo cult was present in the field, one could repeatedly encounter the related ideas in discussions. Unfortunately, these numerous hints, suggestions, and reports have never been systematically analyzed or published by the participants of the research group.

Probably every participant built up a particularly intense relationship with one or several persons of the village during the research. Hauser-Schäublin mentions the name of Sabwandshan; in her she found "as much as a friend" (1977: 17). She remained the only one. In the detailed elaborations by Florence Weiss we come across the name of Meat (also Miat), especially in the later publications. During her second visit to Palimbei she notes: "Her direct and clear way of speaking, her vivacity and warmth fascinates me and when I listen to her now and look at her and notice her serious facial expression, I realize that for Miat our relationship is as important as to me" (1991: 30). About this relationship Weiss has written a whole book – "Die dreisten Frauen." Not all of these components are clearly expressed in the publications. Gisela Schuster, who had indeed received a lot of information as early as 1965 in an Iatmul village, frequently worked with the woman Namburagua, an excellent potter. At the end of my monograph I presented a visual remembrance of the closest contributors to my anthropological work in the village of Gaikorobi. Jürg Schmid categorized his relationship with the villagers under the aspect of "give and take." In the probably smallest village Yenchan on the Middle Sepik, where Schmid (1976) spent ten months, he had a special contact with the so-called village chief Keman, and furthermore to a slightly older and influential man named Bubari. These connections were very often influenced by the choice of the house site in the village. In some cases, it was the so-called "house kiap," a house reserved for patrols of the former colonial officials and built in all the villages as a sort of "official guesthouse." These houses were not on neutral ground, but on the ground of a particular lineage or clan. In general, one did not know at the beginning of one's research much about these special kinship relations. However, they were of central importance for the integration of "anthropologists" in the village structure. The anthropologist group in the village Palimbei had undoubtedly a "pole position," because two anthropologists who could get access to both the female and the male sphere of the community worked there. Stanek has also written in great detail about his main informant Masoabwan, the eldest of the kinship group on whose ground the home of Stanek and Weiss was. With men of his main informant's clan he had the closest links (Stanek 1982: 24).

Meinhard Schuster summed up in a retrospective the similarities between the Frobenius Institute in Frankfurt and the Institute in Basel: "The strong relation between the Institute and the Museum, the strong emphasis on the anthropological fieldwork, the marked interest in the historical dimension, the handicraft and artistic expression and the religious foundation of culture, and the appreciation of the authentic" (Schuster 2003: 29). Nevertheless, he has repeatedly pointed out that he did not want to establish a school. Against his background of studying with Adolf Ellegard Jensen (1899-1965) he did not want his students to follow a particular doctrine.[12] In fact, all monographs that emerged from the expedition of 1972/74 are characterized by a strong empiricism, highlighting direct statements of informants and the approach to a synthetic total view of the village society. Since all monographs were published in German, their reception was very limited in the Anglo-Saxon world. Only the work by Jürg Wassmann "The Song to the Flying Fox" was translated into English and published in 1991. Wassmann also published the results of his investigation in other contributions in English

(Wassmann 2001). But even if no English translation of the results followed, e.g. the study on Sago among the Sawos was extensively used by Deborah Gewertz for her portrayal of "Sepik River Societies".[13] The publication "Geschichten der Kopfjäger" by Milan Stanek, which appeared even before his monograph in 1982, was very widespread among the German public not acquainted with anthropology. Especially the subsequent work by Stanek and Weiss on the ethnopsychoanalytical field made their research on Palimbei very well known and served as the basis for numerous other works.[14] Van der Linden (2008) shows that the ethnographic studies by Stanek and Weiss in Palimbei and the town of Rabaul offer a detailed impression of the gradual incorporation of the Iatmul people in a capitalist system. The studies on children in Palimbei also found their way into a handbook for childhood and youth research (Renner in Krüger / Grunert 2002). Finally, the large symposium in 1984 should be mentioned; the results published by Lutkehaus et al. (1990) included parts of the Basel research in English. In 1978 Christian Kaufmann established a project "for more intensive documentation of Central Sepik cultures. The aim was to collect as much additional evidence as possible [...] from field notes, photographs, films, and tapes" (Kaufmann 1990: 589). Results of the expedition of 1972/74 were also presented in the many films by Hermann Schlenker, in the accompanying booklets and in following exhibitions: "Papua Niugini" 1975 (Kaufmann 1975), "Sepik" 1985 (Greub 1985), the permanent exhibition of the Museum of Ethnology Basel (Kaufmann 1992), "Neuguinea" in Frankfurt a.M. 1987 (Münzel 1987), a photographic exhibition in Zürich 2015 (Flitsch 2015) and most recently "Sepik" in Berlin / Zürich / Paris 2015 (Peltier, Schindlbeck and Kaufmann 2015). What, however, has until now only partially taken place is a new synthesis of the research results obtained in the 1970s. Taking into account different aspects, few attempted a comprehensive view: Deborah Gewertz (1983) on power relations, Christian Kaufmann (1985b) on art, Brigitta Hauser-Schäublin on ceremonial or men's houses (1989) and Ulrike Claas (2007, 2009) on migrations and oral history. A synthesis which arranges the analysis in its temporal contextuality, especially in a diachronic perspective and including other monographs on the Middle Sepik (Manambu, Chambri), should be done.

The years thereafter

It is not possible to discuss all the research carried out in the wake of 1972/74 here, therefore, reference is only made summarily. Gisela and Meinhard Schuster traveled 1987-88 again to the village of Aibom to continue their studies. Almost all of the participants of 1972/74 conducted further fieldwork in Papua New Guinea. Some of them were asked, in accordance with the aims of Meinhard Schuster, to introduce younger students to the fieldwork and find suitable locations for their work. Hauser-Schäublin returned in 1978 with her husband, however, to work in Klabu among the Abelam north of Iamul. They carried out extensive research on ceremonial houses and rituals (first published in 1989, only recently in English translation 2015). She introduced Barbara Greub into the fieldwork; Greub did her research in a neighboring village of the Abelam (Huber-Greub 1988). I myself worked in a neighboring area among the Kwanga in 1979 (Schindlbeck 1990).[15] On this occasion the village Gaikorobi was visited again. I brought back written materials such as name chants, with the intention that the chants should be practiced again. At the same time numerous old village sites in the surroundings were visited and hundreds of potsherds were collected in cooperation with Pamela Swadling for the National Museum in Port Moresby.[16] During this time I was also looking for a suitable research site for the students Brigit Obrist van Eeuwijk and Nigel Stephenson among the northern Kwanga village of Tau. Brigit Obrist van Eeuwijk returned to Tau in 1984 for a full year while Nigel Stephenson started in the same year his repeated field works among the Wam in the north of Kwanga (Obrist van Eeuwijk 1992, Stephenson 2001). Milan Stanek and Florence Weiss also returned to the Sepik, but without introducing younger anthropologists. They began in 1979 with their psychoanalytic studies in the village of Palimbei, together with the renowned psychoanalyst Fritz Morgenthaler and his son Marco. In addition to these psychoanalytic session interviews, the results of which were published in 1984, urban anthropological studies followed in Rabaul in 1988 (Weiss 1999).

Jürg Wassmann was looking for a new field of research outside the Sepik basin, which he found in the Finisterre Range in northeastern New Guinea among the Yupno (Wassmann 1993, 2016). Thus he could continue his focus, already begun in his Iatmul research on space and time, especially with approaches from cognitive sciences (Wassmann 2007). He also maintained the tradition of Meinhard Schuster of introducing young students to anthropological fieldwork, for instance, to villages along the lower Ramu River (Herbst 2016, A. von Poser 2013), to the coast near the mouth of the Ramu River (A. Th. von Poser 2014) and to the Adelbert Range (Meinerzag 2015) of Papua New Guinea as well as to other places in the Pacific (e.g. Walda-Mandel 2016).

Notes
1   Acts of the Ethnological Museum Berlin E 856/09. Acta concerning the relocation and the establishment of the museum's collection Vol. II v. 7 January 1909 until 30 Nov. 1909. Pars I c.
2   All translations of German quotes by the author.
3   For the life of Alfred Bühler see Baer (1982) and Schuster (1982).
4   The collection by his son Dadi could only be recovered because Bühler was ready to transfer it to a public institution, a museum, and not to private dealers. It remains open if among them there were also pieces collected by his father.
5   For the cooperation between Forge and Bühler see Kaufmann (forthcoming).
6   Unfortunately, until today, the new museum has not been built in Frankfurt a.M.
7   The research was funded by the Swiss National Science Foundation.
8   It is remarkable what Bernhard Streck, from 1994-2010 director of the Institute of Ethnology in Leipzig, said in an interview with Dieter Haller of 2008. He had studied in Basel from 1967-69, but then went to Frankfurt a.M. as he found "New Guinea [...] very confusing [and sought therefore] clearer conditions. For me this was Africa. [...] The Sepik is made of many turns and many villages and each village has its own culture and its own language. Anthropology in Basle [...] was just a little narrow. It seemed to me as if Basle was in the shadow of anthropological evolution" (2008: 2-3). However, when he mentions "stationary fieldwork, linguistic preparation, proper questions, patient listening and at least one year in the field was completely new in the German anthropological arena, they had previously only collected and made expeditions" (2008: 6) as a special feature of the Free University of Berlin after 1979, this certainly was more in the shadows of the institute in Basel led by Meinhard Schuster.
9   Additionally I wrote about the following topics: secrecy (1976), hunting ritual (1978), development ideas (1983), oral tradition (1984a, 1993), migration (1984b), men's house and art (1985a), Catholic mission (1985b), ethnomedicine (1988), history of collecting activity (1997), cosmology (2009), photography (2011), and ornament (2013).

10 Before European times the walls were made of palm bark with thin spaces to offer a glimpse of the outside.
11 Kiaps were field officers of the Australian Administration who carried out the initial exploration, brought the people under administration control, maintained law and order, were magistrates, introduced basic services, patrolled from village to village and maintained contact with village officials.
12 This focused and restricted theoretical orientation could be observed at the Berlin University in the 1990's in works on Asia.
13 See my reply to Gewertz in 1985.
14 Mimica 2007.
15 A comprehensive publication of the results on the Kwanga has been repeatedly postponed because of my museum work.
16 Unfortunately, until today they have not been analyzed.

References

Adam, L. 1950. In Memoriam Felix Speiser. *Oceania* 21 (1): 66–72.
Baer, G. 1982. Alfred Bühler zum Gedenken. In: Bericht über das Basler Museum für Völkerkunde und Schweizerische Museeum für Volkskunde für das Jahr 1981. Sonderdruck aus *Verhandlungen der Naturforschenden Gesellschaft Basel* 93: 71–122.
Bodenseh, B., P. van Eeuwijk, S. Hammacher, and C. Kaufmann. 1993. *Fenster zur Welt. 100 Jahre Museum für Völkerkunde und Volkskunde Basel*. Basel.
Bühler, A. 1955/56. *Tagebuch*. Ms. Museum der Kulturen Basel.
Claas, U. 2007. *Das Land entlang des Sepik. Vergangenheitsdarstellungen und Migrationsgeschichte im Gebiet des mittleren Sepik, Papua New Guinea*. Berlin: Lit Verlag. (Göttinger Studien zur Ethnologie Bd. 17).
— 2009. "Fish, Water, and Mosquitoes." The Western Invention of Iatmul Culture. In *Form, Macht, Differenz. Motive und Felder ethnologischen Forschens*, eds. E. Hermann, K. Klenke, and M. Dickhardt. Göttingen: Universitätsverlag Göttingen, pp. 215–226.
Flitsch, M. (ed.) 2015. *Kinder im Augenblick. Florence Weiss – Fotografien vom Sepik*. Zürich: Benteli.
Gewertz, D. 1983. *Sepik River Societies. A Historical Ethnography of the Chambri and their Neighbors*. New Haven, London: Yale University Press.
Haberland, E. 1987. Die Neuguinea-Sammlung des Museums für Völkerkunde in Frankfurt am Main seit 1961. In *Neuguinea. Nutzung und Deutung der Umwelt* (Vol. 1), ed. M. Münzel. Frankfurt a. M.: Museum für Völkerkunde, pp. 29–69.
Hauser-Schäublin, B. 1976. Feldforschung bei den Iatmul. Zwischen Erlebnis und Wissenschaft. *Bulletin de la Société d'Ethnologie/ Bulletin der Schweizerischen Ethnologischen Gesellschaft Sondernummer*: 9–14.

— 1977. *Frauen in Kararau. Zur Rolle der Frau bei den Iatmul am Mittelsepik, Papua New Guinea.* Basel: Ethnologisches Seminar der Universität und Museum für Völkerkunde. (Basler Beiträge zur Ethnologie Bd. 18).

— 1989. *Kulthäuser in Nordneuguinea.* Berlin: Akademie-Verlag.

— 2015. *Ceremonial Houses of the Abelam – Papua New Guinea.* Goolwa: Crawford House Publishing.

Herbst, F. 2016. *Biomedical Entanglements. Conceptions of Personhood in a Papua New Guinea Society.* New York and Oxford: Berghahn. (Person, Space and Memory in the Contemporary Pacific, Vol. 5).

Hinderling, P. 1956. *Basler Forscher bei fremden Völkern.* Basel: Museum für Völkerkunde.

Huber-Greub, B. 1988. *Kokospalmenmenschen. Boden und Alltag und ihre Bedeutung im Selbstverständnis der Abelam von Kimbangwa (East Sepik Province, Papua New Guinea).* Basel: Ethnologisches Seminar der Universität und Museum für Völkerkunde. (Basler Beiträge zur Ethnologie Bd. 27).

Kaufmann, C. 1974. Bericht über die Neuguinea-Expedition des Museums für Völkerkunde Basel (1972-73). *Information S.E.G. / S.S.E. Bulletin de la Société Suisse d'Ethnologie/ Bulletin der Schweizerischen Ethnologischen Gesellschaft* 2: 12–14.

— 1975. *Papua Niugini. Ein Inselstaat im Werden.* Basel: Museum für Völkerkunde und Schweizeisches Museum für Volkskunde.

— 1985a. Südsee – eine Basler Idylle? *Basler Stadtbuch.* Basel: Christoph Merian Verlag, pp. 19–24.

— 1985b. Sepik-Kunst. Ein Essay. In *Kunst am Sepik*, ed. S. Greub. Basel: Tribal Art Centre, pp. 14–18.

— 1990. Swiss and German Ethnographic Collections as Source Materials. A Report on Work in Progress. In *Sepik Heritage. Tradition and Change in Papua New Guinea,* eds. N. Lutkehaus et al. Durham, N. C.: Carolina Academic Press, pp. 587–595.

— 1992. *Ozeanien. Menschen in ihrer Umwelt.* Basel: Museum für Völkerkunde und Schweizeisches Museum für Volkskunde.

— 1998. Ethnologische Forschung am Museum der Kulturen Basel. *Regio Basiliensis, Basler Zeitschrift für Geographie* 39 (3): 259–276.

— 2000. Felix Speiser's Fletched Arrows. A Paradigm Shift from Physical Anthropology to Art Styles. In *Hunting the Gatherers. Ethnographic Collectors, Agents and Agency in Melanesia, 1870s–1930s,* eds. M. O'Hanlon and R. Welsch. New York and Oxford: Berghahn, pp. 203–226.

— Forthcoming. Anthony Forge and Alfred Bühler. From Field Collecting to Friendship. In *Style and Meaning. Essays on the Anthropology of Arts*, eds. A. Clark and N. Thomas. Leiden: Sidetone Press (Pacific Presences, Vol. 1).

Lutkehaus, N. et al. (eds.) 1990. *Sepik Heritage. Tradition and Change in Papua New Guinea.* Durham, N.C.: Carolina Academic Press.

Meinerzag, A. 2015. *Being "Mande". Person, Land and Names among the Hinihon in the Adelbert Range, Papua New Guinea.* Heidelberg: Universitätsverlag Winter. (Heidelberg Studies in Pacific Anthropology, Vol. 3).

Mimica, J. (ed.) 2007. *Explorations in Psychoanalytic Ethnography.* New York and Oxford: Berghahn.

Münzel, M. (ed.) 1987. *Neuguinea. Nutzung und Deutung der Umwelt,* Frankfurt a. M.: Museum für Völkerkunde.

Obrist van Eeuwijk, B. 1992. *Small but Strong. Cultural Contexts of (Mal-)Nutrition among the Northern Kwanga (East Sepik Province, Papua New Guinea.)* Basel: Ethnologisches Seminar der Universität und Museum für Völkerkunde. (Basler Beiträge zur Ethnologie Bd. 34).

Peltier, P., M. Schindlbeck, and C. Kaufmann (eds.) 2015. *Tanz der Ahnen. Kunst vom Sepik in Papua-Neuguinea.* München: Hirmer-Verlag.

von Poser, A. 2013. *Foodways and Empathy. Relatedness in a Ramu River Society, Papua New Guinea.* New York and Oxford: Berghahn. (Person, Space and Memory in the Contemporary Pacific, Vol. 4).

von Poser, A. Th. 2014. *The Accounts of Jong. A Discussion of Time, Space, and Person in Kayan, Papua New Guinea.* Heidelberg: Universitätsverlag Winter. (Heidelberg Studies in Pacific Anthropology, Vol. 2).

Renner, E. 2002. Kulturtheoretische und kulturvergleichende Ansätze. In *Handbuch Kindheits- und Jugendforschung,* eds. H.-H. Krüger and C. Grunert. Opladen: Leske und Budrich, pp. 165–188.

Schindlbeck, M. 1976. Das Gebot der Geheimhaltung und der Ethnologe in der Sicht der Einheimischen. *Bulletin de la Société d'Ethnologie/ Bulletin der Schweizerischen Ethnologischen Gesellschaft Sondernummer*: 15–23.

— 1978. Jagdzauber bei den Sawos in Gaikorobi, Mittlerer Sepik, Papua-Neuguinea. *Verhandlungen der Naturforschenden Gesellschaft Basel* 89: 25–40.

— 1980. *Sago bei den Sawos (Mittelsepik, Papua New Guinea). Untersuchungen über die Bedeutung von Sago in Wirtschaft, Sozialordnung und Religion.* Basel: Ethnologisches Seminar der Universität und Museum für Völkerkunde. (Basler Beiträge zur Ethnologie Bd. 19).

— 1983. Kokospalme und Brotfruchtbaum. Siedlungs-Vorstellungen der Sawos und Kwanga, Sepik-Gebiet, Papua-Neuguinea. *Geographica Helvetica* 38 (1): 3–10.

— 1984a. Über den mythischen Ursprungsort der Sawos und Iatmul (Papua-Neuguinea). *Ethnologica Helvetica* 8: 153–160.

— 1984b. Cargo-Bewegung, Tradition und Migration. Sozio-ökonomische Veränderungen bei den Sawos von Gaikorobi, Sepik-Gebiet, Papua-Neuguinea. *Paideuma* 30: 275–298.

— 1985a. Männerhaus und weibliche Giebelfigur am Mittelsepik, Papua-Neuguinea. *Baessler-Archiv* N.F. 33: 363–411.
— 1985b. Christentum und Ahnenkult. *Missionsjahrbuch der Schweiz 1985*, 51. Jg.: 81–84.
— 1985c. Review of D. B. Gewertz: Sepik River Societies. A Historical Ethnography of the Chambri and Their Neighbors. *Reviews in Anthropology* 12 (2): 166–172.
— 1988. Krankenheilung bei den Sawos. *Baessler-Archiv* N.F. 36: 117–144.
— 1990. Tradition and Change in Kwanga Villages. In *Sepik Heritage*. eds. N. Lutkehaus et al. Durham, N.C.: Yale University Press, pp. 232–240.
— 1994. Formen mündlicher Überlieferung bei den Sawos. In *Geschichte und mündliche Überlieferung in Ozeanien*, ed. B. Hauser-Schäublin. Basel: Ethnologisches Seminar der Universität und Museum für Völkerkunde, pp. 5–14. (Basler Beiträge zur Ethnologie Bd. 37).
— 1997. The Art of the Head-Hunters. Collecting Activity and Recruitment in New Guinea at the beginning of the twentieth Century. In *European Impact and Pacific Influence*, eds. H. J. Hiery and J. M. MacKenzie. London, New York: Tauris Publishers, pp. 31–43.
— 2009. Dualism – A Motif of Thought in Sepik Societies. In *Form, Macht, Differenz. Motive und Felder ethnologischen Forschens*, eds. E. Hermann, K. Klenke and M. Dickhardt. Göttingen: Universitätsverlag Göttingen, pp. 227–236.
— 2011. Fotografie am Mittelsepik in Neuguinea. Inszenierung und Motiv. In *Visuelle Medien und Forschung. Über den wissenschaftlich-methodischen Umgang mit Fotografie und Film*, eds. I. Ziehe and U. Hägele. Münster etc.: Waxmann, pp. 101–111.
— 2013a. Das Berliner Museum für Völkerkunde und seine Mitarbeiter 1933-1945. In *Zwischen Politik und Kunst. Die Staatlichen Museen zu Berlin in der Zeit des Nationalsozialismus*, eds. J. Grabowski and P. Winter. Köln: Böhlau Verlag, pp. 369–386.
— 2013b. Klänge und Düfte. Schmuck vom Mittelsepik in Papua-Neuguinea. In *25 000 Jahre Schmuck*, eds. M. Eichhorn-Johannsen and A. Rasche. München: Prestel Verlag, pp. 331–337.
— 2015. Krieg, Ritual und Kunst. Die kulturellen Besonderheiten der Sawos. In *Tanz der Ahnen. Kunst vom Sepik in Papua-Neuguinea*, eds. P. Peltier, M. Schindlbeck and C. Kaufmann. München: Hirmer, pp. 88–95.
Schmid, J. 1976. Geben und Nehmen. *Bulletin de la Société d'Ethnologie/ Bulletin der Schweizerischen Ethnologischen Gesellschaft Sondernummer*: 25–36.

Schmid, J., and C. Kocher Schmid. 1992. *Söhne des Krokodils. Männerhausrituale und Initiation in Yensan, Zentral-Iatmul, East Sepik Province, Papua New Guinea*. Basel: Ethnologisches Seminar der Universität und Museum für Völkerkunde. (Basler Beiträge zur Ethnologie Bd. 36).

Schuster, M. 1967. Vorläufiger Bericht über die Sepik-Expedition 1965-1967 des Museums für Völkerkunde zu Basel. *Verhandlungen der Naturforschenden Gesellschaft Basel* 78 (1):268–282.

— 1973. Ethnologie in Basel in den Jahren 1971 bis 1973. *Regio Basiliensis, Basler Zeitschrift für Geographie* XIV (4): 668–672.

— 1974. Neuguinea Expedition des Ethnologischen Seminars der Universität Basel. *Information S.E.G. / S.S.E. Bulletin de la Société Suisse d'Ethnologie/ Bulletin der Schweizerischen Ethnologischen Gesellschaft* 1: 13–17.

— 1979. Ethnologische Feldforschung in Papua New Guinea. Alfred Bühler zum 80. Geburtstag. *Geographica Helvetica* 34 (4): 171–180.

— 1982. Alfred Bühler zum Gedenken. Bericht über das Basler Museum für Völkerkunde und Schweizerische Museum für Volkskunde für das Jahr 1981. *Verhandlungen der Naturforschenden Gesellschaft Basel* 93: 109–113.

— 1990. Ethnologische Feldforschung. *Regio Basiliensis, Basler Zeitschrift für Geographie* 31 (3): 237–238.

— 1998. Das Ethnologische Seminar der Universität Basel 1998. Ein Rückblick und Ausblick. *Regio Basiliensis, Basler Zeitschrift für Geographie* 39 (3): 247–257.

— 2003. Studenten- und Assistentenjahre im Frobenius-Institut 1948-1965. *Paideuma* 49: 7–30.

Sepik. Kunst aus Neuguinea. Aus den Sammlungen der Neuguinea-Expedition des Städt. Museums für Völkerkunde. 1964. Frankfurt am Main.

Stanek, M. 1982. *Geschichten der Kopfjäger. Mythos und Kultur der Iatmul auf Papua-Neuguinea*. Köln: Eugen Diederichs Verlag.

— 1983. *Sozialordnung und Mythik in Palimbei. Bausteine zur ganzheitlichen Beschreibung einer Dorfgemeinschaft der Iatmul, East Sepik Province, Papua New Guinea.* Basel: Ethnologisches Seminar der Universität und Museum für Völkerkunde. (Basler Beiträge zur Ethnologie Bd. 23).

Stephenson, N. A. 2001. *Kastom or Komuniti. A Study of Social Process and Change among the Wam People, East Sepik Province, Papua New Guinea.* Basel: Ethnologisches Seminar der Universität und Museum für Völkerkunde. (Basler Beiträge zur Ethnologie Bd. 40).

Streck, B. 2008. Interview vom 27.02.2008 mit Dieter Haller. www.germananthropology.de

Townsend, P. K. 1980. Review of M. Schindlbeck: Sago bei den Sawos. Basel: Ethnologisches Seminar der Universität und Museum für Völkerkunde 1980. *Journal of the Polynesian Society* 89 (4): 548–549.

— 1981. Review of B. Hauser-Schäublin: Frauen in Kararau. Zur Rolle der Frau bei den Iatmul am Mittelsepik, Papua New Guinea. Basel: Ethnologisches Seminar der Universität und Museum für Völkerkunde 1977. *Journal of the Polynesian Society* 90 (3): 409–410.

van der Linden, M. 2008. *Workers of the World. Essays toward a Global Labor History*. Leiden, Brill.

Walda-Mandel, S. 2016. *"There is no place like home". Migration and Cultural Identity of the Sonsorolese, Micronesia*. Heidelberg: Universitätsverlag Winter. (Heidelberg Studies in Pacific Anthropology, Vol. 5).

Wassmann, J. 1982. *Der Gesang an den Fliegenden Hund. Untersuchungen zu den totemistischen Gesängen und geheimen Namen des Dorfes Kandingei am Mittelsepik (Papua New Guinea) anhand der kirugu-Knotenschnüre*. Basel: Ethnologisches Seminar der Universität und Museum für Völkerkunde. (Basler Beiträge zur Ethnologie Bd. 22).

— 1988. *Der Gesang an das Krokodil. Die rituellen Gesänge des Dorfes Kandingei an Land und Meer, Pflanzen und Tiere (Mittelsepik, Papua New Guinea)*. Basel: Ethnologisches Seminar der Universität und Museum für Völkerkunde. (Basler Beiträge zur Ethnologie Bd. 28).

— 1991. *The Song to the Flying Fox. The Public and Esoteric Knowledge of the Important Men of Kandingei about Totemic Songs, Names, and Knotted Cords (Middle Sepik, Papua New Guinea)*. Port Moresby: Institute of Papua New Guinea Studies.

— 1993. *Das Ideal des leicht gebeugten Menschen. Eine ethno-kognitive Analyse der Yupno in Papua New Guinea*. Berlin: Dietrich Reimer.

— 2001. The Politics of Religious Secrecy. In *Emplaced Myth. Space, Narrative, and Knowledge in Aboriginal Australia and Papua New Guinea*, eds. A. Rumsey and J. Weiner. Honolulu: University of Hawai'i Press, pp. 43–72.

— 2016. *The Gently Bowing Person. An Ideal among the Yupno in Papua New Guinea*. Heidelberg: Universitätsverlag Winter. (Heidelberg Studies in Pacific Anthropology, Vol. 4).

Wassmann, J. and Stockhaus, K. (eds.) 2007. *Experiencing New Worlds*. New York and Oxford: Berghahn. (Person, Space and Memory in the Contemporary Pacific, Vol. 1).

Weiss, F. 1981. *Kinder schildern ihren Alltag. Die Stellung des Kindes im ökonomischen System einer Dorfgemeinschaft in Papua New Guinea (Palimbei, Iatmul, Mittelsepik)*. Basel: Ethnologisches Seminar der Universität und Museum für Völkerkunde. (Basler Beiträge zur Ethnologie Bd. 21).

— 1991. *Die dreisten Frauen. Ethnopsychoanalytische Gespräche in Papua-Neuguinea*. Frankfurt a.M.: Edition Qumaran im Campus Verlag.

— 1999. *Vor dem Vulkanausbruch. Meine Freundinnen in Rabaul*. Frankfurt a.M.: Fischer Taschenbuch Verlag.

Weiss, F. et al. 1984. *Gespräche am sterbenden Fluß. Ethnopsychoanalyse bei den Iatmul in Papua Neuguinea*. Frankfurt a.M.: Fischer Taschenbuch Verlag.

Z'graggen, J. A. 2011. *The Lady Daria and Mister Kamadonga. A Legend of Papua New Guinea*. Adelaide: Crawford House Publishers.

Aus dem Blickwinkel der "alten Krokodile" ist also die Initiation nichts Geringeres als die Aktualisierung des urzeitlichen Geschehens, d.h. der Schöpfung der Welt, der Entstehung der Menschen und aller Dinge, und zwar insoweit als die eigenen Vorfahren an dieser Schöpfung beteiligt waren (Wassmann 1987: 553).[1]

PATRICK F. GESCH

3 Thinking Along the Same Lines. Varieties of Initiation and Varieties of Fieldwork in Sepik and Madang

Introduction: Arriving in the field

I come from an initiation tradition. As students in Chicago in 1968, we went through a "marathon." This was a widely employed, voluntary group dynamic, typical of those times in the USA, guided by a psychologist who demanded a psychological break-through from everyone in the group, no matter how long it took, no matter what drama took place. There were real bullet holes in the roof, and post-adolescents wept their hearts out in the process. Added to this, I went through the process of ordination for the Catholic priesthood. There were roughly seven stages to that initiation for everyone to go through, ending with sub-diaconate, diaconate and ordination to the priesthood.

When I received an appointment to the Diocese of Wewak as a member of the Divine Word Missionaries, I was stunned one day in Australia to see a papier-mâché model of the East Sepik Province (ESP) and to realize that the greatest part of the population of ESP was not on the River but in the mountains behind the coast. Only a small population lived on the Sepik River. I was suddenly fearful that I would not be appointed to the Sepik River, so widely known for its colorful culture and initiation customs. And that is the way it turned out. When I arrived in Wewak, my colleagues said, "You are going to Negrie, the cargo cult parish." Since I had Peter Lawrence's *Road bilong Cargo* (1964) in my hand as I arrived, it was hard not to think that one door opened as another closed. I spent two years living in Negrie Parish (the eastern half of the Yangoru Patrol Post) before I was convinced that Yangoru had not only a vigorous cult but also a vivid initiation tradition.

When I got to Negrie I was led by my predecessor in the parish on rounds of the fourteen out-stations, sleeping out in the villages and conducting what was called the Self-Study of the Church. This had the basic format of taking a Church topic, such as the sacraments of initiation, asking what was like this in the tradition, what the villagers were told as new Christian initiates, and what should be done for the future. This was my form of life for the first five years. It occurred to me that it was like a continual boy scout camp as in my growing up days in Australia, going out regularly, and making do for all the necessities of life. Only later did I learn that this could be called "fieldwork," an initiation experience for anthropologists.

Five months earlier than my arrival in March 1973, Jürg Wassmann and the anthropology team from the University of Basel had turned up in the ESP and established their team in Chambri. They were eight people, and under the guidance of their mentors, Gisela and Meinhard Schuster, they went out in different directions to research different aspects of life in the ESP. My impression now is that their very diversity and thorough-going professionalism underlines the great complexity of coming to anthropological knowledge in a cultural region and gives faint hope that we could ever say we have come to know the Sepik, from the islands to the River, from Murik to Drekikir. I enjoyed reading the conundrum of Markus Schindlbeck, also of the group. Imagine, he writes, standing on the edge of the busy bush market with a movie camera in hand, a still camera hung around the neck, a bulky tape recorder of those days with a couple of notebooks and a bilum for necessary things, and then trying to record what was there in front of you (Schindlbeck 1980). Trying to get the whole story was no easy thing. Today a mobile touchscreen telephone might be able to do it all.

Jürg Wassmann took on the task of translating texts used for songs in initiation times, and the quotation given at the start is from a marvellously detailed and graphic portrayal of a resurrected initiation tradition in Kandingei village that took place over the new year period of 1973. The initiation myths tell of the first moments of creation by a crocodile, and this is related to the initiation marks of the boys. It is surely a very religious interpretation of the event, and Wassmann has done a great service to the *haus tambaran* (spirit house) of the Sepik by setting this down.

My own fieldwork followed a different program. For the first five years I was listening to stories of the village traditions and classifying the results according to a church schedule. I was living in the villages about 30% of the time, and the rest of the time was playing a role in the broader community. With the religious sisters we would conduct regular discussions with the men and women, and then we expatriates would come back home and try to recognize the cargo cult filter – "if we said we had an important announcement and they showed they took it as a long-awaited revelation, then what did they hear us say? And if they asked where money came from and we fatuously told them the story of the mint, then what were they saying to us?" This could have been taken as a sign of distrust and miscommunication on both sides, but we thought we had the option to see it as a simple and useful index of cultural difference.

In the following I will present my on-going fieldwork, especially my pursuit of initiation traditions in a few cultures. At first I will present how my eyes were opened to the traces of the religious tradition in Yangoru area behind the coastal mountains of East Sepik Province, where explicit rituals seemed dormant. This rather much climaxed in a year living in three villages in this area, doing my doctorate work for the Religious Studies Department of Sydney University, and looking for stories of the local "cargo cult" against its background in traditional village religion (Gesch 1985). My story will then pass to Madang where I came in contact with communities of the Sawos speaking peoples whose home is just north of the Sepik River. On the strength of these contacts I paid frequent extended visits to the Sawos villages. In 1999 I decided to enter personally into the scarification of the Sepik *haus tambaran* in the hope of sharing the emic viewpoint on this. While in Madang I also took advantage of being there by doing research on an exchange festival and the initiation ceremonies of local villages of the Bel language group. I will then draw conclusions about the religious nature of initiation, as I see it, a form of conversion of life. I will conclude by outlining the functions all this fieldwork served for me.

Pursuing initiation in Yangoru

My interest remained strong in the topic of initiation. For the men of Yangoru, this had died out at least forty years before my arrival. The catechist, Otto Boyu, a reflective and authoritative man, said that, when the rumours of the New Time were coming over the mountains in 1910 (Höltker 1940) then the initiation tradition ceased. This seemed to me to establish a close link between the purpose of the initiation and the New Time. The *hwelempo*, as the spirit house is called in Yangoru, ceremonies were to make competent men, able to handle themselves and the needs of the village in all kinds of circumstances and to direct the customs of the past to the ways of life. If the New Time made the men feel they were lacking mastery, or simply were in awe of what others were doing, then it was time to take a pause in initiation. It was time to accept the leadership of various ritual inventors. Trying to reconstruct the initiation was difficult, although there were a few senior men who had been through a version of the ceremony. Roscoe was more successful than I in drawing up a coherent account of the tradition (1990).

However, remarkably, the women's initiation underwent a revival in Negrie while I was there. Although I showed that I welcomed the revival with great interest, of course I had no role in the revival, about which I knew nothing, but my interest seemed to serve a social purpose. When a girl of a clan group had her first menstruation, she would be enclosed in a hut for five days and come out with great ceremony (Camp 1979). The neighbouring communities would stand on the mountain tops all around and sing in her direction all the nights of the sequestration. It involved the whole surrounding set of communities to honor and admonish this young girl.

At the same time, I gained admission, with considerable difficulty, to the initiation ceremonies of Kiniambu village, who were part of Negrie parish and were outlying speakers of the Yangoru dialect. In the first instance, the catechist let the cat out of the bag, that an initiation ceremony was about to take place. He was led to vehemently deny this information in a short time. I had been deceived and must not come to the village at this time. What was the problem? First someone discreetly pointed to his male member—there was a penis operation involved (consisting of breaking upwards the glans of the penis by the insertion of a cassowary bone into the urethra) which I was not expected to approve of. Then secondly came the story of one of my predecessors as parish priest. When he heard that the village had held a ceremony, he raised a statue of the Virgin Mary, challenged the leaders with "Who started this ceremony? Who? Who?" Then he threw the statue onto the leg of a big man and broke it. He stalked off the five hours of walking back to Negrie. In the following week, three children of the village died. Therefore, I was not welcome to come close to the ceremony. Somehow I talked my way into that one. There were six stages of initiation at Kiniambu together with a number of similar intermediate ceremonies, and I was able to stay close to those events. I did not hear of any evil consequences from this, attributed to my presence.

My fieldwork in Negrie was thus less than full immersion, but it was spread out over a long period (1973 – 1983). I was granted ready access to any kinds of ceremonies, but definitely enjoyed this access on the basis of being eager to learn of the culture. One of my priestly elders said to me eventually, "You give the people nothing to hold on to. You *ask* people about their customs." He meant that I was not doing enough catechetical instruction, and that because I was asking, I was approving the traditions, which were often associated with the old ways identified by St Paul in the New Testament as darkness. When I found out about the Omaha kinship system giving form to the marriage and exchange traditions of much of the East Sepik Province, I made a delivery on the matter to my priestly elders. One said to me in response, "If this were true, we would have heard about it from Fr. X and Fr. Y a long time ago." The Omaha system was the background of Bateson's *Naven* (1936), and it has been made explicit in many publications since then, such as Korn (1971).

After my first five years in Negrie, it seemed to be the agreed time to go for further studies. I went to Sydney University to the Religious Studies department, where my doctoral supervisor was Dr Garry Trompf, who had considerable experience in PNG. Part of my three years of studies was the expectation that I would go back to Negrie and sit down in the villages for a year, the actual anthropologist's initiation in the form of fieldwork.

Participant observation: A year in three villages

I returned to Negrie in mid-1980 and spent equal amounts of time in three villages, knowing that they had been very active in the Movement some ten years earlier. My fieldwork was made easy by residing with families that I already knew, sharing board and lodging with no special effort at rewarding them, and going round the villages. At the beginning of 1973 the Summer Institute of Linguistics representative, Allen Freudenburg, was ready to share his first grammar of the Yangoru-Boiken language and various published short texts of the Bible and texts on local culture (1979). This was a great help to me to make progress in learning the language. I had some good young teachers, and managed to preach a sermon in the local language, but generally could not join in ordinary conversation. My language ability was useful for technical knowledge.

Still in those years (1980-1981) it was possible to see evidence of the "cargo cult" movement. This was not a description accepted by participants in the movement, and I see no reason to force them to accept it, so I adopted the name of Mt Hurun Movement to cover the ritual aspects of this on-going event. This Movement began on 7/7/71 with the taking out of a cement survey marker placed in the top of Mt Hurun in 1962. The expectation had been that a great outpouring of wealth and Western goods would follow (Roscoe 1988).

There was still evidence in Malimbanja village of the incoming flood of enthusiastic members from ESP and further afield who came and built bush material houses. There was the "blue house," a permanent materials house on the top of a hill where the leaders had their offices. One of the main leaders started a utopian commune some kilometres away, along the Sepik Highway. And one afternoon as I was sitting not far from my residential house in the village in 1980, I was informed that when I had made my departure, there would be a "paitim dis" (Tok Pisin: shake the dishes) ceremony. This consisted of boys and girls pairing off in little booths where they would tip K10 worth of coins repeatedly back and forth between dishes, as had already been photographed by *National Geographic* magazine (Kirk 1973). There would be a loud rattling metallic sound and the recount of the money would yield a certain increase. In general, however, there were no more rituals of the

Movement, only stories that could be recounted by everyone in the villages.

In this context I can comment that finding new and thought-provoking information was a feature of this fieldwork phase. I combined the research question of what happened in the Mt Hurun Movement with the more general question of traditional village religion. But it was a time when everyone had a story to tell; the cultural life of the village was on display many days; and the ritual aspect of life was always a topic for observation and enquiry. This was so much in contrast with my six months of fieldwork later in Yamuk village in the Sawos-speaking community where there was little provocation to storytelling. It could be that Yangoru is so much more densely settled that a lot more different communities and individuals were available for observation and interview. It could be that Yamuk simply encountered an event-free season when I was there. There was active opposition to myth-telling at that time. My own private little theory on this is that "cargo cult" is an assay by the tradition into the modern world. It is an attempt to put forth a new idea in answer to the questions of "How do the white people do it? How do we get it all to work for us?" Therefore, everyone had a story to tell me. You are lucky to meet a culture in its new religious movement phase.

In the three villages where I stayed for this year, my hosts were always my best informants. They would let me know when things were going to happen and gave me the comfort of walking together to the events and gatherings. This might be tautologous in the sense that I chose to ask people for residence because they had already showed themselves willing to help me.

Fieldwork in the settlements

After taking care of my doctorate presentation, I returned to Negrie for a year but then heard the call of Divine Word University in Madang. It was there at last that I found the Sepik River communities and the initiation ceremonies I had been expecting. For eighteen years I looked after an urban parish in Madang called Sisiak which was an official squatter settlement with minimal infrastructure. In that time I sought out regular contact with men from villages of the Burui LLG located just off the

Sepik River, in particular from Yanket, Yamuk and Marap. They were visible, with scarification in the form of a crocodile skin cut into their backs. They told stories of seeking out crocodiles, eating them or wrestling with them. When I showed myself too eager for ever more stories I was told, "Oh it's not such a big thing. Pukpuk em i man tasol" ("a crocodile is just like a human"). Which I take to mean that crocodiles are really only proportionate in strength to men of the same size.

The first leaders I followed were men with initiation marks from Yanket village. I went down and stayed six weeks at a time at the end of my teaching year in Madang. But it eventually became clear that there would be no more initiation in Yanket for a long time, because some years earlier an initiate had bled to death. Presumably he was a haemophiliac. On the basis of friendships and acquaintances formed in Sisiak I transferred my attentions to Yamuk, taking whatever chances I had to go there also for a number of weeks at a time at the end of the year. This was the time of the year for initiation ceremonies, when the schooling was out. The whole area was much taken up with initiation and one year I heard reports of ten initiation enclosures being conducted at the same time within easy traveling distance. Yamuk is formed from seven sub-communities and one or two of those sub-communities would have an enclosure every year. Though I was known locally as the visiting Catholic priest in Yamuk which had a long history of association with the Church, it was again not simple for me to gain admission to the enclosure. From my house of residence, I sent a message that I would like to come in to the enclosure and observe the ceremonies but I was not able to pay any large sum of money. I was told to wait a couple of days, as my friends pursued the discussion in the *haus tambaran*. There was a chance to contribute a small payment for kerosene and food for the running of the enclosure, so I did that and was allowed in.

I went with the villagers to the neighboring villages of Korogo, Slai, Miempe and Marap and observed initiations there. Since enclosures lasted about three months, there was a difficulty in seeing ceremonies to their end, but in a non-systematic way I was able to attend a number of closing ceremonies in various villages. I was able to visit Gaikorobi, where Markus Schindlbeck had performed his research and view localities which featured in his report. The stories in Yamuk were as freely flowing as in Negrie previously, but this time the topic of conversation was the active ritual going on or being planned. Some mythical stories were told, and I drew up accounts of the religious identities representing the structure and institutions of the village. This was done by calling the spirit names of totemic animals and plants, of slit drums, of spears and of various implements and positions within the *haus tambaran*. Also frequently I would encounter discussions about *sanguma* (Tok Pisin: witchcraft).

My experience of going repeatedly from Madang to the Sepik Sawos villages lasted over the course of years from 1984 to 2009. In 1999 I decided I should undergo the initiation ceremony of scarification. On the one hand, after viewing about a dozen ceremonies I felt too much like a voyeur of other people's pain and nakedness. On the other hand, I thought it would be a chance to get an insider's point of view on the ceremonies. My chance arose when the Marap community of Madang decided they had enough big men and managers to run their own initiation. The fact that this was only a kilometer from the Madang General Hospital and my own home was not lost on me. I can say that the cutting was about as much pain as a person could voluntarily endure - 1,500 cuts back and front over the skin with a razor blade. This, despite chanted assistance which other initiates say had the effect of putting them to sleep during the operation. The rites concluded with my giving a big pig, which was the right thing to do. I say that the badge I have acquired has been worth my while in becoming a Sepik identity in some areas. Did I get a better insider's point of view? No, I had observed it all before. Translations of texts, as was done by Jürg Wassmann in Kandingei would have revealed more.

From 2010 I went to live in Wewak for four years and decided to conclude my stay there with a visit to Yamuk, doing research on *sanguma* over a six-month period. A Yamuk friend from Madang was ready to host me and to accompany me. But this was a difficult period of fieldwork. There were no major illnesses in the village and no deaths to provide occasion for participation in village interpretations of *sanguma* as an on-going drama. My friend told me that the men I interviewed were saying, "Just talk superficially about the matter."

So what went wrong when I took those six months in 2013 to live in Yamuk to research *sanguma*? I was given a push away. At first, since it seemed to me that I was after a structural knowledge of *sanguma*, how it works and what it is all about, the idea of conducting interviews with a series of big men surrounded by hangers-on seemed sufficient. My assistant wanted more details on who and when and why. But by the end of my time, it seemed that interviews were a very poor substitute for engaging in the unfolding drama of an accusation of *sanguma*. My understanding is that *sanguma* gains its power by talking: serious accusations, the unfolding of hostilities, the threat of revenge attacks and the misery of serious, long-lasting sickness. In the six months of 2013 there was no report of a serious or long lasting illness and no death occurred, apart from that of an old lady who was allowed to complete her life in peace. Nor could I elicit a small fraction of the mythical stories gained by Schindlbeck in nearby Gaikorobi. Finally, some big men of the church had promised me some family totemic stories, but by the time of the telling had decided they had no stories to tell. A young man with me commented, "It looks like time to go." Yes, it was time to give up, which does after all belong to the ethics of research, to allow participants to withdraw whenever they like. I will give Yamuk a rest for a while and return after some years. My contact with them has been over a thirty-year period, and relations with the village continue through some Yamuk families in Madang. I am not likely to miss out on hearing about much that is going on.

The change to Madang

There seemed to me to be a moral obligation to do research in Madang, especially now from a perspective of living here for the last thirty years. Again, I was grateful to be able to approach the cultural events of Madang through my position with the Church, in Riwo, Malmal and Rempi. I was able to follow some *suabul* (a 10-meter-tall diamond shaped display and exchange of packets of food containing sago and galip nuts), which do not seem to have continued after the events of 25 years ago. There were a few initiation ceremonies in the *mulung* (bush enclosure for male initiations) but I was not given access to the full doing of the ceremonies themselves. Two older men took me aside and regularly informed me of all the background of the initiation ceremonies and village rituals. We had a lasting series of discussions together, but they frequently said to me, "You are not allowed to publish any of this." Eventually after one of the two had died, I received a letter while in Germany from a son of the other leader. The letter indicated that the elder felt he was in his last days, and he now granted permission for publication. While I appreciate the action, I have not had the heart to revisit the cold material, and I am sure it would take more consent from the present community to allow general publication. We have all moved on. Nevertheless, I have been invited to go inside the *mulung* and talk to the boys already incised and recuperating in Riwo and Malmal. My presentation to them was always on the expectation that there must be a serious change in their lives.

In 1983 there were at least five villages in the Bel language area around the town of Madang who were having initiation ceremonies for which I went to observe the coming-out ceremonies. These events were very popular with the Sepik youth of town, who often had the idea that a dorsal slit would bring about a desirable increase to the size of their male member. Many Sepik youths of the settlements and the University were doing private versions of this incision. They would typically go down to a private section of the reef foreshore of Madang, armed with razor, some bandages and amoxicillin. One Yangoru student told me mischievously, "I have cut 18 boys, and I am not cut myself." The Sepik youth would claim that this was a traditional initiation from Sepik and they get some measure of support from the older men, but that seems unlikely to me to have been the case for many.

Initiation as religious

With some justification the early missionaries targeted initiation ceremonies in the Sepik region as an opponent to Christian preaching. One German missionary in the Wosera was an agent in causing the destruction of an initiation enclosure, and was taken to court for this. He had to be defended by an Australian Queen's Counsel at great expense, and was eventually cleared because he was not the one who actually handled the axe. Another American missionary in Yangoru discussed the matter with his trusted catechist, who took the initiative of raising his hand to prophesy that this spirit house would not arise. That was the end of the cultural houses in Yangoru. Given that Catholic missionaries themselves belong to a tradition of initiation experiences, what was the precise objection? An answer I received a number of times to this question was the Bible quotation of the First Commandment, "I am the Lord your God. You will not have other gods before me." I responded by saying that I did not see the presence of spirits or images as up front and centre at the time of initiation ceremonies, although the poverty of my language kills was an obvious difficulty here.

The quotation from Jürg Wassmann at the beginning of this essay is a reference to the important role played by religious figures at the time of Sepik initiation. The primeval crocodile divided in two halves, the upper and lower, to provide for the world. By thrashing in the mud down below, all things were created, humans, animals and all other things. The ancestors of the initiates were part of that scene, and now an initiation makes the act of creation real for all the youths—a powerful thing, which should change them from being little boys without their own decisions for life. As such, Christian missionaries might be concerned with a rival creator spirit and a rival creation account. It seems there are two basic responses possible: either one might say, clear out the old and replace it with the new; or one might say, we are thinking along the same lines and religious dependence is the main message in the accounts from Genesis or from Sepik.

There are a number of other ways by which the religious nature of initiation might be recognized. Both in the Old Testament and New Testament of the Bible, the notion of conversion is taken as a key event. Jacob/Israel is attributed with a key conversion by wrestling with an angel and changing his life. No less is Paul of Tarsus a leading religious person who changed his whole orientation of life. I once asked the leaders of the *haus tambaran* in Yamuk: "Do you expect the boys to change with these ceremonies?" Their answer was, "Of course. Why else would we do all this?" The boys are like baby crocodiles coming new born out of eggs. They must be looked after and guided. It should be said then that the nature of initiation is religious primarily because it involves a change in personality and a change in spiritual life, which happens to a person, in the person, but not simply by the person.

Another important idea of religion here is the presentation of knowledge and development as transcendental. This is a word that implies that what is achieved points beyond itself and implies a fulfilment yet to come. A key developer of this theme was Frederik Barth (1975) with his "turnings" in the initiation of the Baktaman. With seven steps in the *haus tambaran*, each level of knowledge and revelation to the initiates was presented with its gainsaying in the next level. Knowledge is always partial and leading to a new framework of knowledge. While this works better in a six step imitation such as that of Kiniambu, it is also a factor for the *baandi* (initiates) in the Sepik River, who are still dependent on their *nyamun* and *alimbandi* (higher grade initiates and experts) as organizers of the *haus tambaran* and resident authorities.

It has long seemed to me that the practice of traditional initiation, in all its forms – for men or for women, for widow's mourning ceremonies or for birth ceremonies – makes a worthy and highly valued cultural attribute for believing Christians. In such a matter it would be a pity to be guided by doctrine meant for elsewhere or a foreign cultural viewpoint. Fieldwork is needed, the full contextual life of the ritual and its derivatives and implications.

Conclusion: a certain type of fieldwork

This is my report on a certain type of fieldwork. As related by Nigel Barley in his *The Innocent Anthropologist: Notes from a Mud Hut* (1983), fieldwork can be at the same time a very exotic and a very boring experience; it can be full of the experiences of alienation and of surprising warmth and fellow-feeling. But it is the only way to get to understand another community of persons when the books and road signs are missing.

My fieldwork has been extended, an approach to multiple and differing communities, diachronic, privileged, a matter of full immersion and backgrounded. This all comes from pursuing an understanding of cultures as an academic, a priest and a long term resident in Papua New Guinea. In recent times I have followed derivative work from the pursuit of culture in doing a record of the national Elections in 2007 and 2012 for Yangoru-Saussia. I have also teamed up to look for the village's point of view on the Pacific Marine Industrial Zone coming to the village in Rempi (Madang). The pursuit of the topic of *sanguma* (witchcraft) has led me to fieldwork of a different kind, relying on reports from communities only lightly known to me first-hand.

What is it that I want to do with fieldwork? It is my wish to meet people, to understand what they are talking about, and why they are doing certain rituals which take up enormous efforts from small communities. Although I need an insight into what is going on, there is the need also, not to make too many basic mistakes. I want to be prepared for the kinds of answers I might get when I propose something as an idea or a project. The students before me in the classroom ask,

"How high?" when I say, "Jump!" but I still need to ask them what the right direction is for the jump and how to make the command communicate well. With my homilies in Church there is always the question of "What do I want to say to these people, here and at this time? Do I have something worth saying?" It is hard to speak to the people over against me without staying constantly in touch, asking for a lot of understanding and building on the shoulders of the giants of anthropology who have gone beforehand.

Note
1 From the viewpoint of the "ancient crocodiles"', the initiation is nothing less than making real now the originating events, i.e., the creation of the world, the coming to be of humans and all things, and indeed it is an indication that your own ancestors were taking a role in this creation.

References

Barley, N. 1983. *The Innocent Anthropologist. Notes from a Mud Hut*. London: Colonnade Books.

Barth, F. 1975. *Ritual and Knowledge among the Baktaman of New Guinea*. New Haven: Yale University Press.

Bateson, G. 1936. *Naven. A Survey of the Problems suggested by a Composite Picture of the Culture of a New Guinea Tribe drawn from Three Points of View*. Stanford: Stanford University Press.

Freudenburg, A. 1979. *Boiken Grammar*. Ukarumpa: Summer Institute of Linguistics.

Camp, C. 1979. A Female Initiation Rite in the Neigrie Area. In *Powers, Plumes and Piglets*, ed. N. Habel. Adelaide: AASR, pp. 68–83.

Gesch, P. F. 1985. *Initiative and Initiation. A Cargo Cult-Type Movement in the Sepik against its Background in Traditional Village Religion*. St Augustin, West Germany: Anthropos Institut.

Höltker, G. 1940. Verstreute ethnographische Notizen über Neuguinea. *Anthropos* 35: 1–67.

Kirk, M. S. 1973. Change Ripples New Guinea's Sepik River. *National Geographic* 144 (3): 354–381.

Korn, F. 1971. A Question of Preferences. The Iatmul Case. In *Rethinking Kinship and Marriage*, ed. R. Needham. London: Tavistock, pp. 99–132.

Lawrence, P. 1964. *Road Belong Cargo*. Melbourne: Melbourne University Press.

Roscoe, P. B. 1988. The Far Side of Hurun. The Management of Melanesian Millenarian Movements. *American Ethnologist* 15 (3): 515–529.

— 1990. Male Initiation among the Yangoru Boiken. In *Sepik Heritage. Tradition and Change in Papua New Guinea*, eds. N. Lutkehaus et al. Durham, North Carolina, pp. 402–413.

Schindlbeck, M. 1980. *Sago bei den Sawos (Mittelsepik, Papua New Guinea). Untersuchungen über die Bedeutung von Sago in Wirtschaft, Sozialordnung und Religion*. Basel: Ethnologisches Seminar der Universität und Museum für Völkerkunde. (Basler Beiträge zur Ethnologie Bd. 19).

Wassmann, J. 1987. Der Biss des Krokodils. Die ordnungsstiftende Funktion der Namen in der Bedeutung zwischen Mensch und Umwelt am Beispiel der Initiation, Nyaura, Mittel-Sepik. In *Neuguinea. Nutzung und Deutung der Umwelt* (Band 2), ed. M. Münzel. Frankfurt am Main: Museum für Völkerkunde, pp. 511–557. (Roter Faden zur Ausstellung 13).

GUNTER SENFT

4 The Coral Gardens are Losing Their Magic. The Social and Cultural Impact of Climate Change and Overpopulation for the Trobriand Islanders

Introduction[1]

Just after I had finished my PhD in linguistics at the Max Planck Institute for Psycholinguistics in 1981, I was invited to join an interdisciplinary research team consisting of an anthropologist, a human ethologist and a physician with ethological and anthropological interests to carry out a research project on "Ritual Communication on the Trobriand Islands of Papua New Guinea (PNG)" at the Human Ethology Research Unit of the Max Planck Institute for Behavioral Physiology in Seewiesen.[2] The Trobriand Islanders have become famous, even outside of anthropology, because of the ethnographic masterpieces on their culture published by the anthropologist Bronislaw Malinowski, who did field research there from June 1915 till February 1916 and from November 1917 till September 1918 (Young 2004). When I first set foot on the Trobriand Islands in 1982, I had the quite romantic feeling that I was stepping right into the picture so vividly presented in Bronislaw Malinowski's books and articles. And having arrived in Tauwema village on Kaile'una Island, I thought I had entered more of a kind of a South-Seas cliché than actual reality. And I started to understand what Robert Louis Stevenson may have meant when he wrote:

> The first experience can never be repeated. The first love, the first sunrise, the first South Sea Island are memories apart and touched by a virginity of sense (1896: 6).

My first two periods of field research on the Trobriand Islands lasted from July to December 1982 and, – after a 6 week break, from January to November 1983. During these two long-term field trips we experienced life on a South Sea island – with its dry and rainy seasons. In the rainy season it really rained cats and dogs and the humidity was extreme. The dry season was often quite hot, but with the trade winds blowing, life was quite comfortable. Thus, there was a clear division between the dry season and the rainy season. However, this changed dramatically in the first decade of this century – a change that was already foreshadowed in the mid-1990s. This paper deals with the dramatic environmental, social and cultural changes on the Trobriand Islands which I experienced during 16 long- and short-term fieldtrips from 1982 to 2012.[3]

I first report on the climate change I experienced there over the years and provide a survey about the demographic changes on the Trobriand Islands – highlighting the situation in Tauwema, my village of residence on Kaile'una Island. I will then report on the social and cultural impact these dramatic changes have had on the Trobriand Islanders and their culture.

But before I do this I will briefly introduce the Trobriand Islanders and their language:

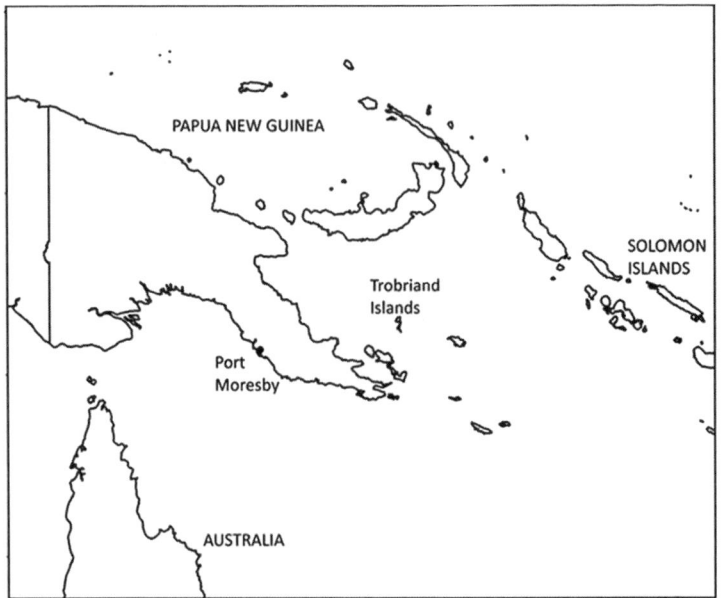

Figure 4.1: Papua New Guinea

The Trobriand Islands

The Trobriand Islanders belong to the ethnic group called "Northern Massim." They are gardeners, practicing slash and burn cultivation of the bush; their most important crop is yams (*Dioscorea esculenta*). Moreover, they are also famous for being excellent canoe builders, carvers, and navigators, especially in connection with the ritualized *Kula* trade, an exchange of shell valuables that covers a wide area of the Melanesian part of the Pacific (see Malinowski 1922; Leach and Leach 1983; Persson 1999). The society is matrilineal but virilocal.

Figure 4.2: The Trobriand Islands

Kilivila, the language of the Trobriand Islanders, is one of 40 Austronesian languages spoken in the Milne Bay Province of Papua New Guinea (see figure 4.1 and 4.2). It is an agglutinative language; the most frequent word order pattern is SVO, but its general, unmarked word order pattern is VOS (Senft 1986). The Austronesian languages spoken in Milne Bay Province are grouped into 12 language families; one of them is labeled Kilivila. The Kilivila language family encompasses the languages Budibud (or Nada, with about 200 speakers living on Budibud Island), Muyuw (or Murua, with about 4,000 speakers living on

Woodlark Island) and Kilivila (or Kiriwina, Boyowa, with about 28,000 speakers; but see below). Kilivila is spoken on the islands Kiriwina, Vakuta, Kitava, Kaile'una, Kuiawa, Munuwata and Simsim. The languages Muyuw and Kilivila are split into mutually understandable local dialects. Typologically, Kilivila is classified as a Western Melanesian Oceanic language belonging to the Papuan-Tip-Cluster group (Senft 1986: 6).

Climate and demographic change experienced between 1982 and 2012

As mentioned above, from the mid-1990s on the dry season was more and more interrupted by rains that in the course of time became heavier and heavier. This was an additional challenge to me and my equipment, like for example my solar cells which provided the energy necessary to run my laptop, my video-camera and my tape-recorders. It was also a challenge for the sun which could no longer bleach coral stone walls any more, walls which were full of moss, lichen and other plants providing a nice biotope for many smaller and some bigger insects. But it was a disaster for the Trobriand Islanders' gardens because yam seedlings and taro plants started to rot away in a soil much too wet and in many places even swampy. This resulted in bad harvests that over the years became so bad that they have been endangering food security on the Trobriand Islands – islands that formerly had been famous for their surplus production of garden products, especially yams. Based on a study by Jane Nancy O'Sullivan which was published in 2008, Michelle MacCarthy pointed out that

> [o]n Kiriwina, the proportion of yams used for gifts or communal meals (feasts) is estimated from survey data at 60-80 percent, with relatively little retained for personal use (…). When necessity demands it, however, it can also be treated as a commodity (…). On average about 5-10 percent of an annual harvest will be sold (2012: 137).

I will come back to this point below. However, I first want to mention that there has been yet another heavy blow to food security on the Trobriand Islands, namely overpopulation.

When I started my field research in 1982, Tauwema had 239 inhabitants. In 1989 my wife and I counted 277 inhabitants. Fifteen years later 550 people lived in Tauwema and in 2012 the village had more than 620 inhabitants. This means that there was an increase in the village population of 258 % within 30 years. This demographic observation is supported by data on the increase of population on all of the Trobriand Islands. In 2008 it was officially announced that 28,784 people live on 321 ha land.[4] However, an unofficial estimate which is based on the 2010 PNG census mentions approximately 40,000 inhabitants on the Trobriand Islands.

This population explosion is not just a local, but a nationwide phenomenon: The first official PNG census from 1970 lists a population of 2.2 million people. The Post Courier, one of the national newspapers of PNG, came out on the 4th of April 2012 with the headline: "Population of PNG is more than 7 million." This means that there was an almost threefold increase in the national population within 40 years (see Kenneth 2012; see also Jarillo de la Torre 2013: 186).

But back to the Trobriand Islands and to reasons for the overpopulation there. First of all, there was a decline in infant mortality on the islands, despite the fact that ever since 1982 the medical care on the Trobriand Islands has been very basic (to say the least). The increase of the island population is also due to the abandonment of the traditional *post partum* sex taboo which prescribed sexual abstinence for mothers until their children could walk (Malinowski 1929: 197).

However, I assume that the most important reason for the present overpopulation is the fact that the Trobriand Islanders neither use traditional forms of family planning anymore, nor do they use modern contraceptives, mainly due to the fact that they are not regularly available everywhere. Traditional forms of family planning do not play any role whatsoever these days, because the local Trobriand missionaries, the "*misinari*" finally won their fight against the "*tomegwa*" – the magicians who knew the recipe for making a contraceptive from a mixture of herbs (for details see Senft 2011: 33-34).

The Trobriand Islanders' society was strictly hierarchically differentiated into four clans. Members of the two lower clans had no chance to exert political influence on societal life on the islands. However, in recent years local missionaries, priests or catechists (*misinari*) have gained more and more status. Most of these *misinari* are members of the two lower clans with little prestige. Magicians are the antagonists of the *misinari*. Since 1989 the *misinari* have been pointing out that there are two ways for living one's life: either the traditional Trobriand life with its beliefs in magic and in the spirits of the dead, or the life with "*Yesu Keriso*" – with Jesus Christ – as a faithful member of (one of) his church(es). These ways were said to be mutually exclusive. This resulted in tensions in families, especially when the husband was a magician and the wife a catechist (or vice versa). The increasing influence of the *misinari* is responsible for the fact that magicians (be they men or women) have lost their political and societal influence. The respect for their magical abilities and their knowledge of the magic with which the Trobriand Islanders formerly believed to control nature, their environment and their society was lost. The magicians, having lost their influence and status in the Trobriand society, could not find apprentices anymore and their maternal relatives were no longer interested in inheriting their skills. Thus, their knowledge, including their biomedical knowledge was lost (see Senft 1997, 2010).

The social and cultural impact of these changes for the Trobriand Islanders

The Trobriand archipelago consists of islands. The Trobriand Islanders are gardeners. The land mass available for gardens is finite. The more people living on the Trobriand Islands the less land is available for gardening. It is obvious that these insights are trivial, but they have terribly severe consequences.

Ever since the turn of the century the bush has been cultivated much more often than before. The fallow period after the slash and burn cultivation to turn bushland into garden land which was then used for two or three years dropped dramatically from six years or more to three or, especially on Kiriwina, even to two years (see Risimeri 2000; O'Sullivan 2008, 2010; MacCarthy 2012; Jarillo de la Torre 2013). This resulted in an impoverishment of soil fertility with the consequence not only of poorer harvests, but also of deforestation. In the long run, this deforestation will result in a shortage of wood, one of the important, if not the most essential resource for the Trobriand Islanders. Wood and timber are not only used as building materials for houses, yams houses, garden sheds, canoes, paddles, masts, tools, furniture and what have you, but also as firewood.

In addition, there has been an obvious rise of the sea level, and the stronger and heavier breakers at high tide have already washed away many sandy beaches like the one of Tauwema, leaving nothing more than the naked coral stone.

Now what about the social and cultural impact of all these dramatic changes for the Trobriand Islanders? Ever since Malinowski we know that

> [t]aytu, the staple food, is to the natives *kaulo*, a vegetable food par excellence, and it comes into prominence at harvest and after. This is the sheet-anchor of prosperity, the symbol of plenty, *malia*, and the main source for native wealth (1935: 81).

Annette Weiner pointed out that

> [t]he small *taytu* yam is both the basic subsistence food and the principal object of exchange. Yams in the latter category open the way to all other avenues of resource control. Kiriwina informants say, "If a man has yams, he can find anything else needed" (1976: 137).

This observation is impressively confirmed by MacCarthy (2012) and O'Sullivan (2008: 51 and 55), quoted above. And Jarillo de la Torre concisely summarizes the importance of yams as follows:

> As is well known, yams in the Trobriand Islands are not only food. They are mostly items of wealth and power (Weiner 1988: 95-96) laden with symbolism (Mosko 2009), associated to magic (Malinowski 1935: 153-154) and instrumental in underlining the social hierarchies and the value of individuals, clans and villages (Malinowski 1929: 442-443) (2013: 159).

The actual fabric of the Trobriand Islanders' social construction of reality (Berger and Luckmann 1966) was YAMS. They played the most prominent role in food exchange rituals, for example, in mourning rituals (Senft 1985) or in communal meals initiated by chiefs or other men of rank as gifts for their fellow villagers as a payment for their support in, e.g. the construction of a new *kula* canoe (see Senft 2016). These yam exchanges had an important bonding function not only for kinspeople, but also for fellow villagers who were members of other clans. Yams were the Trobriand valuta; even the paramount chief had to pay for everything he wanted like, e.g. a new yamshouse, a canoe, or a new village playground with yams.

With the present food security problems that led to a severe food shortage in 2008 which made Trobriand Islanders eat up many of their yams seedlings, which in turn resulted in an even worse food shortage problem in 2009, yams have lost their importance (see MacCarthy 2012: 141f.).

According to MacCarthy (2012), Jarillo de la Torre (2013: 17-23) and O'Sullivan (2008) the fact that yams on the Trobriand Islands have been losing their cultural impact in recent years has already had and continues to have severe consequences for the Trobriand Islanders' social construction of reality – at least on Kiriwina Island:

- Traditional ceremonies lose their importance.
- People steal yams, taro and other crops from the gardens, thus breaking a very severe taboo of old.
- People lose their interest in and their feelings of responsibility for their community.
- People rely more and more on their churches for things that the government and the chiefs of their villages cannot provide any more. They participate more in church activities, which unfortunately also keep them away from their gardens.
- The chiefs lose influence and power, having lost their yams valuta.
- People lose their interest in their gardens and in gardening because of a lack of available garden land and seeds as well as because of a lack of trust in the government and in the chiefs.
- There is a growing reliance on food, especially rice, that can be bought in the stores on the Trobriand Islands.
- The Trobriand Islanders are experiencing a dramatic and fatal loss of pride, self-respect and respect in their culture and tradition.

During my last field trip in 2012 I could not observe such food shortage problems and its consequences on Kaile'una Island, at least not in the villages Tauwema, Koma, Giwa and Kaduwaga. But according to Jarillo de la Torre (2013: 156) the death of a villager in Kaisiga was "followed by only one-off distribution of food" instead of many mortuary rites with many ceremonial food distributions. For Jarillo de la Torre this is the result of food shortage problems in the two villages in the south of Kaile'una, Kaisiga and Bulakwa. I am sure that these food problems will sooner or later reach all the other islands of the Trobriand archipelago – with all the dramatic consequences for the Trobriand Islanders' custom and culture mentioned above. The photographic evidence of the environmental and climate change which I presented in 2014 in a PowerPoint presentation on this topic (Senft 2014) confirms this pessimism. It seems that soon a full yams house will be a rather rare and quite amazing sight on the Trobriand Islands – and MacCarthy's (2012:146) prediction that "the empty yam house" will be a common feature of the Trobriand landscape will come true…

In lieu of concluding remarks

> for the times
> they are a-changin´
>
> The line it is drawn
> The curse it is cast
> The slow one now
> Will later be fast
> As the present now
> Will later be past
> The order is
> Rapidly fadin´
> (Bob Dylan)

Notes
1 This paper is dedicated to my old friend and dear colleague Jürg Wassmann.
2 The applicants for this research project which was funded by the German Research Society (DFG) were Irenäus Eibl-Eibesfeldt, Volker Heeschen and Wulf Schiefenhövel. The team that did field research on the Trobriand Islands over different periods of time consisted of the anthropologist Ingrid Bell-Krannhals, the ethologist Irenäus Eibl-Eibesfeldt, the medical anthropologist Wulf Schiefenhövel and me. In 1983 my wife joined our team and lived with me on the Trobriand Islands. Our village of residence was Tauwema on Kaile'una Island.

3   After my long-term field trips in 1982 and 1983 I continued to do field research (which was sponsored by another DFG grant) in 1989 and stayed with my family for 4 months in Tauwema. In 1991 I left the MPI in Seewiesen and joined Stephen Levinson's Cognitive Anthropology Research Group (now the Department of Language and Cognition) at the MPI for Psycholinguistics in Nijmegen and continued to do field research on the Trobriand Islands in 1992 (3 months), 1993 (2 months), 1994 (2 months), 1995 (2 months), 1996 (2 months), 1997 (2 months), 1998 (2 months), 2001 (2 months), 2003 (1 month), 2004 (2 months), 2006 (1 month), 2008 (2 months) and 2012 (2 months). Besides the DFG and the Max Planck Society who financed my research, I want to thank the National and Provincial Governments in Papua New Guinea, the Institute for PNG Studies – especially Don Niles, and the National Research Institute – especially James Robins, for their assistance with and permission for my research projects. I express my great gratitude to the people of the Trobriand Islands, and above all the inhabitants of Tauwema and my consultants for their hospitality, friendship, and patient cooperation over all these years. Without their help, none of my work on the Kilivila language and the Trobriand culture would have been possible.

4   These data were displayed on a sign in front of the island administration in Losuia on Kiriwina Island.

References

Berger, P. L., and T. Luckmann 1966. *The Social Construction of Reality. A Treatise in the Sociology of Knowledge*. New York: Doubleday.

Jarillo de la Torre, S. 2013. *Carving the Spirits of the Wood. An Enquiry into Trobriand Materialisations*. PhD Thesis. University of Cambridge: Social Anthropology Section.

Kenneth, G. 2012. Population of PNG is More than 7 Million. *Post Courier*, 4th of April, 2012.

Leach, J. W., and E. R. Leach (eds.) 1983. *The Kula. New Perspectives on Massim Exchange*. Cambridge: Cambridge University Press.

MacCarthy, M. 2012. Playing Politics with Yams. Food Security in the Trobriand Islands of Papua New Guinea. *Culture, Agriculture, Food and Environment* 34: 136–147.

Malinowski, B. 1922. *Argonauts of the Western Pacific. An Account of Native Enterprise and Adventure in the Archipelagoes of Melanesian New Guinea*. London: Routledge.

— 1929. *The Sexual Life of Savages in North-Western Melanesia*. London: Routledge.

— 1935. *Coral Gardens and their Magic* (Vol. I). The Description of Gardening. London: George Allen and Unwin.
Mosko, M. 2009. The Fractal Yam. Botanical Imagery and Human Agency in the Trobriands. *The Journal of the Royal Anthropological Institute* 15: 679–700.
O'Sullivan, J. N. 2008. *Yam Nutrition and Soil Fertility Management in the Pacific*. Canberra: Australian Centre for International Agricultural Research.
— 2010. *Yam Nutrition. Nutrient Disorders and Soil Fertility Management*. Canberra: Australian Centre for International Agricultural Research.
Persson, J. 1999. *Sagali and the Kula. A Regional System Analysis of the Massim.* Lund: Department of Sociology, Lund University. (Lund Monographs in Social Anthropology, Vol. 7).
Risimeri, J. B. 2000. Yams and Food Security in the Lowlands of PNG. In *Food Security for Papua New Guinea* (Proceedings of the Papua New Guinea Food and Nutrition 2000 Conference, PNG University of Technology, Lae, 26–30 June 2000), eds. R. M. Bourke, M. Allen, and J. Salisbury. Canberra: Australian Centre of International Cultural Research Proceedings No. 99, pp. 768–774.
Senft, G. 1985. Trauer auf Trobriand. Eine ethnologisch/linguistische Fallstudie. *Anthropos* 80: 471–492.
— 1986. *Kilivila. The Language of the Trobriand Islanders*. Berlin: Mouton de Gruyter.
— 1997. Magic, Missionaries, and Religion. Some Observations from the Trobriand Islands. In *Cultural Dynamics of Religious Change in Oceania*, eds. T. Otto and A. Borsboom. Leiden: KITLV press, pp. 45–58.
— 2010. Culture Change. Language Change. Missionaries and Moribund Varieties of Kilivila. In *Endangered Austronesian and Australian Aboriginal Languages. Essays on Language Documentation, Archiving, and Revitalization*, ed. G. Senft. Canberra: Pacific Linguistics, pp. 69–95.
— 2011. *The Tuma Underworld of Love. Erotic and Other Narrative Songs of the Trobriand Islanders and their Spirits of the Dead*. Amsterdam: John Benjamins.
— 2014. *The Coral Gardens are Losing their Magic. The Social Impact of Climate Change and Overpopulation for the Trobriand Islanders*. Invited Talk (Power Point Presentation) presented at "The Social Impacts of Climate Change. An Interactive Problem-based Workshop hosted by the European Consortium for Pacific Studies (ECOPAS) at the Center for Pacific and Asian Studies, Radboud University. Nijmegen. 9th of April 2014 – 10th of April 2014. [Downloadable at:
http://pubman.mpdl.mpg.de/pubman/item/escidoc:1989770:4/component/esci doc:200 7701/Climate_Change.pdf]

Senft, G. 2016. "*Masawa* – bogeokwa si tuta!" Cultural and Cognitive Implications of the Trobriand Islanders' Gradual Loss of their Knowledge of How to Make a *masawa* Canoe. In *Ethnic and Cultural Dimensions of Knowledge*, eds. P. Meusburger. T. Freytag, and L. Suarsana. Heidelberg: Springer, pp. 229–256.

Stevenson, R. L. 1896. *In the South Seas*. New Introduction by Jeremy Treglown. 1987 Edition. London: Hogarth Press Chatto and Windus.

Weiner A. B. 1976. *Women of Value, Men of Renown. New Perspectives in Trobriand Exchange*. Austin: University of Texas Press.

— 1988. *The Trobriand Islanders of Papua New Guinea*. New York: Holt, Rinehart and Winston.

Young, M. 2004. *Malinowski. Odyssey of an Anthropologist 1884-1920* (Vol. 1). New Haven and London: Yale University Press.

ANTJE DENNER

5 Group Dialogues, Videos and Multilocality in Researching Rituals

Introduction

Anir: a small island group in the Bismarck Archipelago in the blue and turquoise vastness of the Pacific Ocean and the site of the fieldwork on which my doctoral thesis (Denner 2010a, 2012) was based. On my first visit in 2000, I was able to fly in by plane but shortly afterwards the air service was discontinued because it was not profitable enough. From then on transport to and from Namatanai, the nearest town on the east coast of central New Ireland, was limited to small fibreglass outboard vessels. They ran irregularly and – depending on the power of the motor, swells and winds, how heavily the boat was loaded and whether the operators were prepared to speed or not (in view of the fuel costs) – the journey could take anything from five to ten hours. The Anir Islands are remote and the roughly 3,000 people living there call them *las ailand* in Tok Pisin (Papua New Guinea's lingua franca), that is, "last island(s)".[1] The place is also very beautiful – an icon of what stressed-out "Westerners" imagine when they dream of a tropical retreat in the South Seas. The remoteness and beauty go hand in hand with an almost complete absence of introduced building materials, sealed roads, cars, traffic, and, of course, industry.

The very "traditional-looking" settlements with their "bush houses" on the beach and the surrounding palm groves and subsistence gardens imply an equally "traditional" culture, a face-to-face society, and a form of fieldwork that closely corresponds to what has been called the classical or archetypical Malinowskian paradigm of ethnographic research.[2] Indeed, my fieldwork covered practically all the characteristics of this image: I went far away to an "exotic place" to immerse myself (alone) for a long period of time (altogether two years) in a "village" (see

A. von Poser, this volume) to observe and participate in the life of its small-scale community and investigate its beliefs, ritual system and arts.

Not long before I set out on my fieldwork venture, Gupta and Ferguson (1997) pointed out in their often-cited article *Discipline and Practice: "The Field" as Site, Method, and Location in Anthropology* that, although the archetypical Malinowskian image was "often invoked ironically and parodically," this did not mean that it had become an anachronism. Rather, notions of the "real anthropologist" as "real fieldworker" were still deep-seated, ineffable and pervasive (1997:11). In the following years I experienced both sides of what Gupta and Ferguson had meant. On the one hand, the irony of finding myself in situations in which I had to defend my "old-fashioned" research topic of ritual art, and my choice to do fieldwork in a remote location, against critical counterparts engaged in more "contemporary" and "topical" fields such as urban or diaspora studies, and/or colleagues who were investigating or making use of digital and social media.[3] On the other hand, there was the support and appreciation of colleagues who thought highly of my work and for whom I qualified as a good, a "real" anthropologist.

None of the authors I consulted renounce the idea of fieldwork as such, but all prompt us to critically reflect on its conventional construction and the methodologies it involves. And they ask us to examine the role and nature of fieldwork in relation to anthropology as a discipline, that is, its identity-defining, symbolic character and its ideological implications. Critical reviews of fieldwork typically trace changes with regard to research topics, approaches and fieldwork sites. In the process they provide examples of the manifold and heterodox paths anthropologists have taken to depart from the conventions of the canonical Malinowskian model, highlighting aspects such as multi-sited fieldwork in the era of globalization (see Walda-Mandel, this volume), the influence of new technologies and social media, multivocality and multiple subjectivity in view of changing attitudes regarding the relationship between researchers and their respondents, and the significance of experience, immersion, the body and the senses.[4]

James Faubion (2009: 162) assumes that "the anthropological (field) project of the future (…) may well end up looking in fact much as it has looked for several decades." My own fieldwork – as probably many others presently being undertaken in remote areas of the Pacific – at first sight looks quite traditional. In the following I wish to review two aspects of it – engaging Anir islanders in multiple dialogues and the use of videos – to ascertain how they contributed to make my fieldwork an example of up-to-date anthropological research.

Multivocality and focus groups

Having studied in the 1990s, I was, of course, very aware of the Writing Culture debate and the reflexive turn that had taken place within cultural anthropology, that is, with regard to issues such as multivocality and representation. Consequently, going into the field, I did not want to focus or rely upon a single or small number of "key informants." Rather, I intended to establish committed relationships with people from more than one local community to avoid ending up with the views and voices of only a few senior (male) ritual leaders from a single location or social group. In investigating art and ritual, I wished to also include the relevance that ceremonial acts, dances, masks and paraphernalia had for women and younger men. How did they view and deal with ritual actions? Did these mean something else to them? Or did they possibly acquire meaning in other ways?

Prior to arriving on Anir, I imagined that such an approach would entail numerous conversations with diverse individual interlocutors. At the same time, I feared that I might not be able to establish the number and kind of relationships I deemed necessary. My worries were unfounded. The Anir islanders quickly came to terms with the situation and developed their own system of dealing with the themes I was interested in and the questions I had. A key aspect of their "solution" involved conversations that in certain ways resembled focus group discussions as they were first developed in market and medical studies as a method for qualitative, applied research.[5]

According to Powell and Single (1996: 499) focus groups are formed by individuals that meet to "discuss and comment on, from personal experience, the topic that is the subject of the research." Focus groups usually consist of six to ten participants who are selected and assembled by the researcher. While involving a group-interview technique, the interaction among the group members is considered a major aspect, which is why focus groups are deemed a particularly suitable tool to obtain different perspectives and to gain insight into shared understandings, worldviews, beliefs and values regarding the topic under discussion. Another advantage deriving from interaction is that language use and the ways in which individuals influence each other may be observed. But now let us go back to Anir and the circumstances and events that led to the development of a dialogic research tool that resembled focus groups interviews and which in the course of my fieldwork became one of the most effective tools in my "research kit."

The first seeds were cast at the very beginning of my research. Anir is made up of two islands, Ambitlei (87 km^2) and Babase (23 km^2), separated by the one-hundred-metre-wide Salat Strait. Both islands are characterized by villages that consist of numerous, dispersed hamlets, most of which are on, or close to, the beach. Feni Mission on the northern tip of Ambitlei is where the Catholic Church established itself and where the largest church as well as one of altogether three community schools are located.[6] Because the "Mission" had a tradition of accommodating visitors, I spent my first weeks there, exploring the neighbourhood and undertaking day-trips to villages on both islands to introduce myself. These visits usually led to quickly arranged assemblages of members of the community to whom I then (in my still rather limited Tok Pisin) tried to explain who I was and why I had come. This more official part was always followed by a smaller meeting hosted and attended by community leaders and some of their family members. While these more intimate gatherings allowed them to learn more about me and what I had in mind, they gave me the opportunity to find out where and with whom I could or would like to stay more permanently, and to make first enquiries into the ritual system and the arts produced in its context. With hindsight these introductory visits proved very valuable with regard to building up a broad network of contacts and in fact were the first step towards introducing multilocality into my fieldwork. Moreover, as it turned out, the smaller meetings and the conversations had many similarities with the later, more focussed group discussions on ritual themes.

Group dialogues and videos

So, how did these group dialogues develop, and what were their characteristic features? All of them were interview-like and involved several participants, the majority of them usually men. The discussions pivoted on specific features of the Anir cycle of commemorative rituals and its underlying structure. The ritual cycle follows upon the death of a member of a matrilineage and consists of three phases, each of which comprises several steps, that is, separate ritual sequences. The completion of a full cycle requires the activation of numerous individuals, groups and resources and may take more than ten years.[7] Typically, a group dialogue would take place sometime after I had observed a ritual event. In order to explain the purpose of the discussions and how they emerged, some contextual information on how I researched the ritual system might be helpful.

It was clear from the start that, even given repeated visits to the field, I would not be able to witness an entire commemorative cycle carried out by one and the same kin group. Thus I aimed to witness, document and participate in as many ritual events across the islands as possible. At the beginning I frequently asked people in Natong, the village where I settled down after my initial time at Feni Mission, as well as people from other villages whom I visited or who visited me, to inform me about upcoming ceremonies. This mode of procedure proved effective and in the course of my second period of fieldwork notices and invitations from nearby and further away came in without me having to ask.

Usually I tried to arrive early to observe and help with preparations, talk with the organizers about the context and background of the event and, if possible, participate in meetings held to arrange the details of specific ceremonial acts. Apart from my notebook and camera, I also worked with a voice recorder and a video camera. On the whole, my audio-visual recording was focused on the main day and particularly on certain key elements, namely gift exchanges, *am furis* performances that involve the presentation of specific songs and speech acts (Illustration 5.1.),[8] as well as dances. Key moments that required the handling of several devices simultaneously were always a challenge, but also a special (though somewhat unusual) kind of ritual participation and experience. While the audio recordings provided the ground material for analyses with individual persons in one-to-one situations, the videos were the basis of many of the group dialogues. Their length ranged from anything between 60 and 240 minutes, depending on the type of event and the variety of activities and key elements it contained.

Illustration 5.1: *Am furis* performance at the funeral of Paul Munbal; the man heading the choir (left, background) and the man on the right standing in front of the open grave engage in a ritualized verbal exchange. In the forefront, the food to be distributed later at the feast. Nantingi, Kamgot village, March 2002.

In the days after the ritual, back at my "home base," I usually first viewed and analysed the videos on my own, comparing them with the notes I had made on the day, adding new observations, questions and potential interpretations. I then contacted the organizers to ask them for a time when we could meet and discuss their ceremony. Because I attended rituals in nearly all villages on both islands, this usually involved a visit lasting one to three or four days. Naturally, the videos raised curiosity, and often I was asked to first show them to as large a group as possible (using the display of the video camera or my laptop as a screen). The group dialogues took place afterwards. The initial "public" screenings gave those who participated in the following group dialogue the opportunity to view and revisit the event more than once, while for me they provided a chance to observe reactions and listen to comments from a broad range of viewers.

The group dialogues resembled classic focus group interviews in so far as I set the topic, posed previously prepared, open-end questions and probes, and functioned as moderator. The number of participants corresponded with that recommended for focus groups, too. However, there were also marked differences: members of focus groups are selected and assembled by the researcher. I, on the other hand, neither selected nor assembled the group. I always had a fair idea who was likely to participate – men who had been responsible for organizing the ritual, other individuals who had played a prominent role in it, or a trusted friend who was invited for his or her ritual knowledge. Prior to some of the meetings the host and I discussed who would, should or could (not) come, but the exact size and constellation of the group was never decided on by me.

Two other differences concerned the length of the meetings and the way I documented them. According to standard guides on focus group interviews, these should not last longer than two hours. The group dialogues I carried out with Anir islanders normally went on for at least three to four hours, often they lasted even longer – interrupted by breaks, during which we ate, joked and traded small talk – or else they were continued on the next day. This had a lot to do with the content of the interviews, where ritual knowledge is located, and how it is managed and transferred.

The ritual cycle operates as a knowledge system in which numerous messages are communicated, the majority of them ambiguous and multi-layered. They are encoded in many different ways (visually, verbally, acoustically, kinetically, olfactory), to the effect that only senior members of the community who have an intricate knowledge of the diverse aspects of ritual – their structure, spiritual matters, social relations, the history of islands and customary law – are considered to be able to fully understand and interpret them. To further complicate matters, certain elements and performances are subject to traditional rights, which means that only certain people may activate and talk about them. Therefore, whenever I had a one-to-one conversation about aspects of the ceremonial life, my interlocutor would at some stage add that what he/she had just said reflected a personal view or opinion, that he/she did not know about this or that aspect, or that he/she did not have the right to talk about it. And they advised me to see someone else.

The group interviews thus solved a "problem." They were developed by my Anir friends to deal with my questions about the ritual system and considered as an appropriate format to examine and discuss the meaning and significance of ritual activities with me. The organizers arranged meetings, to which they invited participants whom they considered knowledgeable, trustworthy and qualified. During the actual gatherings some questions I posed led to lengthy discussions amongst the group members until they finally gave me an answer that reflected their agreed-upon opinion. This process, that is, the need to cross-check and debate, was also why none of the groups wanted me to document the dialogue with an audio-recorder, a procedure otherwise common when conducting focus group interviews.[9] Instead, I took careful and extensive notes. Often I asked again or read back what I had written down about a particular question or aspect to make sure that my notes reflected their answer. To this I added my own observations and impressions of the discourse, and I am still very grateful for the generosity, patience and perseverance of all those who shared their knowledge in these meetings with me.

The audio-visual, the sensual and the verbal

I am neither a filmmaker nor did I receive any training in producing anthropological documentaries or films. Taking a video camera to the field came almost as an afterthought shortly before leaving for New Ireland. I understood and used the video camera as a device to record moments and activities I deemed relevant with regard to my research topic and interests. And I found it an extremely valuable tool. Essentially, ritual is performance and the Anir ritual cycle gives rise to a multitude of performative acts and various forms of artistic expression (Illustration 5.2). The recordings enabled me to audio-visually document, review and better memorize the proceedings in order to analyze and discuss them with different individuals and groups. The process of viewing and re-viewing the recordings also made me and those I watched them with aware of a lot of aspects we otherwise might have missed, for example, artefacts that were used in the course of a ceremony, details of the performance, the behavior of individual actors or the make-up of participating groups and details of their interactions with each other.

Evidently, the visual, as well as the (separate) audio-recordings were vital in the analysis of dances, songs and oratory. But they also had another effect that I realized only gradually: viewing and listening to recordings always is a form of re-visiting and re-experiencing. In this process, not only visual scenes, rhythms, sounds, movements and smells are remembered, feelings and emotions are evoked and re-lived, and chains of associations are activated.

Illustration 5.2: Ceremonial greeting between two leaders - Patrik Kameta and Anton Tengmil – prior to the start of a dance performed in honor and commemoration of a deceased relative. Verambif, Natong village, December 2001.

The reactions and the ways in which rituals and videos about them were discussed clearly brought to light how much knowledge is based on the interplay of sensuality, emotion and cognition, and is created and passed on through other than verbal channels. Although I had been well aware that rituals are multi-layered events – total works of art or *Gesamtkunstwerke* – and that in their perception, evaluation and interpretation the atmosphere, embodiment, immersion and the interplay of all our senses are vital, it was the work with the recordings – on my own, but particularly together with Anir islanders – that contributed much to my understanding of how aesthetic experience, knowledge acquisition and epistemological processes unfold (Denner 2010b).

Of course, verbal dialogues and conversations about audio-visual recordings were an integral part of this process of understanding. Successful ethnographic fieldwork is always characterized by the combination of different methods. In my case – and this presumably applies to many others as well – participation, observation and participant observation were as important as verbal communications in all their shadings. The fact that Anirians considered the semi-structured group dialogues a particularly appropriate form of sharing ritual knowledge with me neither prevented me from conducting confidential, individual interviews nor from discussing rituals carried out by one group with members of another. Besides, and as all who have had the opportunity to carry out fieldwork know, valuable information and insights often come unexpectedly, for example, during informal conversations when it would probably be inappropriate to take out a notebook or recorder. In the end it was the sum of the numerous and diverse verbal exchanges together with the insights gained through observation, participation, immersion and experience that led to the overall picture I gained of the Anir ritual cycle.

The advantage of the group dialogues was that they enabled the participants to consult with, and ask questions of each other, as well as to re-evaluate and reconsider their understandings of their specific knowledge and experiences in a process of shared sense-making. Together with the fact that it was my Anir interlocutors who took on much of the responsibility for organizing the event, and for selecting those who took part, this had a positive, empowering effect. For me, personally, the group dialogues provided the additional benefit of gaining information and opinions from several people simultaneously as well as exploring or generating hypotheses with them about various aspects of ritual. Furthermore, because interaction (including body language, countenance and demeanor) is a crucial feature of group dialogues, they offered a good forum to gain insight regarding the lacunae between what people say and what they do, and about the variability of practices and how these are interpreted.[10]

Of course, such dialogues also have their limitations. An obvious one is that the participating group members might not be expressing their own, individual views or that they might not trust the situation enough to disclose sensitive or personal information. In this respect, the numerous one-to-one conversations were vital. A particular form refers to the sessions during which the translations of the texts of the *am furis* men's house performances (see note 8) were produced. With only one or two exceptions I conducted these sessions with Christine Sinang, my elder "sister" and one of my dearest friends. For two reasons this is noteworthy: First, because the task was entrusted to a woman to venture with another woman – from outside, that is, me – into a field generally considered to be the domain of men. Secondly, because none of the kin groups on either island, objected to me translating their *am furis* with Christine. On the one hand, this shows how much she was respected across Anir,[11] on the other, it was a sign of something I only slowly came to understand, namely, that knowledge about the structure of the ritual system and esoteric language embedded in it, is, firstly, not per se restricted to men, and, secondly, is common to all kin-groups and connects people living in different localities. The translation and examination of the *am furis* songs and speech acts was as much of an exciting journey into an unknown field of knowledge for Christine as it was for me. Each time we ended up with uncertainties and questions regarding the interpretation. This usually led to Christine consulting with her father or her husband or asking them to join us for a meeting. Later I would discuss the insights gained with those who had organized and performed the respective *am furis*. This often, but not always, happened in a more confidential, smaller meeting separate from the group dialogues.

Conclusion

In his contribution to the reader *Fieldwork Is Not What It Used To Be*, James Faubion asserts what appears to be a truism, namely, that "good anthropology will always take time" (2009: 162). His comment is based on a careful review of changes that have taken place within the discipline in an enquiry into parameters that constitute the craft of up-to-date fieldwork, on the one hand, and what is distinctively anthropological, on the other. Some of the defining features he detects include connectivity paired with open-endedness and an inherent provisionality. They give rise to a seriality that is different from mere reflexivity or recursivity as they are linked to epistemological processes in which the researcher continually problematizes his/her inquiry to generate further questions while conceptualizing and being "acutely sensitive to the actual world, its actual slings and arrows and twists and turns" (2009: 162).

The "good" anthropologist goes again and again, visits and re-visits in a comprehensive sense that goes beyond the classic, narrow definition of fieldwork. It involves steps such as archival research, reviewing and reworking one's own materials and engaging with colleagues and their work and ideas. It may include multi-sited fieldwork or stays in far-away places, but this does not mean that research necessarily or always implies a distinction between "here/home" and "there" or that it needs to be spent in bulk in a physical field site. In the course of four field trips between 2000 and 2011, I spent just a little under two years on Anir, a comparatively long time. It not only allowed me to experience, observe and document a substantial number of ceremonies and ritual events, but indeed to witness all steps of the three phases of the commemorative cycle (albeit relating to different deceased people). Because the various events did not take place in the same village, the information I succeeded in gathering did not come from a single source or a limited number of "key informants." Although I did not explicitly conduct multi-sited ethnography in the sense of George Marcus (1995; see the contribution by Walda-Mandel in this volume), my fieldwork was characterized by working in more than one community. Some of them, or rather the friends I had made there, I visited regularly and accordingly I spent much time with them. This kind of multilocality, being able to rely on a wide network of amiable relationships, traveling to different parts of the islands and staying in diverse communities for longer periods, was an important aspect of my research. It contributed as much to my well-being as it helped to yield valid, representative and reliable data.[12]

Seriality, as Faubion understands it, came into play while conducting research on Anir, in processes such as the shared sense-making between myself and my respondents as described above, but also applied to the times that lay between the actual field visits while analysing my data, comparing and supplementing it with archival and other sources, discussing it, writing it up, and linking it with other projects. Faubion calls for intellectual continuity in an on-going extension and elaboration of the questions one pursues. My fieldwork on Anir was closely connected with questions about the relationship between ritual and art, perception and aesthetic experience, and links between anthropology and art history. These concerns continue to be central to my work. And while I am moving into the field of contemporary Pacific Islander art, which has little resemblance with the way I did "traditional" research on Anir, I am convinced that a thorough consideration of what is distinctly Pacific –

what links urban artists to their individual heritage and locales – will be as important as questions regarding pan-Pacific relationships and globalization.

Notes
1 Anir is one of several island groups that lie east of the much larger, long and narrow island of New Ireland. Anir is the southernmost, thus the "last" of the island groups belonging to the province. On some maps one finds the name Feni. This actually is the correct term in the local language. However, because Anir became the dominant and more common term in the province, and beyond, the islanders asked me to use Anir rather than Feni.
2 See for example Stocking (1992: 57-59), Gupta and Ferguson (1997: 7-8), Marcus (2009: 1, 34).
3 Even now, at the time of writing this article, the Anir Islands neither have mobile phone coverage nor electricity.
4 See for example Amit (2000) and Marcus (2009), as well as the different aspects covered in the reader published by Robben and Sluka (2012).
5 See Krueger (1988) and Morgan (1997 [1988]). Gibbs (1997) gives a concise outline of the main features of focus groups while Cronin (2011) provides a summary of important literature and resources on focus groups.
6 The majority of Anirians (approximately 70-80%) are Catholics.
7 The last phase of the cycle encompasses the construction and inauguration of a new men's house, which is accompanied by the presentation of specific songs, dances and masked performances. This phase, and thus the full cycle, is only staged in honor and memory of prominent persons. The organization and successful staging of the commemorative rituals allow for the transmission of rights to resources such as land from one generation to the next, but are also the means by which roles of leadership are gained or consolidated.
8 *Am furis* performances are presented during many rituals of the commemorative cycle. They are staged in and around the men's house and involve various previously selected actors who perform a lineage song, speech acts and dramatic actions. Many are metaphorical and thus carry multi-layered messages and symbolic meanings most of which point to the organizing lineage's history, their relationship to other groups, and to rights to land and other resources.
9 The arguments my Anirian counterparts raised against recording were that finding the correct answer often took a lot of time (hence I would waste my mini-discs) and that they often switched from Tok Pisin (in which the interview was to be conducted) to the local language (which I could only follow in parts). In the background, however, there also stood something else. Anirians are proud of the complexity and multivocality of their ritual

performances with their rich array of allusions and visually or verbally transmitted metaphors and tropes. Many stressed that *finailim*, that is, revealing hidden or implicit information and knowledge, is a pivotal characteristic of the ceremonial cycle. However, it is equally important to maintain the ambiguity and multi-layeredness of this system – the possibility to see and understand things differently – to leave room for flexibility and future negotiation. This explains why all groups asked me for copies of the videos (which they received), but did not want me to record our discussions, as they feared this would lead to an immobilization or fixation of the system.

10 See Mauksch and Rao (2014) for a very different example of processes of shared sense-making between researchers and research-subjects (and amongst them), and how such dialogues may produce new insights about social practice.

11 Christine, who sadly passed away, was not only the eldest daughter of an acknowledged, senior leader, but also the mother of ten children, a school teacher and the wife of an up-and-coming leader.

12 Accordingly, I felt happy and reassured when I returned to Anir in 2011 to bring back my PhD thesis and learnt that, apart from a few minor corrections, everyone was satisfied with the way I had represented them and their ritual system.

References

Amit, V. 2000. Introduction. In *Constructing the Field. Ethnographic Fieldwork in the Contemporary World*, ed. V. Amit. London: Routledge, pp. 1-18.

Cronin, K. 2011. *Focus Group Resource Guide*. Available from https://inside.fammed.wisc.edu/sites/default/files/dmt/focus-group-resource-guide.pdf [30 January 2016].

Denner, A. 2010a. *Under the Shade Tree – Mortuary Rituals and Aesthetic Expression on the Anir Islands, New Ireland, Papua New Guinea*. PhD Thesis. Norwich: University of East Anglia. Available from https://ueaeprints.uea.ac.uk/19418/1/PhDthesis_ADenner_whole_thesis.pdf [30 January 2016].

— 2010b. Aesthetic Experience and the Power of the Artwork. In *After the Event. New Perspectives in Art History*, eds. J. Potts and C. Merewether. Manchester: Manchester University Press, pp. 90–104.

— 2012. *The Anir Islands. Religious Beliefs, Ritual Practices, and Aesthetic Expression in the South of New Ireland, Papua New Guinea / Les îles d'Anir. Esprits, masques et spectacles dans le sud de la Nouvelle-Irlande*. Geneva: Fondation Culturelle Musée Barbier-Mueller.

Faubion, J. D. 2009. The Ethics of Fieldwork as an Ethics of Connectivity, or The Good Anthropologist (Isn't What She Used to Be). In *Fieldwork Is Not*

What It Used to Be. Learning Anthropology's Method in a Time of Transition, eds. J. D. Faubion and G. E. Marcus. Ithaka: Cornell University Press, pp. 145–163.

Gibbs, A. 1997. *Focus Groups. Social Research Update 19.* Available from http://sru.soc.surrey.ac.uk/SRU19.html [30 January 2016].

Gupta, A., and J. Ferguson 1997. Discipline and Practice. "The Field" as Site, Method, and Location in Anthropology. In *Anthropological Locations. Boundaries and Grounds of a Field Science,* eds. A. Gupta and J. Ferguson. Berkeley: University of California Press, pp. 1–46.

Krueger R. A. 1988. *Focus Groups. A Practical Guide for Applied Research.* London: Sage.

Marcus, G. E. 1995. Ethnography In/Of the World System. The Emergence of Multi-Sited Ethnography. *Annual Review of Anthropology* 24: 95–117.

— 2009. Introduction. Notes Toward an Ethnographic Memoir of Supervising Graduate Research through Anthropology's Decades of Transformation. In *Fieldwork Is Not What It Used to Be. Learning Anthropology's Method in a Time of Transition*, eds. J. D. Faubion and G. E. Marcus. Ithaka: Cornell University Press, pp. 1–34.

Mauksch, S., and U. Rao 2014. Fieldwork as Dialogue. Reflections on Alternative Forms of Engagement. *Zeitschrift für Ethnologie* (Special Issue: Current Debates in Anthropology) 139 (1): 23–38.

Morgan, D. L. 1997 [1988]. *Focus Groups as Qualitative Research.* London: Sage.

Powell, R. A., and H. M. Single 1996. Focus Groups. *International Journal of Quality in Health Care* 8 (5): 499–504.

Robben, A. C. G. M., and J. A. Sluka (eds.) 2012. *Ethnographic Fieldwork. An Anthropological Reader.* 2nd edition. Chichester: Wiley-Blackwell.

Stocking, G. W. Jr. 1992. *The Ethnographer's Magic and Other Essays in the History of Anthropology.* Madison: University of Wisconsin Press.

STEPHANIE WALDA-MANDEL

6 "I didn't know that there were other worlds out there". Inside a Multi-Sited Ethnography

Introduction

Today, not less than every second Pacific Islander lives far away from his or her home island (Mückler 2006: 64) – a tendency that will even increase with the looming developments. More and more people feel at home in different worlds: They migrate, some in the course of step migration to more than one place, and sometimes they return to their original home – a permanent flow, permanent mobility. Globalization and diaspora do not only change the lives of the migrating people and the ones of the relatives staying back, but also the essential scientific method of anthropology: fieldwork. Since the 1990s it therefore has been discussed intensely how anthropologists can meet the requirements of people's mobility in space and cognate subjects adequately.

By migration and transnationalism, for migrants the perception of nation and the one of people as "identifiable as spots on the map" (Gupta and Ferguson 1992: 7) are no longer linked in the same way as they are for people who have never left their home. Even cultures are no longer simply assigned to only one single place. In the course of this development, it is arguable whether the classic method of the single-site ethnography where the anthropologist stays in one single place to do research is still sufficient.

The traditional pattern of fieldwork is to stay in one site over a longer period of time to live with the people one wants to do research on, to share their daily routines and to establish close ties with them. By this means, one intends to collect numerous and reliable information. Bronislaw Malinowski – seen as the father of fieldwork by many – has first formulated standards in the 1920s that, from his point of view, defined ideal fieldwork. By doing so in his book *Argonauts of the Western Pacific*, he was able to establish participant observation as a professional norm. It was introduced in the beginning of the 20th century in contrast to the so-called armchair anthropology, and one of its most important features and minimum standards for Malinowski was the one-year-long field research in the community. This long stay in the observed society is often regarded as a kind of initiation or also rite of passage for the incoming anthropologist. It is also considered as the biggest advantage of the anthropological research that sets it off against other disciplines like sociology, for example. The standards imposed by Malinowski were in his times a crucial professionalization of the discipline, which was still in its beginnings. And on these standards the science still leans on, even when it has developed tremendously since then.

Anthropology and multi-sited ethnography

Anthropology is thanks to its subject matter a living science that is in a permanent state of flux. The crisis of ethnographic representation, for instance, which reached its climax in 1986, contributed greatly to changing the way of how anthropological groups of themes were presented. In that year, James Clifford and George Marcus published their collective volume *Writing Culture: The Poetics and Politics of Ethnography* and put up for discussion how knowledge about others is gained and reproduced. As part of criticizing the anthropological methods at that time, new ways developed to collect, process and analyze data. The controversy about the multi-sited ethnography that has come up lately is a similar innovation or an extension of methodological fundamental work within a scientific discipline of our time.

A science that deals with human culture needs to be responsive to the changing social circumstances and conditions, like, for example, globalization and also migration that gets intensified by it. One possibility is to include the new worldwide developments in a multi-sited ethnography. It leads anthropologists not only to one, but to a number of study relevant research sites, where they collect data by participant observation as well as by interviews. According to Marcus (1995: 95), the multi-sited ethnography has developed with the discipline as an answer to "more complex objects of study." Intensively, Marcus discusses the idea of multi-sited ethnography in his essay from 1995 and emphasizes that it is not about just adding sites, however, it has to do with a general "theoretical rethinking of field work itself" (Marcus 2009: 185). Even before Marcus' methodological approach on multi-sited ethnography, it had been practiced. By him it just got a label and has been discussed among experts, however, not appreciated by everybody.

The multi-sited approach is not suitable for every research topic. However, some aspects simply require a multi-sited approach to obtain the best results. This is specifically research addressing aspects of transnationalism, transmigration, migration and diaspora, and a multi-sited approach is suitable to capture people's networks adequately: "In sum, applying multi-sited methods enables us to study the field as a network of localities which are linked to each other through various types of flows" (Horst 2009: 120).

Variety is the foundation of every society. The previously existing picture of self-contained societies can by no means be upheld and even in the past it did not satisfy the complexity of any form of human cohabitation. What is more, small island societies that also may be organized pluralistically, they manifest themselves as complex networks of human relationships. Differentiated systems can hardly be comprehended by analyzing only one location. This problem intensifies in a great measure when social movement as, for example, migration comes in addition – complex networks by itself, now become transnational and create links with wide distances between the society of origin and residence. The essence of a multi-sited research consists of establishing connections between the people and the different sites that are relevant to them. The more people are involved, the more connections emerge.

To analyze these, the scientist needs to invest a lot of time and energy into his or her project. Even before Malinowski, there existed standards and expectations when it came to the course of anthropological research. According to Malinowski, besides fluency in the local language and living with the local population, a one-year stay in the studied society is of essential importance. The aspiration at that time was also to give a full overview of the whole culture. In so doing, the annual cycle was essential, since scientists at that time strived to witness all celebrations and activities of the whole year.

Today, it is usually not the defined goal of anthropological research to portray a culture in its entirety, like numerous anthropologists did in the past for various societies. To describe a culture only by aspects of geography, religion, or kinship relations as a whole, appears today more and more presumptuous regardless of whether it is based on single-site or multi-sited research. The Swedish cultural anthropologist Ulf Hannerz points out that nowadays, for instance, people of many societies are less dependent on seasons, harvest etc. (Hannerz 2003: 209). Instead of following the claim of portraying a society in its totality, scientists usually choose a specific aspect that they survey.

Sonsorol Island:
A multi-sited approach to migration and cultural identity

Mobility has been a feature of the people of Micronesia for hundreds of years (see also Keck and Schieder 2015). Part of the cultural and ecological life has also been the use of outrigger canoes to travel long distances to explore other islands or "other worlds" as a young Sonsorolese describes it in the title of this chapter. When it comes to geographic mobility, today's inhabitants of Sonsorol, an island in the Palauan archipelago, are no exception.

To demonstrate the importance of a multi-sited approach, I would like to use my own research among the Sonsorolese people, which analyzes the effects of migration on the cultural identity of the Sonsorolese and is a study that deals with the Sonsorolese in different places (Walda-Mandel 2016). It is embedded in Jürg Wassmann's interdisciplinary project *Person, Space, and Memory in the Contemporary Pacific* which focuses on the tradition and transformation of local perceptions of identity and person in the Pacific region.[1]

My approach is aimed to study the exterior social conditions as migration and social transformations and its effects on the cultural identity of the inhabitants of Sonsorol Island. What constitutes Sonsorolese identity, and how far and in which form is it passed to the children in the migration situation far away from Sonsorol?

Sonsorol that is called Dongosaro ("Place where strong currents exist") in the indigenous language, is a 1.36 m² coral island that belongs to the archipelago of Palau and where there are less than 20 people living together. To get to Sonsorol it takes a 22-hour boat ride from the main island of Palau. Palau is the westernmost group of the Caroline Islands and consists of 241 islands, of which 11 are inhabited. If one also counts the very tiny islands, it is even 343 (Mückler 2009: 219). These are located over a maritime area of about 130,000 km², what is approximately a third of the area of Germany. Part of the Palauan archipelago are also the so-called Southwest Islands that are found 300 km southwest of Palau's main islands. These remote Southwest Islands, namely Sonsorol, Fanna, Pulo Anna, Merir, Helen Reef and Tobi, have their own language and culture, which is completely different from the one of the rest of the Palauan islands. Due to its remoteness and the linguistic and cultural differences, Sonsorol's inhabitants represent a minority that in the past had to deal with more or less visible discrimination by some inhabitants of the main islands of Palau. However, by now there are also many friendships and relationships, especially between the younger Sonsorolese and Palauans.

Sonsorol does not offer the people who live there many future prospects. That is why numerous Sonsorolese are leaving their island to pursue their education or find work in Echang, Saipan, Guam and the USA mainland. One can observe different migration steps: The first step leads the Sonsorolese away from Sonsorol to Echang, a village that is located on one of the main islands of Palau. Here live only the people from different Southwest Islands together in a migrant community. The next step lets them take the plane to the Micronesian islands of Saipan or Guam in the South of the Marianas. Even more ambitious Sonsorolese (or the ones in a later phase of their migration career) further migrate to the west coast of the USA, most end up in Portland and Salem in the state of Oregon. This is due to the fact that in 1979 the first migrating Sonsorolese woman settled down in Portland to become a trained nurse. Here one can see the phenomenon of a chain migration: Even today, the young Sonsorolese follow her and find a home away from home in her household until they can build their own life there.

To portray the process of migrant identity adequately, in my fieldwork I followed the footsteps of the Sonsorolese migrants from the island of origin to the different migration sites in form of a multi-sited ethnography. With only the methodological means of a single-site fieldwork on Sonsorol I possibly may have got much information of the island dwellers about the life and tradition on the island; however, the topic of migration and its impact on the Sonsorolese identity makes it imperative that the research spreads over several sites.

Multi-sited ethnography in the field: challenges and potentials

The multi-sited ethnography is a relatively young method, which got applied increasingly in the course of globalization to realize multi-local research projects since the 1990s. It is specifically suitable to investigate complex research sites. The interconnectedness of people and organizations across national borders challenged the standard stationary fieldwork: "The single-sited methodology, its sensibility and epistemological presuppositions, were no longer felt to be adequate to the realities of an increasingly mobile, shifting and interconnected world" (Candea 2009: 26).

It is not only "Western" societies that are pluralistic, but also little island societies. Given the structural complexity that results from the coexistence of the people and is therefore part of every society, even with a smaller population, it is also found in island societies. Social diversity needs to be considered in every anthropological research. It needs to be the goal to see cultural life and the handling of migration as a whole, and if the respective community spreads over different places, these places should be incorporated to collect sufficient empirical data. If one does not integrate them, one is at risk of developing an empirical cognition that is too reduced for the necessary conclusions. A society is like a puzzle and is never made from only one piece. The pieces are spread to specific sites, and its description never comes to an end. If the particular research locations are perceived by critics as separate worlds, then the everyday reality of people obviously is not reflected in its totality.

In anthropology the object of investigation are people and the societies they constitute. Each person as a separate subject encounters others also as individual subjects. The complexity of the network of only two people regarding their origin, expectations, interests, fears, hopes etc. potentiates with every additional person. Therefore, each society is by its structure not only highly complex and sparsely predictable in its mobility and characteristic, in the study of social phenomena we are dealing with a rarely ponderable relativity that, moreover, is in constant motion.

To begin with the problem of the relativity of knowledge, the methodological question of the form of the right field research we are facing here, touches a difficult epistemological initial situation in general. We cannot evade the problem, that (in the field) because of the relativity of the (cognitive research) subject and the subject (to do research on), we never generate objective knowledge, however, we are always constrained by the relativity of our own findings. Nobody can circumvent his or her own subjectivity. The relativity, complexity, and mobility allow merely getting close. We can only face this dilemma by merging as many aspects of the relation as possible, and by circumscribing them, so that we little by little come to a fairly informative picture. With scientific integrity we admittedly cannot gain objectivity. The strongest base of cognition is therefore the inclusion of many subjectivities that are linked with each other in some way. These enable an understanding between subjects, a framework of references and connections. The appropriate term for this is intersubjectivity. Scientifically we only reconstruct what is the nature of societies.

The second difficulty in the study of people and society is caused by the constant flow, the instability and the development of these phenomena. When, in addition to that, the everyday reality of the studied agents and the society changes beyond the normal for the long-term, for example, by migration, it is all the more a necessary competence of an anthropologist to reconsider and modify the research design even during fieldwork. Two qualities anthropologists should therefore bring to the field are openness and flexibility. That requires them to adapt their own research design to the mobility and dynamics of the people, when the circumstances in the field demand that. The same applies to the timeline of the project.

In the traditional anthropological conception, the one-year fieldwork on the spot fulfills an ideal to which the idea of witnessing a full annual cycle is tied. The theoretical ideal case of a multi-sited fieldwork would be then to spend a full year in each of the locations visited – de facto hardly possible. Therefore, it is a solution, when it comes to topics that require research on several locations, to choose one place as the center of the research. Then only during fieldwork will this focal point reveal itself.

In my research this was the Sonsorolese migrant community in Echang, since here is the biggest community of Sonsorolese in the whole Pacific. Here you can also find living what my informants considered the oldest knowledge carriers of the Sonsorolese culture, whereas I was told that on the island of origin one cannot find them anymore. Besides the lack of jobs and further education, the most important reason for the strong movement of people away from Sonsorol lies in the non-existing medical facilities, since there is neither a nurse nor a doctor. The island is approached by ship only about three times a year, so that the people need to plan visits to the Palauan main islands ahead (Illustration 6.1).

Illustration 6.1: Women from the Southwest Islands celebrating the new year in Echang together

To illustrate the necessary flexibility in the field: Since I had little information about the anthropologically underexplored island available before my departure, I only became aware of the full extent of the depopulation of Sonsorol when I arrived in Palau. If I had put the focus of my research only on the less than 20 people on Sonsorol, I would have missed important information from the elderly people now living in Echang. It is not always possible to name all research destinations during preparations for the fieldwork, since they in some cases may only follow the dynamics and the interactions with the local population. Therefore, even Sonsorolese people themselves advised me more than once when I had asked them questions to also address them to the older Sonsorolese in Echang. They also urged me to talk to the ones who migrated to Saipan or Guam: "Now, that you've come all the way here from Germany you need to go to Saipan also to talk to them!" The ones living

6 Inside a Multi-sited Ethnography 93

in Echang volunteered information about relatives in Saipan and offered contacting them for me. This way, they became very important gatekeepers for my stay there. Even when the people themselves are no scientists in the field of cultural anthropology, however, they would have been very puzzled if I had not talked to the migrated knowledge carriers in their new home. As a consequence, they possibly would have questioned the seriousness of my research agenda, what would have had consequences for my further stay there. Therefore, it was not only the case that both, theory and practice, suggested to adapt my method in the form of multi-sited ethnography to the given conditions, but the point was also not to damage my credibility and the trust the people had put in my research.

Naturally, a research project that includes several localities bears a logistical, financial, personal and in some cases also linguistic challenge. This begs the following question: "[I]s there a reasonable balance between the extra effort and the returns?" (Nadai and Maeder 2009: 242). On the other hand, it would be pointless to address migration, which touches sending and (often several) receiving countries, however, investigating merely the island of origin. Nevertheless, in the field it can lead to difficulties to find the appropriate sites and to get access to them (Tomlinson 2010: 168).

By including different localities the multi-sited approach is often understood as if one would do research completely contextless in geographical autonomous places. If that was the case, critics sure were right with their postulation to do research in one single place only. However, this is not up to reality when it comes to topics such as migration – on the contrary: By migration, for example, a network of the different destinations is created by the migrating people. In different places one deals with members of a common cultural background. In the case of the Sonsorolese, it was like this that before I left to go to Saipan and Guam I had already acquired extensive knowledge about Sonsorolese life and related practices and values by living with the Sonsorolese in Echang and on Sonsorol. On this I could build upon. Furthermore, prior to my arrival in the migration destinations I was announced by the Sonsorolese people as "the adopted daughter of the former governor of Sonsorol State, Laura Ierago," because I was living with her family. This way, the migrated Sonsorolese knew how to locate me in the system of Sonsorolese families. This embedding in the Sonsorolese family network helped me to create trust. The perception as a trustworthy person is even reinforced by Sonsorolese family members giving notes or presents to the anthropologist, so that she can pass them to the migrated people.

The inclusion of new research sites offers another advantage: Even when my arrival was announced in the migration destinations in Saipan and Guam over the phone, the extended research in a different place offered the possibility to reposition myself with my role in the society in a new place. Potential difficulties, conflicts etc. which the anthropologist might have experienced in the first research site, he or she can leave behind for a short period of time and get a fresh start.

That is why it would be a mistake to see the multi-sited ethnography merely in terms of its deficits from the view of the single-site ethnography. Instead, one should see it as the proper method for specific issues. After half a year staying with the Sonsorolese community in Echang, I had the opportunity to fly to Saipan and Guam to get to know Sonsorolese life there. After about one month, I returned to the village in Echang. This temporary distance from the Sonsorolese home community helped me to find new approaches to my topic and to widen my perspective after I returned. At the same time, doing research in archives in the migration destinations gave me new insights in my subject, which I could call attention to in my interviews. By this means, different perspectives of migrated and other Sonsorolese developed in my issues.

Since many Sonsorolese migrated beyond the Micronesian region, I wanted to include the Sonsorolese who have migrated to the USA. I solved this problem in practice by adding a three-month stay at the west coast of the USA to my one-year research in Micronesia. There I had the opportunity to experience Sonsorolese life in the state of Oregon.

Linguistically for my multi-sited approach I did not need to make great extra efforts, since the Sonsorolese I met, regardless of where they lived, communicated in Sonsorolese, as well as in English and Palauan. In this context, Ferguson (2011: 203) submits that the linguistic skills of many "Western" anthropologists, also when it comes to traditional stationary fieldwork projects, were represented grossly overstated in the past.

The traditional idea of classic anthropological research of culture as self-contained is hurdled. When the anthropologist goes to the field, the term conveys the idea of the impression of a closed, definite geographic space, where he or she stays to do research on a culture. However, reality shows that the field originally perceived as coherent, spans beyond borders. Its particular reference points result from the fact that the people who move within it build transnational networks. What is more, the Indian cultural anthropologist Arjun Appadurai (1990: 19) points out that culture takes place in a translocal, globalized space. In this context, he minted the term "scapes" and differentiates in his model the different forms of cultural flows in form of five spheres, where cultural pledges disperse across borders: ideoscapes (ideational ideas), financescapes (translocal trade currents), technoscapes (means of communication, e.g. the internet), mediascapes (worldwide media), and ethnoscapes (migration, tourism). Thus, Appadurai ignores the outmoded concept of static culture homogeneity in an increasingly deterritorialized world. At the same time, a conjunction of the local and the global takes place. By this idea of unbound scapes, one can link Appadurai with Marcus' concept of multi-sited ethnography.

Marcus (1995) suggests in his interpretation of multilocal research to follow people, objects (money, presents), metaphors (discourse), life histories, plots and conflicts on their particular way of distribution. On the described path, meanings and valences of the latter may change for the people or can be perceived by them differently. To capture this global perspective, it needs a multi-sited approach, and "following the people" described by Marcus presents the direction of thrust of the multi-sited ethnography.

The different fields influence and cross-fertilize each other, a circumstance the anthropologist needs to accommodate. Instead of getting wedged in rigid boundaries, it would seem the thing to acknowledge this development. Purely isolated fields that stand just for themselves hardly exist anymore, and maybe they have never existed. Even the case of the remote island of Sonsorol shows strong interconnectedness, since it is in touch with the rest of the world in many aspects. Also the studied sites in the multi-sited ethnography are no random collection of different places, but rather the sites are chosen carefully along the migration paths of the people and track their network. If and only if this is the case, a multi-sited approach is reasonable: "Multi-sited ethnography is not just something that helps us add together perspectives from multiple sites, but instead it forces us to change perspective" (Hovland 2011: 105).

Nevertheless, the single site approach still is the more common method, which surely lies in the fact that only a fraction of the research projects deals with topics that give point to multi-sited ethnographies.

Research themes like Yapese massage techniques, for example, is an aspect of research that certainly cannot be studied appropriately without intensive single-site research.

Which difficulties lie in the multi-sited approach? The most abrasive criticism targets the lack of depth the multi-sited ethnography sometimes is associated with. This idea is strongly linked to the notion of "thick description" that has been used by Clifford Geertz (1987). Geertz is considered to be the founder and most important exponent of the interpretative anthropology and he understands culture as an ensemble of texts. According to his (also criticized) theory, in these texts in which symbols manifest themselves and the anthropologist can read their meanings when reading those texts over the shoulders of the people they were meant for. Each society has its own interpretation and by using his or her imagination and creativity the anthropologist can bypass the fragmentary access to a foreign cultural setting. This is possible by means of the so-called "thick description."

Critics of the multi-sited ethnography assume that by splitting the anthropologist's attention in several places this kind of depth cannot be achieved, since in their eyes, it is hardly possible to build close links in these localities, if one has the same one-year time frame. This can lead to superficial observation: "If I work in several places over the time period when previously I would have been in only one place, is my fieldwork necessarily more superficial and lacking the richness of context that traditional ethnography claimed?" (Miller and Slater 2003: 51). Yet, how exactly is this depth defined and does a single-site approach automatically mean depth? Thus Gallo concludes: "I do not think here that 'depth' is the diagnostic distinction between traditional and multi-sited fieldwork, not least because what 'depth' is is subject to contestation" (Gallo 2009: 91-92).

Furthermore, it should be brought into question, in how far a single-site research that claims to be deep, is able to study and describe networks and bonds. One could therefore also see a "thick description" of networks and flows in the multi-sited ethnography (see also Horst 2009: 126). In addition to that, too much depth involves the risk of too much closeness. Several localities put statements made in different places into perspective, reveal a bigger picture based on greater scientific evidence.

Final considerations and perspectives

Today, we hardly find self-contained societies, which exist untouched by the rest of the outside world. More and more people, states, and corporations are linked in an increasingly globalized world and, therefore, also the requirements for anthropologists become more challenging. It goes without saying that the core ideas defined by Malinowski of a stay as long as possible, the participant observation, as well as the acquisition of language skills, are still relevant today. Nevertheless, the anthropologist nowadays is supposed to satisfy the dynamics of transnational everyday practice. For this purpose, anthropology needs to open up to new approaches like the multi-sited research, even when the scientist needs to brace him- or herself for additional bureaucratic effort. It is important to choose sites that push the research forward and to explain why these sites are relevant for the people and the research. Ideally, by doing so, one manages to combine the core standards of a single-site research with the multilocality of the multi-sited approach.

Berg (2008: 15) points out, that it is important to address eventual limitations of the multi-sited ethnography and that it is possible to approach potential problems methodologically also by different research practices, like, for example, team-based research, fieldwork in transit (moving with migrants) and interdisciplinary work (see the contributions by Völkel and by Dasen in this volume). Horst (2009: 122) sees the advantage of team work in the fact that one can approach the different sites simultaneously while a single researcher can do this in a multi-sited ethnography only step by step. However, in so doing, it is necessary to consider that different researchers, for example, study the lives of migrants in different localities and each of them only gets the impression of just one site.

The search for new methods that satisfy the latest developments does not mean that the traditional single-site fieldwork with its underlying principles is obsolete: "Novelties are useful when they solve specific problems, but they should not be expected, in any through-going way, to replace the old" (Ferguson 2011: 204).

The point is to complete the existing classic method – namely in these cases when it is conducive to the scholarly interest, to get to better research findings that way. Therefore, the multi-sited ethnography is a relatively new way to perceive and understand links and networks across borders. As in every academic discipline, also in anthropology the leading question and the object of research should require the choice of methods.

Note
1 I would like to express my gratitude to the Volkswagen-Stiftung which funded my fieldwork.

References

Appadurai, A. 1990. Disjuncture and Difference in the Global Cultural Economy. *Public Culture* (2): 1–24.
Berg, U. D. 2008. Practical Challenges of Multi-Sited Ethnography. *Anthropology News* 49 (5): 15.
Candea, M. 2009. Arbitrary Locations. In Defence of the Bounded Field-site. In *Multi-sited Ethnography. Theory, Praxis and Locality in Contemporary Research*, ed. M.-A. Falzon. Farnham [u.a.]: Ashgate, pp. 25–45.
Clifford, J., and G. E. Marcus (eds.) 1986. *Writing Culture. The Poetics and Politics of Ethnography*. Berkeley and Los Angeles: University of California Press.
Ferguson, J. 2011. Novelty and Method. Reflections on Global Fieldwork. In *Multi-Sited Ethnography: Problems and Possibilities in the Translocation of Research Methods*, eds. S. Coleman and P. von Hellermann. New York and London: Routledge, pp.194–207.
Gallo, E. 2009. In the Right Place at the Right Time? Reflections on Multi-sited Ethnography in the Age of Migration. In *Multi-sited Ethnography. Theory, Praxis and Locality in Contemporary Research*, ed. M.-A. Falzon. Farnham, [et al.]: Ashgate, pp. 87–102.
Geertz, C. 1987. *Dichte Beschreibung. Beiträge zum Verstehen kultureller Systeme*. Frankfurt am Main: Suhrkamp.
Gupta A., and J. Ferguson 1992. "Beyond Culture." Space, Identity, and the Politics of Difference. *Cultural Anthropology* 7 (1): 6–23.
Hannerz, U. 2003. Being there...and there...and there! Reflections on Multi-Site Ethnography. *Ethnography* 4 (2): 201–216.
Horst, C. 2009. Expanding Sites. The Question of "Depth" Explored. In *Multi-sited Ethnography. Theory, Praxis and Locality in Contemporary Research*, ed. M.-A. Falzon. Farnham [et al.]: Ashgate, pp. 119–133.
Hovland, I. 2011. "What Do You Call the Heathen These Days?" For and Against Renewal in the Norwegian Mission Society. In *Multi-Sited*

Ethnography. Problems and Possibilities in the Translocation of Research Methods, eds. S. Coleman and P. von Hellermann. New York and London: Routledge, pp. 92–106.

Keck, V., and D. Schieder 2015. Introduction. Special Issue: *Contradictions and Complexities – Current Perspectives on Pacific Islander Mobilities*, eds. V. Keck and D. Schieder. *Anthropological Forum* 25 (2): 115–130.

Malinowski, B. 1922. *Argonauts of the Western Pacific. An Account of Native Enterprise and Adventure in the Archipelagoes of Melanesian New Guinea.* New York: Dutton.

Marcus, G. E. 1995. Ethnography in/of the World System. The Emergence of Multi-Sited Ethnography. *Annual Review of Anthropology* 24: 95–117.

— 2009. Multi-sited Ethnography. Notes and Queries. In *Multi-sited Ethnography. Theory, Praxis and Locality in Contemporary Research*, ed. M.-A. Falzon. Farnham [et al.]: Ashgate, pp. 181–196.

Miller, D., and D. Slater 2003. Ethnography and the Extreme Internet. In *Globalisation. Studies in Anthropology*, ed. T. Hylland Eriksen. London [et al.]: Pluto, pp. 39–57.

Mückler, H. 2006. Unwanted Neighbours – Implications, Burdens and the Instrumentalization of Migration: Relations between American Samoa and the Republic of Samoa. In *Migration Happens*, eds. K. Ferro and M. Wallner. Wien: LIT, pp. 63–81.

— 2009. *Einführung in die Ethnologie Ozeaniens*. Wien: Facultas.

Nadai, E., and C. Maeder 2009. Contours of the Field(s): Multi-sited Ethnography as a Theory-driven Research Strategy for Sociology. In *Multi-sited Ethnography. Theory, Praxis and Locality in Contemporary Research*, ed. M.-A. Falzon. Farnham [et al.]: Ashgate, pp. 233–250.

Tomlinson, K. 2011. The Anxieties of Engaging in Multi-sited PhD Research. Reflections on Researching Indigenous Rights Processes in Venezuela. In *Multi-Sited Ethnography. Problems and Possibilities in the Translocation of Research Methods*, eds. S. Coleman and P. von Hellermann. New York and London: Routledge, pp. 161–173.

Walda-Mandel, S. 2016. *"There is no place like home". Migration and Cultural Identity of the Sonsorolese, Micronesia.* Heidelberg: Universitätsverlag Winter. (Heidelberg Studies in Pacific Anthropology, Vol. 5).

ANITA VON POSER

7 "Houses Jumbled Everywhere"? Visions of a "Village" in Papua New Guinea

Introduction

My contribution aims at exemplifying the fluid, ever-changing character of one ethnographic field in particular, which featured prominently in traditional anthropology as *the* ethnographic site per se. The site which I have in mind is the one that is usually called the "village" in our discipline, referring, as it were, to a small-scale societal and spatial arrangement in which a fieldworker's traditional anthropological endeavor is situated (see Denner, this volume).

Rather than addressing a particular method as a facet of fieldwork, I have decided to direct an analytic lens on the field in which my own research was undertaken by bringing together the different visions of the "village" which I gradually came upon. "Houses jumbled everywhere," for instance, can be found among the descriptions which were used by a patrol officer during the colonial era to describe "villages" in the Bosmun area of Papua New Guinea. I use this phrase in order to discuss Bosmun perceptions of place, as I became aware of them during phases of my ethnographic fieldwork in Daiden and other Bosmun places between the years 2004 and 2010. I focus in particular upon people's ideas about what contributes to the formation of a "proper village" and how these ideas have been influenced throughout colonial and post-colonial history. As I will show, most people have not freed themselves from a rather negative view of local, ancestral village forms, a view which was imbued by the work of colonial officers in the area who were convinced that these local village forms were lacking in structure and cleanliness and therefore needed to be improved. I also suggest that only very recently a few individuals, especially those who have experienced the outside world on a more long-term basis, have begun to re-establish a local sense of self-esteem by weighing up the advantages and disadvantages of rural and urban lifestyles.

My approach is both empirical and historical. I present data which I gathered during extended anthropological periods of fieldwork in Daiden. I also relay data from historical colonial sources relating to the formation of "villages" in the Bosmun area. By means of repeated fieldwork, during which I would also bring with me historical sources of knowledge found in the National Archives of Papua New Guinea, I was able to explore Bosmun visions of the "village." This exploration, in turn, also deeply fostered my understanding of the field to which I had come to in order to conduct my research.

A conceptual note on the term "village"

"Daiden is a Bosmun village in Papua New Guinea." There is something about this sentence that does not sound appropriate in my ears. When talking or writing about my fieldwork experiences in and around Daiden, I feel rather uncomfortable using the term "village." I do not completely avoid it but often prefer to speak of Daiden as a "place," a "location," a "locality," or an "area in which a particular group of people dwells." Why is this so? Such ambiguity can certainly be traced back to Appadurai's warnings of a "spatial incarceration of the native" (1988: 37). It may also be traced back to a current trend, at least among some colleagues in anthropological academia, to deconstruct "traditional fieldwork" in rural settings due to globalization, as if rural settings no longer existed (cf. Stasch 2010: 42; Mines and Yazgi 2010: 26). General answers to the question raised above may also be found in the debates concerning the *Anthropology of Landscape* (Hirsch and O'Hanlon 1995; Feld and Basso 1996; cf. Casey 2009) or the *Phenomenology of Landscape* (Tilley 1994; cf. Bender 1993; Ingold 2000). Triggered in the mid-1990s, these debates revealed the cultural, political, and embodied dimensions of people's relationships with places. Finally, a few recent articles, dealing in particular with notions of the village in the Southwest Pacific (Stasch 2010; Dalsgaard 2011; Van Heekeren 2011), may provide answers as to why the term "village" needs more conceptual clarification. In his article *The Category "Village" in Melanesian Social Worlds*, Stasch claims: "Rather than take 'village' for granted as a pre-existing category, we need to work out inductively the particular shape and life of this category in given locations" (2010: 43).

It is this emically-based approach to space, as grounded in Bosmun understandings of place and of "village," which my contribution is concerned with. I follow Hirsch's (1995: 4) usage of the terms "space" and "place." Whereas "space" refers to the sheer physical surrounding and functions as a "background potentiality" for different social actors, "place" is the lived and, individually as well as culturally, shaped experience of that physical surrounding that is its "foreground actuality." Villages are often "assumed to be the same thing everywhere" (Stasch 2010: 43) filled with "scenes of primordial *Gemeinschaft*-style social experience," as Stasch (2010: 48) points out by referring to German sociologist Tönnies' (1957) ideas on *Gemeinschaft*, that is to say, the ancient and primal face-to-face community (*Gemeinschaft*) as based on family life.

By exploring Bosmun notions of place, I hope to be able to show that Daiden is much more than what the term "village" often suggests in blurred and indeed superficial ways. Between 2004 and 2010, when I repeatedly lived and worked in Daiden, Bosmun visions of what they call <u>vunis</u>[1] in the local vernacular and which I variously translate as "place" / "inhabited space" / "social space" (including areas of work, where social action takes place) basically consisted of three images: of a pre-colonial, a colonial, and a post-colonial place. This "periodization" of time is not my bias. Though there certainly has been some conceptual impact from outside on how time is now being perceived, my interlocutors themselves preferentially divided time into a *taim blo tumbuna* ("time of the ancestors"), a *taim blo kiap* ("time of colonial administrators"), and a *taim blo nau* ("present time").

After describing the Daiden scene in a general ethnographic way, I show that Bosmun ideas and narratives of place, including narratives about the formation and deformation of a "proper village" across time, are ideational reflections on and assessments of life. After all, "[a] village form (…) is not self-evident or natural but is an incarnation of specific values, ideas, narratives, feelings, political and moral projects, and visions of what social life should be" (Stasch 2010: 43).

Daiden: A place on the move

Daiden is located at the lower banks of the Ramu River in the Madang Province of Papua New Guinea. It is part of the wider Bosmun region, which comprises approximately 1500 residents. A Papuan vernacular as well as Tok Pisin (Papua New Guinea's Pidgin English) are spoken. Children also learn English in local schools. When I first worked in the area in 2004-5, Daiden was inhabited by approximately 200 people.

The surrounding environs of Daiden are dominated by sago palms and the river Ramu. Heavy rainfalls keep the area extraordinarily humid and swampy for almost three quarters of the year. Although to an outsider life in such an environment may appear harsh, my interlocutors appreciatively spoke of it as a nurturing and benevolent country (von Poser 2013), a country regularly providing people with sago and fish. Most of my interlocutors made their daily living through subsistence-based economic activities. Due to regular floods, gardening as a means of producing food is not predictable. For this reason, gardens are not very present in the physical landscape, but if a garden is made, people today also plant cash crops such as cocoa and vanilla. Men sell these crops together with copra in town. Women sell river offerings on coastal markets.

More regular contact with coastal areas and towns started in the 1970s when the first inland road was built. Among the colonial reports which refer to the building of this road (e.g. Calderwood 1970/71: 4; Douglas 1970/71: 6), the following account can be found:

> The Bosman [Bosmun] people (...) have been over the past year or two working on a road which starts at Nubia plantation on the coast going inland to Sepen Village and coming out near the new airstrip at Bunapas (...). They have been working on the road without any assistance or supervision and having walked along the road I have been impressed by the efforts of the Bosman people. The road itself travels along very flat country with hardly any hills to worry about. There are three rivers but they appear to be slow [sic] moving and can be easily bridged. However, this road may be subject to flooding during the wet season. Nevertheless it opens up another possible route to the Ramu River which may be well worth considering (Browne 1968/69: 12).

Although in the past Bosmun regularly moved far beyond their home territory by taking part in either huge trading networks (cf. Tiesler 1969, 1970) or headhunting raids, this road linked the entire Lower Ramu region to a new social and economic space. Prior to today's custom of traveling with buses on roads, Bosmun traveled less frequently on ships to urban areas. The ships could be reached at Bogia, the nearest town, via a day's march. Interestingly, the colonial report indicates that the road was built without any clear instructions from the colonial agenda, thus apparently showing the local population's enthusiasm for moving Daiden closer to the outside world and hinting, as it were, at an understanding of the "road" as prevalent in the thoughts of people living elsewhere in Papua New Guinea. In his discussion of the mutual constitution of the categories "village" and "town," Dalsgaard argues that roads on Manus Island are seen to be "both a concrete connection and a symbolic or metaphorical expression for connectedness" (2011: 232), and that they are "typical examples of what people regard as 'real development' in third world countries. Like bridges, hospitals and schools, they are visible and tangible effects of the delivery of government service" (2011: 237). Since the Bosmun road is made of gravel, which means that it is easily damaged during the heavy rainfalls each year, the feelings of connectedness and the delivery of government services are sometimes limited.

Bosmun life, as decreed by ancestral lore, is organized following egalitarian, patrilineal, and virilocal rules. Apart from gender segregation in ritual activities, people adhere to gender-complementarity in labor and in daily social living. The group is split into four clan-associations: Ŋgoinmbaŋ and Ndoŋon belong to the moon-moiety (*karvi*), Rom and Maŋgai to the sun-moiety (*raao*). Most members of the clan-association Rom are residents of Daiden, Ndenekaam (a place half an hour to walk from Daiden and similar in size) as well as several adjacent clearings where single families regularly or temporarily dwell. An early report by botanist Gehrmann (1916: 29) of the German Gogol-Ramu-Expedition provides evidence for the emergence of a new living space around 1913, at a spot where Daiden or at least parts of Daiden are to be found. Gehrmann's observation correlates with what I was told about the creation of Daiden. My middle-aged and elder interlocutors mentioned that a residential shift had happened during their parents' parents' times.

If we look at the linguistic encryption of the name "Daiden," we can in fact also trace its emergence historically and socially. According to Stasch, an important methodological approach to understanding village formations is "to document the terms by which villages are spoken of in vernaculars, linguae francae, and languages of colonial and post-colonial rule mediating the creation and ongoing life of villages as concrete spatial forms" (2010: 44).

The place name Daiden is an alteration of Ndennden, which stems from the Bosmun vernacular and which literally translates as "grasslands." The name Daiden, I was explained, was chosen to make it sound more like Tok

Pisin and more modern, as well as more easily comprehensible for the *kiap*, as the patrol officers of colonial Papua New Guinea are called in Tok Pisin. Such linguistic alteration may also be understood as an attempt to obscure the fact that the ground on which Daiden is built was grassland before it was made inhabitable. When asking about the physical shape and the historical formation of Daiden, several interlocutors said in Tok Pisin: "*Daiden em ples kanaka ya ...mipela stap lo bus*" ("Daiden is a backward place...we live in the bush") or "*mipela stap lo kunai*" ("we live in the grasslands") – as if a residential space erected on former grassland was not a proper place to live in.

Ndennden is actually just a descriptive place name. Its social place name is Romo vunis, the "place of the Rom clan-association." Members of the other clan-associations address themselves in similar ways. They add the word <u>vunis</u> to their respective clan name. The name Romo vunis does not only embrace a single "village" understood as "a certain density of dwellings standing in one place for an extended time" (Stasch 2010: 46). It covers all residential areas of Rom and the pathways which link these areas as well as those parts of the forest, the sago swamps, and the river where members of the Rom have ancestral rights to work and obtain materials for food and shelter. Further, the name also embraces the pathways which lead to exchange partners of the Rom outside Bosmun territory (cf. Van Heekeren's [2011: 212] description of the complex meanings of the term "kwalu" as understood by the Vula'a people living in the Hood Point area of Central Province in Papua New Guinea). In Daiden, the forest is generically called <u>ruaŋ</u>, the sago swamps <u>osnis</u>, and the river <u>xoaam</u>. In local understandings, these spaces are part of people's <u>vunis</u>. Romo vunis denotes a social space inhabited by familiar and sociable actors, where good interpersonal relationships based on regular food-exchange exist. Whereas "village" suggests a clearly separated, bounded spatial entity with a clearly defined population, <u>vunis</u> has a broader and more dynamic connotation.

If we are to speak of a particular Bosmun "village form," we have to speak of it as less bounded, although not without boundaries altogether. Spatial boundaries do exist, yet they have to be discerned according to local schemes of organizing space. As said earlier, Ndenekaam, the other Rom "village," is a half-hour walk from Daiden / Ndennden. Ndenekaam literally means the "end of the grasslands." My interlocutors used <u>kaam</u> to refer (1) to a "sound" / "language," (2) to a "sign," and (3) to a "spatial marker," a distinct topographic feature, which delineates a visual border between two areas. From Bosmun perspectives, Ndenekaam is a part of Ndennden; it is both its extension and its limitation, at least in one specific direction. What to a person without local spatial expertise may appear as two distinct places constitutes, in fact, a single spatial entity.

The Tok Pisin term *ples* ("place") seems to grasp the ideational meaning encoded in the term *vunis*. Although it is a language that developed during the colonial era, most of my interlocutors considered Tok Pisin the nation's proper idiom and an equivalent second local language. To my knowledge, people rarely applied the term "village" in conversations since most did not regularly converse in English. Being familiar with the word through school education and mass media, however, they had their ideas about what a "village" is. The English term "village" was associated with ongoing Western "improvements" of everything local. This "improvement" was first prompted by colonial and missionary agendas and continues to be prompted by representatives of state and church, by expatriate business people, by media and tourists, and by NGO workers trying to set up health-care projects or programs for the protection of the environment.

I close this section with a note on a topographic particularity and its relevance for livelihood in this part of Papua New Guinea. A highly visible obstacle to Western "improvements" is the Ramu itself. Its strong currents regularly erode at the ground and thus keep people and their dwelling areas constantly moving. My interviewees often said: "*Mipela sa bihainim Ramu tasol*" ("we just follow the Ramu"). In biographical interviews, people explained to me: "*Taim mi pikinini, mi stap namel lo wara yet*" ("I spent my childhood in the middle of the river"). The changing river was a recurring topographic mnemonic device and a time trajectory in the narration of people's biographies. During my first visits to Daiden in 2004-5 and 2006, I did not fully grasp the dimensions of the above statements. I had no experience to compare different states over time. This was different in 2008 and 2010. In 2004-5, the house where I was allowed to live stood approximately 30 meters away from the riverbanks. In 2008, the distance was ten meters, and in 2010 only three meters. The houses surrounding my house were not there anymore, and my neighbors had moved to a safer area elsewhere on clan ground.

People relocate their dwelling sites only when living in a house next to the river becomes extremely dangerous. Direct river access is extremely important. Abandoning such an access is therefore postponed for as long as possible. People fetch water, catch fish, and travel to their sago swamps by canoe on a daily basis. Passing through unfamiliar households is uncommon according to Bosmun rules of movement through social space. Therefore, when looking for a new place to reside, people not only look for the shortest path to the river but for a path that is used by other kin-members.

Bosmun houses shift in geographical space with a regularity which on more solid ground would probably not be the case, but I gained the impression that people have adopted a positive attitude to this transience. The single components of a household might be used in different ways. Houses are built near the water, and people dwell there until the Ramu forces them to move. A household is made up of a sleeping house, a cooking house, a utility house, and a resting platform. If the Ramu breaks the ground where, for instance, the sleeping house stood, it may leave the site of the cooking house unaffected. In such a case, the cooking house turns into the sleeping house. As with the category of the "village," the category of the "house" may differ from one cultural context to another (cf. Fox 1993a).

The people who spoke with me appreciated the Ramu because of its creative and nurturing force. Although the river forces people to move, I was told it provides them year after year with sandbanks during the dry season where they find fresh water mussels, a welcome culinary alternative to the continuous diet of fish. Moreover, it turns parts of the soil into swamps, where sago palms can grow.

Bosmun visions of a pre-colonial and colonial place

The anthropology of villages raises the question: "What's in a village?" (Stasch 2010: 56). My first answer to this question relates to the material aspects of village formation under colonial influence. My second answer addresses the ideational, moral, and emotional aspects implied in shifting place-aesthetics.

With the arrival of Australian patrol officers in the Ramu region in the mid-1940s, huge spatial "improvements" began, which, in fact, were also considered to trigger social "improvements." Areas were regularly patrolled, usually for one or two days per month. The patrol officers radically changed local place-aesthetics, and their ideas of what a "proper village" should look like do not differ much from how extra-local agents

7 "Houses Jumbled Everywhere" 109

today imagine a prototypical Papua New Guinea village. According to *kiap* opinions, "structure" needed to be introduced into places such as Papua New Guinea. In an analysis in *Walkabout*, a journal which promoted Australian patriotism for over 40 years, Quanchi shows how patrol officers and other authors "frequently depicted the dependent territories as possessions benefiting from benign colonial rule" (Quanchi 2003: 77). Patrol officer Douglas (1969/70: 3, 1970/71: 5) notes that especially the younger generations in the Bosmun area were open-minded toward colonial reforms. In fact, my interlocutors above the age of 60, who were children, youth, or young adults at that time, commonly spoke of the officers with respect and gentle admiration (von Poser, forthcoming), especially of *Mista Siki* and *Mista Braun*, probably Sheekey (1962) and Browne (1968/69), two officers working in the area in the 1960s. In retrospect, the people of Daiden seem to have positively picked up the administrators' visions.

As elsewhere, the past is often drawn in more colorful ways than is the present. It could also be due to my presence as a *mese viar*, "white woman," as I was referred to in Daiden at the beginning of my research, that such a positive assessment was made of the patrol officers. For my interlocutors, I belonged to another category of "white people," along with missionaries, researchers, business people, and expatriates living in the country. On the other hand, my consociates never hesitated to tell me their opinions of contemporary "whites" in Papua New Guinea, commonly labeling them as greedy characters who rely on a cash-based life and who lack social skills such as sociability and empathy.

According to *kiap* perspectives, several material changes had to be made. I was told, for example, that the *kiap* complained about the layout of the houses. He demanded that buildings should stand in line and, when broken down, be rebuilt on the same spot. From my own experience of having lived next to the banks of the Ramu I know that such "improvements" were not always practical: aligning houses is not feasible in an ecological setting where, as previously stated, strong river currents regularly rearrange ground and water. In order to get a quick overview of the actual population and to collect head taxes, a familiar spatial structure may have facilitated the officers' work. In the beginning of the 1950s, Officer Dyer assessed the local housing pattern and recommended changes:

> The striking feature about the housing was that there was evidence that houses had been constructed in the past that were really first class but have been allowed to fall in disrepair. The same applied to village areas generally – shrubs had been planted out with good effect but the general appearance was one of untidiness on the arrival of the patrol. After some old houses were removed and the grounds tidied the villages looked much better. The Bosman villages are poorly laid out – houses jumbled everywhere. They have a large rebuilding program and advice was given as to how best they could lay out houses (Dyer 1952/53: 6-7).

"Houses falling in disrepair" is but one etic way to describe the Daiden scene. I also saw several abandoned areas, but I learned that there is an emotional and political reason for not immediately removing houses. A single house post, pieces of bark for the floor or woven leaves for the roof – the distinct parts of a Bosmun house are charged with emotional value. They may have been contributions by beloved kin who provided material when the house was built. In either reusing house parts or leaving them as they are for a considerable time, people express their appreciation. Politically, people maintain their rights to a piece of land for as long as the remnants of their former houses are still there. Even if they have decided to rebuild their household elsewhere, they may return in the future; especially if the old residential spot lies closer to the water.

"Houses jumbled everywhere" is another etic way to describe spatial arrangements in Daiden. A more emic way would be to say that houses are laid out so as to link them to the houses of kin and separate them from the houses of non-kin. Structurally, Bosmun housing mirrors the extensions as well as the limits of kinship ties. When families grow bigger, households start to stretch in different directions. With adulthood, the male members of a family build their own sleeping houses – always in close vicinity to the parental house and to the houses of (biological and / or classificatory) brothers. After marriage, further buildings are erected where one's own nuclear unit can properly reside, and where meals can be prepared and things can be stored.

Despite colonial assumptions of a missing spatial structure, pre-colonial "village-scapes" were highly structured. Local spatial structures were dictated by local lifestyles and philosophies of life and by the environment in which people live. According to interlocutors who either remembered or knew from narratives what it had looked like before, the pre-colonial spatial arrangement was a "clanscape" (Bender 1996: 323), systematically divided into areas inhabited by the clan-associations and the individual clans belonging to them.

Moreover, the houses had a particular, ancestral design. I saw parts of this ancestral house design when I first lived in Daiden. There were at least four different ways to weave the sago leaves which are used as roofing materials. There were at least two different ways to shape the roof. There were two entrances into the sleeping house at front and back, one for men and one for women; front and back of the house were walled with bark materials whereas the sides were made of bundled sago leaves. The remaining structural parts of a Bosmun household – the cooking house, the utility building, and the resting platform – had no walls. By customary convention, only the sleeping house was built with walls because the sleeping house was considered the proper place for spouses to share sexual intimacies without having to fear gossip or attacks by bush spirits.

The installation of walls (made of bamboo) on local houses in general, the division of the house's interior into distinct rooms, and the bordering of houses with flowers and plants were all material alterations which ignored important social dimensions inherent to conventional Bosmun schemes of spatial formation. For example, there is no word for "room" in the local language. Fox has pointed out that "[f]rom a physical structure – a particular arrangement of posts and beams – one can begin to trace the ideals and social values of a society" (1993b: 2). In fact, the style introduced by the patrol officers did not correlate with the notions of sociality which were in existence and which were not immediately abandoned. After all, as Bender has put it, "[t]he forces of modernity may rework a landscape, but they may also be reworked in response to a local sense of place, a particular way of being-in-the-world" (2001: 85).

As I have argued elsewhere (von Poser 2013), the people in Daiden who told me that they were following the ways of their ancestors engaged in a particular mode of transparent personhood. Individuals linked through long-standing, regular, food-related activities such as joint food production and consumption have the right and the duty to emotionally enquire into each others' lives (von Poser 2011). From childhood on, people internalize the idea that they constantly have to watch others, and that they are constantly being watched. Ideally, subjectivity is negotiated in intersubjective encounters, including the articulation among social consociates of feelings such as jealousy, resentment, or anger. It is believed that a person runs the risk of developing severe hatred if he or she keeps such feelings exclusively to him- or herself. A person who refuses to let others assess his or her character is likely to become suspected of sorcery.

In order to adhere to this kind of moral empathy, a more permeable spatial formation is needed which allows individuals to watch social interaction taking place around their households. Households whose residents have no social linkages with each other are usually separated by spatial distance, not by some sort of material enclosure. In this way, household members can easily spot people. Interestingly, night-time is said to start once one is no longer able to distinguish people approaching one's household.

Furthermore, according to Bosmun rules of movement in social space, people need to make themselves known when they arrive at a household. By ostensibly moving slowly when coming closer or by making "'noise' to announce their presence" (LiPuma 1998: 70), for instance, by audibly telling others who live nearby that they have come for a visit, they allow the residents of a household to catch sight of them. A person sneaking off to places is variously regarded as a messenger for secret lovers, a suspect of sorcery, or a spirit haunting somebody.

A further important aim of the colonial administrators was to "improve" existing health and sanitary conditions. As a result, the area was provided with several new, place-related signs of "cleanliness" in the eyes of the colonial administration: the village had to have a community-serving aid post, toilets for each family, and a communal well for "good" drinking water.

People only reluctantly adjusted to the communal use of an aid post that was first opened at Ndoŋon, another Bosmun place, around 1952 (Healy 1951/52: 9, Frawley 1953/54: 10). Curing used to be a matter of "family based care" (cf. Welsch 1986). Only in specific cases of illness were experts beyond the family consulted. I gained the impression that people who had no kin-relation with the person responsible for primary health care were still hesitant to ask for help. Frequently, they complained about the man's preferential treatment of his kin when giving medical advice and distributing medication.

I also observed that in terms of taste people still preferred to drink water from the Ramu, which was said to be special because of the soil it contains. My adoptive father in Daiden, who was born shortly after World War II, and others of the same generation described the *kiap* as a hot-tempered man who did not hesitate to burn down buildings which showed the slightest sign of neglect.

Another place-related sign was added to the colonial reformation of local space by the missionaries who started to proselytize in the Bosmun area around 1935 (Höltker 1937: 1570): a Christian landscape emerged with a communal cemetery and a church building. A church was erected with the establishment of the Catholic Mission's headquarters in 1958/59 in Ndoŋon (Kahler 1959/60: 3, 7). With increasing religious conversion to Christianity, the burial of the deceased of all families together at the periphery of the residential space began to substitute the customary burial amidst the living kin, directly underneath the dwelling house (cf. Van Heekeren [2011: 219-221) about the influence of the formation of a Christian space on Vula'a residential arrangements). The location of the cemetery in Daiden gives more evidence for the regular rearrangement of ground in the Ramu River region. Thirty or forty years ago the cemetery was located where cemeteries should be located according to Christian ideas – at the periphery of Daiden. Now, however, graves are once again located amidst the living with the cemetery marking the border between *vunsi xuur* ("the old [and diminishing] place") and *vunsi ŋgaam* ("the new [and growing] place").

Finally, the *kiap* said that people should plant rice around their villages. A letter accompanying a patrol report from 1957/58 refers to this project: "The goal to aim for would be the gradual divorcing of the people away from the traditional staple of sago and replacing it with rice and other root grobs [sic] as it is obvious that the land will lend itself to this" (Johnston 1957). The processed starch of the sago palm provides people with carbohydrate; it is New Guinea's second most important energy source after sweet potato (Townsend 2003: 4). To outsiders, sago often appears to be a low-quality food and even among sago-eating peoples it may rank as a monotonous or famine food (Tuzin 1992: 104; Barker 2008: 48). Although several patrol reports comment on the continued growing of rice in the area, I gained the impression that people in Daiden and other Bosmun places have not forsaken sago.

To my knowledge, people have left the project of rice fields largely undeveloped. This may be due to the fact that the soil in this humid lowland climate did not "lend itself" as easily as envisioned by the administrators. Another reason could be that, in customary understandings, sago is the only food that is said to keep the human body growing properly. People only abstain from sago in order to express feelings such as sorrow caused by the loss of beloved kin or disagreement over certain social issues. At birth, a sago seedling is planted for a newborn child, and it is ready to be processed when the child reaches adolescence. Moreover, following an ancestral taboo, no one is allowed to eat sago he or she planted. Therefore, sago has to be exchanged on a regular basis, and since it is the staple diet, this taboo urges people to engage in social networks. Interlocutors still adhering to the taboo frequently said to me: "*Mipela kaikai saksak! Yupela kaikai rais!*" ("We eat sago! You [people who prefer a modern / urban lifestyle] eat rice!"), thereby implying that "generous characters" consume sago, whereas "greedy characters" consume rice (von Poser 2013).

Although the consumption of rice has this negative implication, it is becoming important in Bosmun cuisine, and so are the ideational values attached to it. My interlocutors admitted that they were increasingly becoming ŋgumu mbakmbak ("faces covered with spoiled sago"), which is a conventional Bosmun idiom to describe a greedy person. Rice cannot be exchanged to the same extent as sago. Sago is locally obtained, on a regular basis and in large amounts, whereas rice is occasionally bought in town and in small amounts. Since over time the attitude of greed has been gaining ground, the traditional open structure of local living space is being replaced by a more closed structure, apparently mirroring a new lifestyle of social concealment. Most of the people who spoke with me considered this culinary and structural change to be a necessary step in order to adjust to a modern, capitalist-oriented, and progressive life.

Contemporary visions of the "village"

In order to understand how people in Daiden perceive and assess the rural parts of their country, one has to keep in mind their knowledge of the place-making practices of colonial officers in the past. As said earlier, these strategies were not only vividly remembered by the elder generations whom I talked to in Daiden, but are also being reinforced by contemporary extra-local agents such as representatives of the state and NGOs. The media, too, plays its part in the visual transmission of new place-aesthetics. Daiden is not connected to the electricity grid but movies or documentaries are occasionally screened if people provide fuel for generators. Apart from that, people also grasp different senses of place when visiting kin who live in town.

7 "Houses Jumbled Everywhere" 115

Paradoxically, despite more than fifty years of what might be called a "local improvement history," most of my younger and middle-aged interviewees looked at their "village" in rather negative ways, thinking of it as a poor and underdeveloped place. I gained the impression that they were looking through "auto-orientalistic" lenses (Wardlow 2006), as do people elsewhere in contemporary Papua New Guinea. Wardlow, for example, writes that the people of Tari, in the Southern Highlands, have imposed upon themselves a

> brand of "auto-orientalism" – representing themselves as excessively desirous, too easily failing each other, and too easily embittered by others' similar failures. First, one should note that this discourse always has a temporal dimension – Tari is a *jelas* [desirous] place *now*; the past is portrayed as a more disciplined, orderly, and relational era. Second, self, place, and material environment are imbricated in this discourse: the desiring self has become more difficult to manage, but this change has occurred as Tari itself has changed. Tari is said to be a place where commodities are on display, eliciting desire within people; thus, the emotional terrain has changed in synchrony with the material lifeworld (Wardlow 2006: 35).

With Papua New Guinea's independence in 1975, the patrols of colonial times were not replaced by new government services. Thus, people have been left with a number of visions of what a developed material lifeworld should look like but without appropriate access to the resources and materials to build this world; as said earlier, people in this part of the country still mainly survive by self-subsistence.

The "local sense of place," to which I referred earlier by quoting Bender (2001), has therefore continued to "rework modernity." Unfortunately, the on-going forces of such a local sense of place appeared deficient in the eyes of many of my interlocutors, leading, as it were, to the emergence of a distinct collective inferiority complex. Especially my younger interviewees used a rhetoric which rests upon "Western" visions of wealth. To cite but one such opinion expressed about Daiden by one of my interlocutors, a man in his early thirties:

> "*Em ples nogut ya. Yu lukluk ya! Ol haus i bagarap...nogat neil...gras i wok lo karamapim ples...nogat lonmoa...na planti ol lain lo ples...ol wok lo kaikai saksak yet!*"

("This is a bad place. Look! The houses are broken down...[because they have] no nails...grass covers the place all over...[because there are] no lawnmowers...and many people of this place...they still eat sago!").

Obviously, from this quote, a "proper village" should have housing structures that are held together by nails. The grass should be cut with lawnmowers, and the residents' diet should be based on something other than sago, the traditional staple food in the area. The man who told me this had spent some years in town during his early adolescence, living with a sister of his father in a semi-urban part of Madang. Before finishing high school, he had to return and thus brought back his impressions of "life in town." Since he was looked after by his father's mother, he did not himself experience what it meant to earn and spend one's wage for the provisions that are required to maintain a proper life in town. This may have led to a somewhat "idealized" image of life in a seemingly developed place such as the town. My consociates often complained about their fellows who had left the home area for an education and a wealthier life in town, never returning, never bringing back their outside expertise. They anticipated that if these fellows were to come back and share their knowledge, local life could be greatly improved. Only very recently have some educated and wage-earning migrants returned, bringing with them their own visions about what their "village" should look like. It is worthy to note that only those migrants who have managed to maintain proper moral relationships with kin while they were away have the right to a say in local social, political and economic affairs (cf. Dalsgaard 2011: 236; Van Heekeren 2011: 215; von Poser, forthcoming).

For example, I interviewed a man in his fifties from Ndoŋon, who had been trained as an agriculture scientist and who had spent almost thirty years outside his home area. Since he was related to members of the family who looked after me in Daiden, I had the chance to meet him quite regularly. After having experienced the advantages and disadvantages of outside life, the man had come up with his own ideas about combining modernity and tradition. Upon his return to Ndoŋon, where he had grown up, he had built himself a permanent, generator-driven house (at a considerable distance from the river banks). Such houses are still rare in the Lower Ramu region; only few people can afford them. In fact, as Cox (2014: 2) has shown, many Papua New Guineans who belong to today's "working class" in the country must actually be classified as the "working poor." For, often, ordinary wages are inadequate to meet basic costs. Due to his profession, my interlocutor luckily was in a very good position. Wishing to keep the standard of living he had adjusted to during his years in town, the man preferred this kind of house to the traditional constructions which are made of local materials. Considering the nutritional preferences, however, the man wanted to make the younger generations aware of the health-threatening consequences of fast food, which can be obtained in the towns of Papua New Guinea, and has therefore started to propagate the importance of local food, including sago. In doing so, he has also started to create an awareness of the dangers of exploitative land extraction. For instance, he has provided information to the Bismarck Ramu Group which seeks to help customary land owners in the area (cf. Sullivan 2010), and has been raising his voice in Papua New Guinea internet blogs and YouTube sites as well as in a short documentary called *Guardians of the River* filmed by the Sacred Land Film Project (2010). Also, he has been successful in joining larger environmental protection projects that bring together different "indigenous voices" (Letman 2016). In re-evaluating various modes of "improvement" and finding solutions which are more suitable for the locality, he and others have begun to recreate a positive perspective of local life. Also, being proud of his ancestry, including the stories of mythical origin he had listened to as a youngster, the man was confident that he would convince others to lead their lives in a way that would allow for the integration of traditional values into contemporary social, economic, and political contours of life.

Local actors with long-term outside experience are still few but are gaining importance in their society with new and thoughtful ways of ameliorating their lifeworld by re-incorporating distinct ancestral visions of a "good village," thus developing their own opinions about whether "houses jumbled everywhere" should be described this way or not.

Conclusion

My engagement with the different visions of a "village" in Papua New Guinea was based on my exploration of empirical data, on the one hand, and the screening of historical sources, on the other. It helped me in shaping and re-adjusting over time my own understanding of the place to which I had come to in order to conduct fieldwork. I did not only realize that the field which I had first visited in 2004 was, upon my returns, physically as well as ideationally ever-changing. I also realized that, upon my first arrival, this field had already been saturated with different layers of meaning and evaluation and that, if I were to properly understand my interlocutors in "my field," I would need to detect these different layers. As a former doctoral candidate of Jürg Wassmann, I am aware that he considers the long-term immersion into the life of a particular "village" by means of a "second socialization" to be instrumental in gaining the kind of qualitative data which anthropologists call ethnographic knowledge. As I hope to have shown with my exploration of Bosmun visions of the "village," this socialization process never ends because there is no presumed given, stable nature of the field. Therefore, there are many more steps involved in a fieldworker socializing her- or himself into a particular field, and this might be the reason why Jürg Wassmann has kept returning to the field a major premise in his own academic life-course.

Notes

1   Words in the Bosmun vernacular are italicized and underlined. Words in Tok Pisin, the Melanesian Pidgin English, are italicized.

References

Appadurai, A. 1988. Putting Hierarchy in Its Place. Place and Voice in Anthropological Theory. *Cultural Anthropology* 3 (1): 36–49.

Barker, J. 2008. *Ancestral Lines. The Maisin of Papua New Guinea and the Fate of the Rainforest*. Peterborough et al.: Broadview Press.

Bender, B. (ed.) 1993. *Landscape. Politics and Perspectives*. Oxford: Berg.

— 1996. Landscape. In *Encyclopedia of Social and Cultural Anthropology*, eds. A. Barnard and J. Spencer. London & New York: Routledge, pp. 323–324.

— 2001. Landscapes on-the-Move. *Journal of Social Archaeology* 1 (1): 75–89.

Calderwood, B. R. 1970/71. *Patrol Report Bogia No.20 of 1970/71 (Situation Report)*. Sub-District Office, Bogia, Madang District. Port Moresby: National Archives.

Browne, R. C. 1968/69. *Patrol Report Bogia No.7 of 1968/69*. Sub-District Office, Bogia, Madang District. Port Moresby: National Archives.

Casey, E. S. 2009. *Getting Back into Place. Toward a Renewed Understanding of the Place-world*. 2nd Edition. Bloomington/Indianapolis: Indiana University Press.

Cox, J. 2014. "Grassroots", "Elites" and the New "Working Class" of Papua New Guinea. *SSGM In Brief* 6: 1–2.

http://bellschool.anu.edu.au/sites/default/files/publications/attachments/2015-12/SSGM_IB_2014_6_0.pdf [accessed May 27, 2017].
Dalsgaard, S. 2011. The Battle for the Highway. Road, Place and Non-place in Manus (Papua New Guinea). *Paideuma* 57: 231–249.
Douglas, M. A. 1969/70. *Patrol Report Bogia No.11 of 1969/70*. Sub-District Office, Bogia, Madang District. Port Moresby: National Archives.
— 1970/71. *Patrol Report Bogia No.4 of 1970/71 (Situation Report)*. Sub-District Office, Bogia, Madang District. Port Moresby: National Archives.
Dyer, K.W. 1952/53. *Patrol Report Bogia No.8 of 1952/53*. Sub-District Office, Bogia, Madang District. Port Moresby: National Archives.
Feld, S., and K. H. Basso (eds.) 1996. *Senses of Place*. Santa Fe, N.M.: School of American Research Press.
Fox, J. J. (ed.) 1993a. *Inside Austronesian Houses. Perspectives on Domestic Designs for Living*. Canberra: Research School of Pacific Studies, Australian National University.
— 1993b. Comparative Perspectives on Austronesian Houses. An Introductory Essay. In *Inside Austronesian Houses. Perspectives on Domestic Designs for Living*, ed. J. J. Fox. Canberra: Research School of Pacific Studies, Australian National University, pp. 1–28.
Frawley, J. W. 1953/54. *Patrol Report Bogia No.10 of 1953/54*. Sub-District Office, Bogia, Madang District. Port Moresby: National Archives.
Gehrmann, K. 1916. Die Gogol-Ramu-Expedition in Kaiser-Wilhelmsland. September und Oktober 1913. Tagebuch über die Gogol-Ramu-Expedition. *Mitteilungen aus den Deutschen Schutzgebieten* 29: 2–30.
Healy, J. P. 1951/52. *Patrol Report Bogia No.6 of 1951/52*. Sub-District Office, Bogia, Madang District. Port Moresby: National Archives.
Hirsch, E. 1995. Landscape. Between Place and Space. In *The Anthropology of Landscape. Perspectives on Place and Space*, eds. E. Hirsch and M. O'Hanlon. Oxford: Clarendon Press, pp. 1–30.
Hirsch, E., and M. O'Hanlon (eds.) 1995. *The Anthropology of Landscape. Perspectives on Place and Space*. Oxford: Clarendon Press.
Höltker, G. 1937. Die Kinder der Kopfjäger. *Wochenpost* 9 (50): 1570–1571.
Ingold, T. 2000. *The Perception of the Environment. Essays in Livelihood, Dwelling and Skill*. London and New York: Routledge.
Johnston, W. J. 1957. *Comments to the Patrol Report Bogia No. 9 of 1956/57*. Sub-District Office, Bogia, Madang District. Port Moresby: National Archives.
Kahler, S. P. 1959/60. *Patrol Report Bogia No.3 of 1959/60*. Sub-District Office, Bogia, Madang District. Port Moresby: National Archives.
Letman J. 2016. Asia's Indigenous Voices, Defending Sacred Lands. *The Diplomat* http://thediplomat.com/2016/12/asias-indigenous-voices-taking-a-stand-for-sacred-lands/ [accessed January 9, 2017].

LiPuma, E. 1998. Modernity and Forms of Personhood in Melanesia. In *Bodies and Persons. Comparative Perspectives from Africa and Melanesia*, eds. M. Lambek and A. Strathern. Cambridge: Cambridge University Press, pp. 53–79.
Mines, D. P. and N. Yazgi 2010. Introduction. Do Villages Matter? In *Village Matters. Relocating Villages in the Contemporary Anthropology of India*, eds. D. P. Mines and N. Yazgi. New Delhi: Oxford University Press, pp. 1–28.
von Poser, A. 2011. Bosmun Foodways. Emotional Reasoning in a Papua New Guinea Life-world. In *The Anthropology of Empathy. Experiencing the Lives of Others in Pacific Societies*, eds. D. Hollan and C. J. Throop. New York and Oxford: Berghahn, pp. 169–192.
— 2013. *Foodways and Empathy. Relatedness in a Ramu River Society, Papua New Guinea*. New York and Oxford: Berghahn. (Person, Space and Memory in the Contemporary Pacific, Vol. 4).
— Forthcoming. Care as Process. A Life-Course Perspective on the Remaking of Ethics and Values of Care in Daiden, Papua New Guinea. *Journal of Ethics and Social Welfare*. doi: 10.1080/17496535.2017.1300303.
Quanchi, M. 2003. Contrary Images. Photographing the New Pacific in *Walkabout* Magazine. *Journal of Australian Studies* 79: 77–92, 230–233.
Sacred Land Film Project 2010. *Guardians of the River. Bosmun, Ramu River, Papua New Guinea*. Film, 5 min. http://www.sacredland.org/guardians-of-the-river/ [accessed February 9, 2017].
Sheekey, D. P. 1962. *Comments to the Patrol Report Bogia No.6 of 1961/62*. Sub-District Office, Bogia, Madang District. Port Moresby: National Archives.
Stasch, R. 2010. The Category "Village" in Melanesian Social Worlds. Some Theoretical and Methodological Possibilities. *Paideuma* 56: 41–62.
Sullivan, N. & Associates LTD. 2010. *Middle to Lower Ramu Subsistence, Household and Culture Study*. 2nd Revision. For Phil Shearman and Bismark Ramu Group. http://www.nancysullivan.net/companyreports.htm [accessed October 5, 2012].
Tiesler, F. 1969. Die intertribalen Beziehungen an der Nordküste Neuguineas im Gebiet der kleinen Schouten-Inseln (I). *Abhandlungen und Berichte des Staatlichen Museums für Völkerkunde Dresden* 30: 1–122.
— 1970. Die intertribalen Beziehungen an der Nordküste Neuguineas im Gebiet der kleinen Schouten-Inseln (II). *Abhandlungen und Berichte des Staatlichen Museums für Völkerkunde Dresden* 31: 111–195.
Tilley, C. 1994. *A Phenomenology of Landscape. Places, Paths and Monuments*. Oxford and Providence: Berg.
Tönnies, F. 1957. *Community and Society*. East Lansing: Michigan State University Press.
Townsend, P. K. 2003. *Palm Sago. Further Thoughts on a Tropical Starch from Marginal Lands*. Canberra: Research School of Pacific and Asian Studies (Resource Management in Asia-Pacific, Working Paper No. 49).

Tuzin, D. F. 1992. Sago Subsistence and Symbolism among the Ilahita Arapesh. *Ethnology* 31 (2): 103–114.

Van Heekeren, D. 2011. From Trading Canoe to "Village Citizen." The Place of Vula'a Identity. *Paideuma* 57: 209–230.

Wardlow, H. 2006. *Wayward Women. Sexuality and Agency in a New Guinea Society*. Berkeley, Los Angeles and London: University of California Press.

Welsch, R. 1986. Primary Health Care and Local Self Determination. Policy Implications from Rural Papua New Guinea. *Human Organization* 45 (2): 103–112.

HERMANN MÜCKLER

8 The Chase for Archival Material and Biographical Information in the "Field" of Archives. Remarks about a Research Project, carried out in Chile, Rapanui and Other Places

Introduction: The stimulus

In the late 1990s I noticed a book, existence of which I knew nothing about until then. An Austrian antiquarian bookseller had Walter Knoches book *Die Osterinsel. Ergebnisse der chilenischen Osterinselexpedition 1911* on offer. This book is indeed very rare; from the early 1950s up to the 1990s only one original copy of this book appeared on an international auction. Consequently, the price of the book was exorbitantly high. Nevertheless, it was – after long negotiations with the bookseller – finally possibly for me to acquire the book. This book is rare and also widely unknown. It was published in 1925 in Concepción in Chile in the German language. In Chile hardly anyone knows it as it was written in German; in the German speaking countries of Europe hardly anyone knows the book as it was released in Chile as a limited edition that scarcely found its way to Europe. This is the reason why this book is truly rare and often cannot be found even in prestigious scientific libraries. Since the 1990s only one other copy was auctioned at an international book auction in the USA, and the price for an original copy of the book has even climbed significantly since. Until today, no one has edited or published it in a commented version to make it available for a broader, interested public. Also *google books, Projekt Gutenberg* and other internet platforms who offer the full texts of books do not provide access to the contents of this book.

Walter Knoche's book of 320 pages describes the first Chilean Easter Island expedition which took place in 1911, and provides detailed aspects on the meteorology, physical anthropology, ethnology and archaeology of Easter Island as well as characteristics of the Easter Islander's material culture, which he illustrated with numerous images. Only some Easter Island experts know about this book, and only some few have read and reflected on its content. The Norwegian archaeologist Thor Heyerdahl was one of the few who had read some of Walter Knoche's articles and his book on Easter Island; he even dedicated to Knoche a subchapter in his popular-scientific book *The Art of Easter Island* from 1975 (Heyerdahl 1975). Heyerdahl also mentioned Knoche several times in his bulky two-volume *Archaeology of Easter Island* (Heyerdahl and Ferdon 1961) which he edited together with Edwin Ferdon. Also the linguist Steven Roger Fischer (1997) paid tribute to Walter Knoche and his achievements in a subchapter of one of his books. But Knoche and some of his early articles related to Easter Island, which appeared already in 1912 shortly after the expedition, are not mentioned by Katherine Routledge Scoresby (*The Mystery of Easter Island*) who did research on Easter Island only three years after Knoche's visit to the island, and also John Macmillan Brown (*The Riddle of the Pacific*) gives no reference to Knoche, although he published in his own book a photograph of Knoche's ethnographic collection. If you ask Pacific Islands experts "who is Walter Knoche?" only a few might have heard about him.

What could be better than to devote oneself to this person and his work? Although an anthropologist by profession, I have a strong inclination to work as a historian and with historians, and would rather call myself an "ethnohistorian" or an anthropologist dealing with historical questions in relation to anthropological/ethnological findings. In 2008 I started to trace back Knoche's life and oeuvre, and his importance for natural and social sciences.

After many years of historical and biographical research, the search for traces of different kinds and the effort of putting together many small pieces of the mosaic, I have fulfilled this desire with the publication of a book offering a re-edition of Knoche's book, accompanied by a detailed account on Knoche's biographical background and a closer look at the circumstances of the Chilean Easter Island expedition of 1911 (Mückler 2015, 2016). The collection of material for this book started in 2008 and was finalized in early 2015. Research trips, supported by a grant from the Federation of Austrian-Foreign Societies – PaN (Partner aller Nationen) brought me during these seven years to many European and overseas cities and their scientific archives. Can such research be called a form of "fieldwork"?

Disappointment and ambition – obstacles and coincidences

The ambition to find out more about Walter Knoche met with limitations immediately after an immediate Google search. When I started investigations on Walter Knoche, I soon found out that there was little information on hand to shed light on his biographical background. There was no Wikipedia entry about this scientist and also the Chilean Easter Island Expedition of 1911 does not have a separate entry up to now in Wikipedia or other similar internet information gathering platforms. This aroused and increased my ambition to find out more about the person and his personal and scientific background.

A first hint was that many articles by him on meteorology, geophysics and climate exist, proving his professional expertise in these disciplines. An enquiry at the Leo Baeck Institute in New York, which specializes in the history of German Jews in exile, finally brought the first facts to light. A dossier consisting of six documents included an obituary for Walter Knoche and for the first time gave a rough idea of his paths of life. Investigations in the library of the Ibero-American Institute in Berlin finally revealed a list of publications by Knoche in connection with his research on Easter Island. I traveled to Chile twice and once to Argentina in search of material. The first time that I went to Chile was in the summer of 2009, where I had the chance to visit, amongst others, the large Chilean exhibition on Rapanui *Kuhane Rapa Nui. En Las Islas Del Pacífico* on the premises of "La Moneda" (the "mint"; Fundación Centro Cultural Palacio La Moneda) in Santiago de Chile. This was the largest and most comprehensive exhibition to date that Chile had ever devoted to the history and culture of Easter Island (Gómez and Rauch 2009). Among the exhibits there were some important objects from Walter Knoche's Easter Island collection. A few months later I went to Santiago for a second time, together with the cultural and social anthropologist Gabriele Weichart from the University of Vienna, this time for a longer stay to visit all the sites where Walter Knoche had been active. In the course of many weeks we visited libraries, university institutes, museums and companies which were associated with Knoche's work. Gabriele

Weichart acted not only as an interpreter and translator but also played her part as a cultural and social anthropologist in our investigations and had many good ideas as to how to obtain information on Knoche's biographical background. Among others, we went to the Dirección Meteorológica de Chile in Quinta Normal, Santiago, which had been co-founded and built up by Walter Knoche. Curiously enough, his is the first name on a list on a copper plate next to the door of the head office. We made it clear to the manageress who Knoche had actually been and that he was one of her predecessors and the founding father of modern meteorology in Chile. Similarly, we received substantial support from the Institute of Meteorology and we were able to reconstruct an important chapter in Knoche's life. Our visit with the Chilean pharmaceutical company "Instituto Sanitas S.A." on the outskirts of Santiago, in an industrial park near the airport, was also fruitful. In 1920 Knoche had been one of the founders of this enterprise, which devoted itself to medical research, diagnosis and to the manufacture of drugs and the development of therapies. We visited this enterprise, now a good deal bigger than in Knoche's day, hoping to find documents on the beginnings of this company. The managing director Gonzalo Amenabar Vives was obviously delighted not to have to talk shop for once and proved very helpful. His staff were not quite so enthusiastic about having to search in the basement for dusty and forgotten records and having to take them upstairs to the head office for inspection. Next we went to Valparaiso where the logbooks of the Chilean Easter Island Expedition are held by the local Naval Museum and Archives (Museo Naval y Marítimo Nacional). Even though we became the victims of a robbery only a few hundred meters away from the Museum on the occasion of one of our many visits there, this visit to the research institution was still worth it. Knoche had sailed to Easter Island as the scientific leader of this expedition on the Chilean naval vessel "General Baquedano." The logbooks gave evidence of the planning details of the beginning and end of the voyage and provided information on the stay on Easter Island from the Army and Navy points of view. From there we proceeded to Viña del Mar, where exhibits are held of the material culture of Easter Island from Knoche's collection in the Museo Francisco Fonck, which is also one of the centres of Chilean Easter Island research.

Eventually we went to Easter Island itself, and for a whole week we gathered material not only in the Biblioteca William Mulloy des Museo Antropológico Padre Sebastián Englert (MAPSE), but we were also able to visit all those places on the island that Knoche had visited and documented. Knoche had set up a meteorological station near the present day airport of Hanga Roa in 1911. Nowadays, the same site boasts its modern successor, which transmits data on the current (flight) weather to Santiago. And finally we traveled to Argentina where Knoche spent the final years of his professional and private life. In Buenos Aires, the last place where he worked and where he died in 1945, we were able to find out what he did last, and who the persons were with whom he worked and exchanged letters. Regrettably it was not possible to find his grave before the book was completed, since a lengthy search of many weeks would have been necessary; there were over twenty-five cemeteries in Buenos Aires and additionally five German and five Jewish cemeteries. All of them had no digitalized data and some of them did not even have written documentation about the graves and their occupants. In spite of this, the six weeks of fact finding during the second journey to Chile and the journey to Argentina yielded a wealth of useful material. This was evaluated and utilized in the past four and a half years, frequently interrupted on my part by teaching and research as my academic profession required it, and additional investigations were made by mail and email.

Only towards the end of my research was I so lucky as to track down a descendant of Knoche's family in Chile. Carlos Berliner, a distant relative of Knoche, helped me to make contact with Walter Knoche's great-nephew Peter Gross and his mother, a cousin of Walter Knoche's. And so I had indeed found people who had actually known Walter Knoche! It was a very moving moment for me to talk on the phone to the already 93-year-old cousin of Walter Knoche's by the name of Marian Ansten, who lives in the US State of Arizona and whose sister, Ursula Vera Knoche, had lived with Walter Knoche in Buenos Aires for quite some time. The personality of Walter Knoche finally came to life through these contacts with people who had known and experienced Walter Knoche personally. Additional material which I received from Mrs. Ansten not only illustrated the findings, but also opened up the opportunity to get a visual impression of the person and his lifetime.

Some findings

Although at the beginning almost no personal information about Walter Knoche was available, the years of research evolved successfully. To provide an overview of the results I shall summarize the findings:

Walter Alfred Knoche was born on 7th of March 1881 in Berlin, Germany, as the son of the factory owner Moritz Knoche and Anna Ehrlich; he was one of seven siblings. After graduating from school in 1902, he devoted himself to scientific studies. After one term at the University of Geneva he switched to the Friedrich Wilhelm University in Berlin where he attended the lectures of the German physicist and meteorologist Wilhelm von Bezold as well as the geographer and meteorologist Wilhelm Meinardus. On the 31st of July 1905 Walter Knoche obtained his doctoral degree with a dissertation with the title *On the spatial and temporal dispersion of warmth in the lower air layer* at the Berlin Royal Meteorological Institute. Afterwards Walter Knoche started geographical and meteorological field research in the Mediterranean region, particularly in Turkey, in several North African countries and on the Canary Islands to intensify his studies. Afterwards he went to South America on an expedition into the Bolivian cordillera to explore the micro-climatic and aero-electric conditions at an altitude of above 5,200m sea level. The results of this expedition were later published by the Instituto Central Meteorológico y Geofísico de Chile, whose control and reorganization was offered to Knoche (and accepted by him) during the Chilean government of prime minister Pedro Montt in 1910. This job opportunity prompted Knoche to emigrate to Chile; he settled in the capital Santiago and later also became a Chilean citizen. In the following decades, Knoche undertook several educational journeys to most South American countries as well as to Europe. Following his great interest in medical problems, he worked together with famous Chilean medical doctors such as Aldunate, Muenich, Cadiz, Cruz Coke and others and founded together with them the Instituto Sanitas (Institute for Health) which was (and still is) a scientific and commercial enterprise with the aim of developing new medications and therapies. In 1937 Knoche moved from Chile to the neighbouring country Argentina where he settled himself in Buenos Aires.

On the 3rd of July 1945 Walter Knoche died of heart failure. At the time of his death he was the head of the Climatologic Department of the

8 The Chase for Archival Material

Direction for Meteorology, Geophysics and Hydrology in Buenos Aires. Walter Knoche left behind an oeuvre of 270 publications, among them 163 scientific articles and books dealing with meteorological, climatological, geo-physical, geographical but also medical-anthropological topics. 36 of the articles dealt with Easter Island and aspects of Rapanui's cultural world.

It cannot be clarified if Walter Knoche already knew that he was chosen to be the conductor of a planned Easter Island Expedition when he arrived in Chile. It is certain that he knew about it in 1910 and that he was involved after that in the preparatory work. The aim of the expedition was to establish a first-order meteorological station and a seismological station on the island; to survey the health situation and hygienic situation of the indigenous inhabitants of Easter Island and finally it was Knoche's privilege to do further investigations and research surveys on the island on his own. Presumably, in the preparatory meetings Knoche had already mentioned his ethnological and anthropological interest in the inhabitants of Easter Island and their cultural life. On the official Chilean side, the top commander of the navy Jorge Montt and the deputy head of the Department of the Chilean Ministry of Education (Ministerio de Instrucción Pública) Moisés Vargas were the driving forces and substantial supporters of the expedition. Knoche was accompanied by three other scientists on the trip: Francisco Fuentes, a botanist of the Lyzeum in La Serena in the northern part of Chile; Edgardo Martinez, a scientific assistant at the Central Station for Meteorology and Geophysics, Santiago de Chile; and Juan Calderon, a mechanic at the Seismological Service, Santiago de Chile. For the expedition that took place under the direction of the Chilean Navy, the training ship "General Baquedano" was chosen as the means of transport.

On 26th of March 1911 the passage started from the Chilean naval port Talcahuano with the commission on board. On the 13th of April they reached Easter Island and anchored in Hangaroa Bay. The stay on the island lasted until 25th of April 1911. The 9th of May 1911 is quoted as the date of return to Talcahuano, which meant at the same time the end of the journey. Therefore, the passage to Easter Island took eighteen days, the stay on the island twelve days and the return passage another fourteen days. One member of the scientific commission stayed on Easter Island: Edgardo Martinez, who was Knoche's assistant. He then lived on Easter Island until the beginning of June 1912 to accomplish meteorological measurements and observations over the course of a whole year. The logbooks do not provide any indication about what the scientists actually did on Easter Island. In his book and articles, even Walter Knoche gives only little information about the procedure of the observations on the island. He mentions that the overall conditions for the setup of the meteorological station and the introductory trainings for its proper use were difficult (Knoche 1913a: 2). It is striking that, so far, Chilean researchers have paid little attention to the Easter Island expedition 1911. To the present day there is no oeuvre that explicitly deals with the expedition and its findings. Even though in some Chilean contributions to the knowledge of Easter Island as well as in books about Chilean history this enterprise is repeatedly mentioned, the information is often incomplete or incorrect. Knoche brought along ethnographic objects from Easter Island that are on display in Chilean and several European museums. The exact number of objects of the material culture of Rapanui that Knoche brought with him is unknown. Knoche's book, his successively published 36 articles on Easter Island, and the results of his colleagues traveling with him make up the findings of this expedition. As Knoche later noted, one unintentional and negative result of the Chilean Easter Island expedition was that the weevil (*curculionidae*) found its way to Easter Island in 1911 in the wooden boxes which the members of the expedition left behind. These boxes were used to transport the potatoes which made up part of their provisions (Knoche 1925: 137).

Subsequent scientists saw Knoche's surveys with ambivalence. On the one hand, the Norwegian Thor Heyerdahl examined Knoche's collection of objects more precisely and used them as a basis for his research on his own expedition to Easter Island (Heyerdahl 1975: 72-73). On the other hand, the New Zealand scientist Steven Roger Fischer sees Knoche's ethnographic findings first of all in the light of his own interest and research in the rongorongo panels and their graphic characters; for Fischer, Knoche was not able to contribute any additional or interesting findings for the advancement of research on the tablets. Nevertheless, Fischer classifies Knoche's book on Easter Island from 1925 as "a model of sober and precise scholarship, one of the best to appear about the island in the first half of the twentieth century" (Fischer 1997: 123). Certainly this is one of the reasons why Knoche's enthusiastic surveys have in part only limited significance: He only had eleven days to accomplish the meteorological and geophysical duties that he had been instructed to do by the Chilean government, and in addition to accomplish the tasks he personally was interested in. It was inevitable that he could not do everything. Limitations in his research also occurred due to the fact that Knoche's translator Juan Tepano indeed spoke Spanish but in dealing with the indigenous Rapanui he spoke a Rapanui-Tahitian idiom that differed clearly from the original Rapanui language only spoken by a few old people. For this reason, the accuracy of the translations needs to be brought into question. Presumably Tepano was not able to understand and translate everything that the ancients told him about "old" traditions (Fischer 1997: 123). Nevertheless, in 1911 Knoche was chronologically the first person who worked systematically, tried to get information on all aspects of the life of the Rapanui and later wrote a monographic book on his findings.

Knoche's book on Easter Island

Walter Knoche's Easter Island book combines his own observations and surveys as well as conclusions derived from these. When reading the introductory part, it becomes clear that Knoche also processed events that took place after 1911. He mentioned, among other things, Katherine Routledge's expedition to Easter Island only three years after his own visit, and the German encounters with the inhabitants of Easter Island during World War I. This shows that Knoche considered and incorporated in the book – published in 1925 – also developments and the advanced insights that had resulted since 1911. The book was published by the Publishing Company of the Scientific Archives of Chile, which is located in the Chilean city of Concepción. The exact size of the edition cannot be determined anymore; presumably the edition comprised around 100 books. What is so exceptional about this book? Knoche did his research even before Katherine Routledge and others who devoted themselves to an intense acquisition of the still remaining "old" elements of Rapanui culture. He was still able to observe and ask for things that three years later – when Routledge came to Easter Island and stayed a lot longer than Knoche – did not exist any longer. Knoche still had the opportunity to ask two old men about traditional customs, feasts, dances, ceremonies and other cultural manifestations and they roughly informed him. When Knoche was on Easter Island, the indigenous populations' living conditions were extremely difficult due to the problematic Chilean exercise of power. In his book Knoche criticizes this. Knoche was aware of the dramatic consequences that the appearance of Europeans and Chileans caused on Easter Island. He certainly knew about the problematic role of the Chilean government that permitted the local indigenous population to become marginalized and to have to endure the most adverse living conditions due to economically motivated exploitation. Out of deference to his Chilean employers Knoche did not criticize this in his articles and also in his book he only refers in a general critique to these aspects. Knoche's cultural pessimism has to be seen from the perspective of the early 1920s when it was even clearer than in 1911 that the old times on Easter Island were irretrievable and there was no more connection to the past through contemporary witnesses. Steven Roger Fischer called this pessimistic attitude "cynicism of the embittered German expatriate" (Fischer 1997: 122). In 1911, the native population's medical conditions were disastrous. Knoche paid attention to the diseases found and especially to leprosy. It can be assumed that this infectious disease had found its way to Easter Island around 1900, coming from Tahiti in Central Polynesia. Knoche not only mentions this situation in his book but also in two separately published articles, one of which was published straight after the expedition in 1912 and the second one year later (Knoche 1912; 1913b). In the subchapters, Knoche tries to address nearly all aspects of the life of the Rapanui. The individual issues listed in the table of contents are the following: Discovery of Easter Island; Further visits to Easter Island; About the geography of Easter Island; Volcanoes and seismicity; The climate on Easter Island; Health issues; The flora on Easter Island; Statistics; Anthropology; Tattoos, Jewellery, Hairstyles; The nature of the inhabitants; Dwellings; The cuisine of the Easter Islanders; Fishing; Trade and transport; The married life; Midwifery; Medications; Funerals; Music, Dance, Games, Sport; Religion; Vendettas; Stone sculptures and wood carvings; About certain paintings on Easter Island; Statues on Easter Island; Remarks on the graphic panels; Linguistics and Grammar; Folklore; History; Annex to the music of the Easter Islanders.

It has to be annotated that Knoche did not use the then typical and "zeitgeisty" methods of measurement when he was in contact with the indigenous population on Easter Island. Knoche himself never did any anthropological measurements of heads or bodies that seemed to have been taken for granted at this time and that were conducted almost automatically by scientists during their expeditions around the beginning of the 20th century. Contrary to many of his contemporary colleagues from anthropology, Knoche does not express any judgmental comments on race, which shows that he set himself apart from certain trends and cut his own path. There is also evidence that many topics only got touched on and would have required more intense attention to come to more sustainable conclusions. Due to the serious time pressure under which Walter Knoche had to do his surveys, this was impossible. Maybe this is one of the reasons why his oeuvre still has not gained the attention it should have. Actually, Knoche has not only stated his position on single aspects in this book but also in, as already mentioned, 36 professional articles that were published before and after the expedition. This should make clear that Knoche 1.) had a personal and relentless interest in Easter Island throughout his life (his last article was published in 1939) and 2.) participated actively in the growing number of recently arisen professional discussions on the island and the culture of the Rapanui. There are no private statements of Knoche's where he explicitly expresses his sympathy for the Easter Islanders but his cautious socio-critical comments are an indication that he was unhappy about the conditions that he discovered on site in 1911. In any case, he helped to memorialize the indigenous Polynesian inhabitants of this island by writing down details of the traditional but already lost culture of the Rapanui as were told to him upon his requesting them. His book on Easter Island reflects his interdisciplinary and transdisciplinary method as well as his ability to link several sciences to obtain more profound results. Knoche's book is not only a description of the Chilean Easter Island Expedition but also affirms Knoche's multifaceted scientific expertise.

Some theoretical considerations

Although some contact could be established via email and some copied material sent at my request, during the period of research on Walter Knoche and the collection of material it was necessary to go to Knoche's birth place, Berlin, and to follow him from there to Chile and Easter Island, as well as to Argentina, where he died. The amount of financial investment in this project was considerable, the investment of time over a span of seven years obviously even more. The research was carried out at a methodological intersection of life history and biographical research, archival research, library research, and the contextualization and assessment of a scientific book; its contemporary and present scientific framework was examined through reviewing, reediting and adding comments. In this way, the project combined methods and theories from different scientific fields: life history research, to some extent biographical research, and particularly archival as well as library research – the last mentioned being rather fitting to describe the core research done about Knoche.

Whereas biographical research, generally spoken, can be seen as part of the broader practice of qualitative methods, typically the topic constitutes the study of a single life, focusing primarily upon an individual (Garraty 1957; Oates 1986). Other research methodologies are often bundled within the descriptor of biography and include life history writing, oral history, memoir, autobiography, and life narrative (Josselson and Lieblich 1993; Roberts 2002). For instance, life history is a method of qualitative research, frequently, but not exclusively, used in history, anthropology, but also in recent times in health sciences. It provides an alternative to empirical methods for identifying and documenting life patterns of individuals and groups. Life history also allows the researcher to explore a person's micro-historical, or better, his individual experiences within a macro-historical, a so-called "history of the time" framework. Life history information thus challenges the researcher to understand an individual's attitudes and behaviors and how they may have been influenced by initial decisions made at another time and in another place. Usually a life story is the story a person tells about the life he or she has lived. As I was dealing with a person already deceased and only available as a "historic person," things changed considerably. The "life story" had to be distilled from the remaining detectable primary and secondary sources. The primary sources found in different archives in the USA, Israel, Chile, Rapanui and Germany enabled me to get as close as possible to what actually happened during the respective historical events and time periods. Unpublished manuscripts and records, printed and published materials, maps, plans, visual materials, including photographs and ethnographic artefacts were the record formats which I could collect during a period of seven years.

So I reconstructed a "life story" out of archival material, keeping in mind that archival records exist to be used and not merely saved for their own sake. Remembering the words of Robert Atkinson (1998: 8), that a life story is "(...) a fairly complete narrating of one's entire experience of life as a whole, highlighting the most important aspects," I tried to document and bring the different tesserae together to create as "lively" an image as possible. Also remembering that in social science, life (hi)stories exist in many forms: specific and general, long and short, surface and deep, fuzzy and focused, realistic and romantic, I kept in mind that all of them have a slightly different emphasis and meaning, but all focus on the first persona accounting of a life; a life history is first of all an overall picture of the informant's biography. As life history is a method of qualitative research, we have to admit that qualitative research usually has a number of features stemming from its philosophical and theoretical approach to the social world. Those can be summarized, following Alan Bryman, as "viewing events, action, norms, values etc. from the perspective of the people who are being studied, (...) to provide detailed descriptions of the social settings, (...) commitment to understanding events, behavior, etc. in their context, (...) to view social life in processual, rather than static terms, (...) a research strategy which is relatively open and unstructured" (Bryman 1988: 61-68, cf. Roberts 2002: 2-3). These points can be applied even to historic persons via a multi-layer approach that incorporates different forms of biographical research. These include, for instance, single aspects of an intellectual biography which forsake the need for basic chronological structure and develop a narrative of a life through the conceptual analysis of the subject's motives and beliefs within the world of his or her ideas. Another aspect was the use of some motives and tools of narrative biography for interviewing contemporary witnesses ("Zeitzeugen") who either knew Walter Knoche personally (only one person), or had some specific relationship to one of Knoche's life and work contexts. One might feel relieved that no definitive listing of biographical types can ever be constructed since new forms, both content and process oriented, are continually being conceived and explored. Of course, acting as a biographer, I was during my engagement in the research on Knoche constantly examining the interpretive voice, my voice, as much as the life of the biographical subject.

Archival research on the other hand lies at the heart of most academic and other forms of original historical research, but it is frequently also undertaken in conjunction with parallel research methodologies in other disciplines within the humanities and social sciences. Archival research is usually more complex and time-consuming than library and internet research, presenting challenges in identifying, locating and interpreting relevant documents. For example, the days spent at the Naval Archive of the Chilean Navy in Valparaiso reading and photographing the logbooks of the Chilean Easter Island expedition not only took considerable time, but also showed the limits of archival research in a country with an "archive culture" whose collecting practices differ significantly to those in European archives. In other words, apart from the logbooks no other material related to the Easter Island expedition was archived (or remained in the archives). Other sources had to be found, new ways had to be found. Archival research has, more so than library research, at least one similarity to classical fieldwork: the tracing and hunting of the desired information embedded in a context which could best be compared with the strategies of a criminal profiler, who has to put him- or herself in someone else's position to obtain useful and valuable information.

An anthropologist in the field often employs strategies close to those of a criminal profiler. In the field we do thorough analysis of the type and nature of the social behavior of people; this is then compared to the types of people who had and/or have similar patterns of behavior. An in-depth analysis of the actual social and political scene is made and the people's background and activities are analyzed to look for possible motives for (daily life, ritual, political) actions and connections to other aspects of organized social entities. Thus possible factors for the motivation of the people's actions are analyzed, and a description of the main players (e.g. a Melanesian Big Man) is developed and founded on the detected characteristics, which can be compared to previous examples (or shall we call them "cases"?). Profiling can thus be seen as a behavioral and investigative tool that is intended to help investigators, in our case the fieldworker, to accurately predict and profile the characteristics of unknown subjects. Fieldwork as an anthropological method, and particularly participant observation, are core aspects of anthropology as a discipline. Participant observation enables the social anthropologist to undertake detailed, lengthy and often complex observations of social life in fine detail. Jürg Wassmann's extensive fieldwork in Papua New Guinea may act here as a good example of the importance and the potential which lies in the traditional form of anthropological fieldwork and which lead to classic ethnographies (Wassmann 1982; 1988). As we know, the practice of "fieldwork" can be done in a variety of different settings such as an urban or virtual environment, a small-scale society, a museum, a library, a cultural institution, etc.

Conclusion

What is, or what can fieldwork (also) be? As Jan Blommaert (2006: 3) once stated:

> [It is] trying to accomplish a task initially formulated as a perfectly coherent research plan with questions, methods, readings and so on – and finding out that the "field" is a chaotic, hugely complex place. Fieldwork is the moment when the researcher climbs down to everyday reality and finds out that the rules of academia are not necessarily the same as those of everyday life.

You can have such an experience in the highlands of Papua New Guinea as well as while practising historical biographical research in archives, libraries and in sometimes precarious interviewing contexts.

Of course "traditional" fieldwork cannot really be compared with "digging" in archives, libraries, institutions and museums – a discussion of these aspects would fill several books – but the latter are also "fields" in which you can investigate, collect and document, in which you are faced with disbelief and confronted with obstacles, and in which you have your subjects whom you have to handle with kid gloves.

References

Atkinson, R. 1998. *The Life Story Interview*. Thousand Oaks: Sage Publications.
Blommaert, J. 2006. *Ethnographic Fieldwork. A Beginner's Guide*. London: Institute of Education, University of London.
https://www.jyu.fi/hum/laitokset/kielet/tutkimus/hankkeet/paattyneet-hankkeet/fidipro/en/courses/fieldwork-text. [accessed 26 October 2015].
Brown, J. M. 1926. *The Riddle of the Pacific*. London: T. Fisher Unwin Ltd.
Bryman, A. 1988. *Quantity and Quality in Social Research*. London and New York: Routledge.
Fischer, S. R. 1997. *Rongorongo. The Easter Island Script. History, Traditions, Texts*. Oxford: Clarendon Press.
Garraty, J. 1957. *The Nature of Biography*. New York: Knopf.
Gómez, C., and M. Rauch (eds.) 2009. *Kuhane Rapa Nui, en las islas del Pacífico*. Santiago de Chile: Fundación Centro Cultural Palacio La Moneda.
Heyerdahl, T. 1975. *The Art of Easter Island*. New York: Doubleday and Company.

Heyerdahl, T., and E. N. Ferdon, Jr. (eds.) 1961. *Archaeology of Easter Island. Reports of the Norwegian Archaeological Expedition to Easter Island and the East Pacific, Volume I*. London: George Allen and Unwin. (Monographs of the School of American Research and the Museum of New Mexico, No. 24, Part 1, 1961).

Josselson, R., and A. Lieblich (eds.) 1993. *The Narrative Study of Lives*. Thousand Oaks: Sage Publications.

Knoche, W. 1912. Die Lepra auf der Osterinsel. *Zeitschrift für physikalische und diätische Therapie* 1 (1): 8.

— 1913a. *Observaciones Meteorológicas en la Isla de Pascua Mayo 1911 – Abril 1912*. Con estudios de F. Montessus de Ballore, F. Fuentes, W. Knoche. Instituto Central Meteorológico y Geofísico de Chile. Publicaciones bajo la dirección del Dr. W. Knoche, No. 4, Santiago de Chile.

— 1913b. Der Lepraherd auf der Osterinsel. *Medizinische Klinik* 1 (1), 5th January: 13.

— 1925. *Die Osterinsel. Eine Zusammenfassung der chilenischen Osterinselexpedition 1911*. Concepción: Verlag des Wissenschaftlichen Archivs von Chile.

Mückler, H. 2015. *Walter Knoche. Die Osterinsel. Die chilenische Osterinsel-Expedition von 1911. Herausgegeben, eingeleitet und kommentiert*. Wiesbaden: Harrassowitz Verlag. (Quellen und Forschungen zur Südsee, Vol. 6).

— 2016. Der vergessene Osterinsel-Forscher Walter Knoche, wissenschaftlicher Leiter der chilenischen Rapa Nui-Expedition 1911. *Jahrbuch für Europäische Überseegeschichte* 15: 89–111.

Oates, S. B. (ed.) 1986. *Biography as High Adventure*. Amherst: University of Massachusetts Press.

Roberts, R. 2002. *Biographical Research*. Buckingham: Open University Press. https://student.cc.uoc.gr/uploadFiles /1110-004K/BIOGR1_Biographical%20research.pdf [accessed 26 October 2015].

Routledge, K. S. 1919. *The Mystery of Easter Island. The Story of an Expedition*. London: Hazell, Watson and Viney/Sifton, Praed.

Wassmann, J. 1982. *Der Gesang an den Fliegenden Hund. Untersuchungen zu den totemistischen Gesängen und geheimen Namen des Dorfes Kandingei am Mittelsepik (Papua New Guinea) anhand der kirugu-Knotenschnüre*. Basel: Ethnologisches Seminar der Universität und Museum für Völkerkunde. (Basler Beiträge zur Ethnologie Bd. 22).

— 1988. *Der Gesang an das Krokodil. Die rituellen Gesänge des Dorfes Kandingei an Land und Meer, Pflanzen und Tiere (Mittelsepik, Papua New Guinea)*. Basel: Ethnologisches Seminar der Universität und Museum für Völkerkunde. (Basler Beiträge zur Ethnologie Bd. 28).

RAYMOND AMMANN

9 References to Time and Space in Melanesian Music

Introduction

During a stay in 2002 on Toman Island just off Malakula in central Vanuatu, I was sitting on the beach with Longdal Nobel, a local Cultural Center field worker. He suddenly told me, "You know, Ambat has now some bad habits." I knew that Ambat is the local cultural hero. There are many legends explaining how Ambat, the smallest of five mythical brothers, brought actual culture to the region and there are just as many legends telling about the various ways Ambat died. So I did not understand Longdal's remark and asked what he meant. Longdal explained that a few days before he and other people had found some empty bottles of alcoholic beverages and a hat in the forest of this little island. Toman Island is so small that everybody living there is familiar with all the belongings on the island. And nobody possesses a hat like the one they found. I thought that probably a sailing boat had passed by and that the wind had blown the hat from the boat to the island, and that somebody had smuggled alcoholic beverages from town to the little island. For Longdal and his friends, however, it was clear that only Ambat could have gotten drunk and forgotten his hat - a bad habit of his. That means that according to the people of Toman Island, Ambat the mythical protagonist, can now be here in the present as well as in mythical times. This short conversation inspired me to investigate the Melanesian notion of time and space more deeply, especially in relation to music and dance. But first I wanted to know what "Western" philosophy's latest concept of time and space was.

Concepts of time and space

In 1908, three years after the publication of Einstein's article on the special theory of relativity, the idealist metaphysician John McTaggart published *The Unreality of Time* in which he stated that our view of time is an illusion and purely ideal. To explain his point of view, he introduced two interpretations of time: the A-series and the B-series. The A-series is "the series of positions running from the far past through the near past to the present, and then from the present to the near future and the far future" (McTaggart 1908: 458). Thus the A-series represents the events in time in moving relation to the temporally moving observer. The B-series, on the other hand, declares that events are ordered from earlier-than to later-than relations. The supporters of the B-series would not talk of past, present and future. Rather, they would refer to a tenseless ordering of events, where the all times are real. B-theorists maintain that the future is no less real than the past; we just know less about it.

There are more philosophical interpretations of time and space but most are based on one of these two series. A few might start from a different time concept all together. For example, the "growing block universe theory" (Broad 1923) says that the past and present exist and the future does not exist. Supporters of this theory say that time is related to space and, as the universe is expanding, by the passage of time more of the world comes into being and with it space and time.

In short, these theories reflect the current state of Western philosophical ideas of time and space. For anthropologists and ethnomusicologists it is equally important in this discussion to include the way people experience and think about time in their daily lives. For human beings there is a general discrepancy in their idea of time. On the one hand there is the time period which is repetitive, like day and night, the seasons etc., which Evans-Pritchard (1940) refers to as ecological time, and on the other hand there is the undeniable reality that living beings get older, which he calls structural time. Alfred Gell (1996) tried to resolve this contradiction by talking of lineal spirals in progressive time: ecological time embraces the micro-layer with its seasons and repetitions of time events, while structural time in the macrocosm encompasses time as part of the social structure. We can conclude that "time" does not simply exist and that the calculation of time is not natural, but socially and culturally created – which means that there are various ways of thinking about time in this world.

However, there is apparently one universal principle. In order to estimate or imagine the lapse of time, people all over the world conceptualize and visualize time as positions in space. As a rule, time lies along an egocentric axis of opposite directions with the future in one direction and the past in the other. But where this line is situated and on which side the future and the past respectively lie depends on the individual society.

The Yupno in the Finisterre mountain range in Papua New Guinea have yet another understanding of time. According to Jürg Wassmann, the past is below; the Yupno river flows down; flows in the invisible ravine, continues flowing down; there is *omodeñ* (downhill, east); in the past (most) Yupno came from there and all the dead return there. Down there, in front of the river's mouth, on Nomsa Island, all of them are assembled. Being in the canonical position, a person can look down at them; and would know everything about them. It is the time of the ancestors (personal communication with Jürg Wassmann 2016).

So far we know that each society has its own way of thinking about the time line, but they always use space either as a line or a reference to topography to imagine and talk about time. Furthermore, these examples illustrate that space is not only a reference point to explain the lapse of time, but the combination of time and space is a necessary element in the concept of life. Einstein made that clear for us.

However, in pre-Christian Melanesian thought there is also the world of the ancestors and the mythological world, and to solve the question about Ambat's time travel we must ask if the concept of time is the same in these mythical worlds. We are familiar with the Melanesian idea that the spirits or souls of the deceased move to the world of the ancestors, where they continue their existence in spiritual form. As we know for the Yupno, their mythological place is a small island at the mouth of their river (Wassmann 2016: 15). For the Tannese in the south of Vanuatu the world of the ancestors is the sea around their island (Bonnemaison 1994); the people on the volcanic island of Ambrym in central Vanuatu, who have strong cultural bonds to their neighbors on South Malakula and Toman Island, believe that the entrance to the ancestors' world is in the crater of the volcano, and in the north of New Caledonia's main island (Grande Terre) I was shown a large cave which is thought to be the entrance to the ancestors' world. I will present and analyze a few legends, songs and dances that might help to find an answer to the question of Ambat's time travel.

New Caledonia

For an introduction to the idea of how time and space are conceptualized by the Kanak, the Melanesians of New Caledonia, I start from a general legend on the creation of the world. The anthropologist Emmanuel Kasarhérou, also co-initiator of the exhibition *Kanak, l'art est une parole* at the museum of Quai Branly in Paris in 2014, presents this legend in the exhibition catalogue. I will not cite the entire version, only the part that refers to the world of the ancestors. For the Kanak, nouns and verbs are referred to as Nô – in the language of Paicî, one of the more than 25 languages in New Caledonia. Nô has an important mythological meaning and it is at the origin of the life of beings and objects. The myth says that the first human beings did not grow old and had a good and happy life. Then the lizard (an important mythological protagonist in Kanak belief system) was jealous and persuaded them to make space in the world for a younger generation and so human beings became mortal. With this step they changed their world, where time and death did not dominate their lives, into the actual and real existing world with the diachronic situation of ecological and structural time, as explained by Evans Prichard and Gell.

According to Melanesian worldviews, it is possible to communicate in the everyday language with the ancestor spirits and the mythological protagonists during certain rituals and ceremonies, for example, in the ceremony called *pilou-pilou,* which unfortunately was given up by the Kanak some hundred years ago. In this ceremony the ancestors are called and when they arrive, their spiritual presence is felt by the participants. The principal course of events in such ceremonies was a meeting of matrilineal and patrilineal clans, with the exchange of food and materials, combined with celebrations and dances. To create an occasion to unite with the ancestor spirits was a subsidiary motivation, but a very important one, as a ceremony is only thought to be successful when the presence of the ancestor spirits is felt by the participants. Out of the large range of music, dances and exchange activities I will refer to the ritual speech *popai görö upwârâ* and the spiritual round dance *cäbu tabéa*.

First, there is the *popai görö upwârâ*, a ritualized speech delivered by a speaker who is standing on a small tree. Each group invited provided a speaker who presented the group's origin and its relation to other social groups in a poetical language rich in symbols. The subject of the speech is a recounting of mytho-historical events concerning the group which owns the speech. It starts with the presentation of the clan founder, who might be a semi-human, semi-animal or even semi-geographical being, and is followed by narrations of important weddings, adoptions, wars, as well as alliances created and recalled. The major part of this ritualized and song-like speech is a listing of names which refer to the places where these mytho-historical events took place.

While the speaker on the tree delivers his account, the men of his group stand on the ground in a circle around the speaker and make long backwards sliding steps while remaining on the spot. Asking them about the meaning of the steps, I learned that they refer to time and space in reference to the names of the places told by the speaker. These are sliding steps and not walking steps – the men do not walk – and with these sliding steps the dancers seem to create space and time for the events told by the speaker. The content of this song-like narration passes the periods of the first human beings in mythical times to the time of the living people today – or in simpler words from mythological to historical time, and for that journey space and time is created with the sliding steps of the dancers.

The *cäbu tabéa*: this round dance takes place on the last night of that ceremony. While today the *cäbu tabéa* is simply a joyful communal dance, some hundred years ago and more it was not trivial. It was a means making contact with the ancestors and of dancing with their spirits. The central pole, around which the dancers move, was essential to relate the living dancers to the dead ancestors. It was not merely the hub of the dance but also its spiritual centre. The French missionary and ethno-linguist Maurice Leenhardt (1980: 171) refers to the pole as "le corps de la danse" (the body of the dance) and goes on to say that it is the dance of the gods, the spirits of the dead, and in the minds of the dancers it is the ghostly ancestors themselves who dance.

The early missionaries to the Grande Terre declared that the round-dance – which they called the night-dance – was the "most debauched feast of Bacchus imaginable" (letter of Pierre Rougeyron of the 3, September 1846 quoted in Rozier 1990: 175). Besides sexual licence, the occasion of the round-dance could also mean that long-suppressed interpersonal or inter-group disputes could surface. It was reported several times that, at the conclusion of the ceremony with the final round-dance, deadly fights broke out.

These "excesses" may have been the reason why the missionaries wanted the round-dance to be stopped. However, the dance was important to the Kanak because it involved spiritual relations with the ancestors and it is thought that their ancestor spirits perform the same dance of sexual liberty and fights in their world. Leenhardt (1986: 169) writes: "For, in the invisible world, the deified ancestors are still dancing; those newly arrived in the after-world join in the round in the same way as one joins in that around the pole with the ribbons."

The round-dance, or *cäbu tabéa*, is accompanied by songs performed by two singers in alternation and accompanied by percussion instruments beating a constant dual pattern. As this dance continues through the entire night, the singers must know a large number of songs to last for about twelve hours. Most of them are without mythological references. However, one such song, again from the same linguistic region, is called *Tchamba*, and its content has an interesting relation to mythological time.

This song takes the listener back to the time when the island came into being, when neither the island nor the places had names, as *nô*, the word of the beginning, was not yet spoken and apparently time did not exist. The song refers to the journey of the mythological founders of the Dui and Bai moieties northwards along the east coast of the island. The journey starts at Tchamba and ends at Poyes. The two places are about 50 miles away from each other.

On this mythological journey, some of the protagonists or clan founders stay at certain places like valleys, mountains, rivers etc. and give names to these places when they settle there and so they name the region's geographical features from Tchamba to Poyes. The song divides the journey into several legs, from one geographical feature to the next, and each of these legs corresponds to a verse and its repetition in the song. The first strophe and the strophe after a break consist entirely of neutral or non-meaningful syllables, as is common for all of these *ae-ae* songs. At the beginning of the other strophes the name of the place where the leg of the journey begins is recited followed by neutral syllables. The first strophe begins with Tchamba, the next strophe begins with the topographical name Wiindö, which lies only about seven miles north of Tchamba, then Tié, which again lies further north and then Wagap and finally Poyes, which are the names of the places in the order in which a traveler encounters the places traveling from the south to the north. The five mythological protagonists started the journey and each one stayed at a certain place and gave a name to that place and so created the geography of the island in its actual and current form. And by moving through the island these clan founders created time.

This song identifies a region and at the same time reminds of mytho-historical events on which present land claims are based. With only a few names it refers to an ancient migration by naming toponyms in the order of the migration's route. This migration also created the island as it exists today with the actual structure of time. And as the song refers to the border between the world of the ancestor spirits and the world of living beings, it refers to the border of the world with ancestor time and the world where time of the living exists. Thus, with migration on the island, the clan founders not only created the geography and named it but also created time.

Conclusion

I mentioned Evans-Pritchard's and Alfred Gell's ideas to distinguish two concepts of time, ecological time with its repetitive character to explain the seasons etc. and structural time which explains growing older. These few examples from New Caledonia indicate that there is a third concept of time in the mind of the Kanak, namely time in the world of their ancestor spirits. This is a world in which the inhabitants do not grow old and time is thought to be ecological and repetitive. In ceremonies and dances the necessary creation of time is symbolized by movements in space, such as sliding steps or a migration. We also learned that mythical protagonists are able to travel from one of these time zones to the other. I showed this using the example of New Caledonia, but there is more ethnographic knowledge from Melanesia available that would allow this issue to be brought to a more general level in Melanesia. In particular, the research results from Jürg Wassmann (1982, 1988) with their detailed information on time, space and mythology would allow for an examination in this direction. Wassmann reported detailed myths of the creation of the world as conceived by the Iatmul, where movements by either mythical dogs or mythical crocodiles create space as well as time – ecological and structural time.

And among the Iatmul again the ancestors are able to move from their world to the world of the living when they are called by songs and music. This is comparable to the story that I told at the beginning of this text, where the cultural hero, Ambat, moved easily from the world of the ancestor spirits to the world of the living to have a quiet drink.

References

Bonnemaison, J. 1994. *The Tree and the Canoe. History and Ethnography of Tanna*. Honolulu: University of Hawai'i Press.

Broad, C. D. 1923. *Scientific Thought*. London: Routledge and Keegan Paul Ltd.

Evans-Pritchard, E. E. 1940. *The Nuer. A Description of the Modes of Livelihood and Political Institutions of a Nilotic People*. Oxford: Clarendon Press.

Gell, A. 1996. *The Anthropology of Time. Cultural Constructions of Temporal Maps and Images*. Oxford: Berg.

Leenhardt, M. 1980. *Notes d'ethnologie néo-calédonienne*. Travaux & Mémoires VIII. Paris: Institut d'Ethnologie. (Fac-similé de 1930).

— 1986. *Gens de la Grande Terre, Nouvelle-Calédonie*. Nouméa: Éditions du Cagou (Fac-similé de 1937, Paris: Gallimard).

McTaggart, J. 1908. The Unreality of Time. *Mind. A Quarterly Review of Psychology and Philosophy* 17: 457–474.

Rozier, C. 1990. *La Nouvelle-Calédonie Ancienne*. Paris: Librairie Fayard.

Wassmann, J. 1982. *Der Gesang an den Fliegenden Hund. Untersuchungen zu den totemistischen Gesängen und geheimen Namen des Dorfes Kandingei am Mittelsepik (Papua New Guinea) anhand der kirugu-Knotenschnüre*. Basel: Ethnologisches Seminar der Universität und Museum für Völkerkunde. (Basler Beiträge zur Ethnologie Bd. 22).

— 1988. *Der Gesang an das Krokodil. Die rituellen Gesänge des Dorfes Kandingei an Land und Meer, Pflanzen und Tiere (Mittelsepik, Papua New Guinea)*. Basel: Ethnologisches Seminar der Universität und Museum für Völkerkunde. (Basler Beiträge zur Ethnologie Bd. 28).

— 2016. *The Gently Bowing Person. An Ideal among the Yupno in Papua New Guinea*. Heidelberg: Universitätsverlag Winter. (Heidelberg Studies in Pacific Anthropology, Vol. 4).

DON NILES and EDWARD GENDE

10 The Early Field and Commercial Recordings of Kuman Music. Research Using Repatriated Music in Papua New Guinea, and Recent Threats to Cultural Diversity

Introduction

A couple years after I (Niles) began work at the Institute of Papua New Guinea Studies, we received a copy of Jürg Wassmann's *Der Gesang an den fliegenden Hund* (1982), a masterful exploration of the world of the Iatmul through the texts of their totemic songs. Such an important study to ethnomusicology, other academic disciplines, and essential to the understanding of traditional cultural expression had to reach a wider audience. I was thrilled that we could publish an English translation of that book less than a decade later (Wassmann 1991), in a series that was launched precisely to more widely disseminate knowledge about Papua New Guinea music traditions.

In the intervening years, I had the opportunity to correspond with and meet Jürg and his wife/colleague Verena, and even do some collaborative research with them in the Yupno area in 1987 (Niles 1992b). In addition to the wonders of email to our communications, being based in Port Moresby enabled me to frequently meet up with them at the beginning or end of their Papua New Guinea visits. Our contribution here celebrates that friendship and Jürg's dedication to long-term research and the sharing of knowledge. *Amamas gut, poro!*

In this paper Edward Gende and I intend to demonstrate how repatriated collections of music from one part of Papua New Guinea complement other collections and contribute to a better understanding of continuities and potential differences between practices today and those up to eighty years ago. While such efforts reflect the goals of the Institute of Papua New Guinea Studies, recent neglect of other archives in Papua

New Guinea and moves by fundamentalist Christians to distance the country from ancestral traditions threaten to severely affect these activities and attitudes towards such collections.

IPNGS origins

The Institute of Papua New Guinea Studies (IPNGS) was established in 1974, one year before Papua New Guinea's independence from Australia. Ulli Beier had previously spent 1967–71 at the University of Papua New Guinea teaching a very influential course in creative writing (Beier 2005) and also collaborating with Michael Somare, who would eventually become the country's first prime minister. Beier returned to live in Nigeria, where his primary work had been, but was asked to return to Papua New Guinea to establish the IPNGS. He was director from 1974 to 1978.

The types of cultural research and archival activities in which IPNGS was meant to engage were undoubtedly influenced by similarly named institutions found in other parts of the world, such as the Institute of African Studies (e.g., one established in 1962 at the University of Ghana, with others at other African universities) and the Australian Institute of Aboriginal Studies (1964). Indeed, Beier himself was at one point director of the Institute of African Studies at the University of Ife, Nigeria.

Papua New Guinea is a country of great cultural diversity, and it has experienced many changes since it was first divided amongst overseas powers in 1884, until its independence just ninety-one years later. Cultural traditions are of tremendous variety and are widely respected. The Preamble of *Constitution of the Independent State of Papua New Guinea* (1975) clearly acknowledges the essential contribution of ancestral traditions and more recently obtained Christian ideals in defining the nation:

> WE, THE PEOPLE OF PAPUA NEW GUINEA–
> - united in one nation
> - pay homage to the memory of our ancestors—the source of our strength and origin of our combined heritage
> - acknowledge the worthy customs and traditional wisdoms of our people—which have come down to us from generation to generation

- pledge ourselves to guard and pass on to those who come after us our noble traditions and the Christian principles that are ours now.

IPNGS was established by the government to focus on cultural research, with the goal of archiving such materials and making them available to those concerned with development of the arts. In the most recent legislation concerning IPNGS,[1] the relevant sections concerning its music work make it responsible for:

> (a) carrying out research into, recording and interpreting all aspects of the traditional culture of the indigenous inhabitants of the country; and
> ...
> (c) making all its records available for the development of literature, drama, music and the visual arts; and
> ...
> (e) the systematic recording of the music of the country with a view to establishing a tape and record library of such music ... (*National Cultural Commission Act* 1994, sec. 20)

From the beginning, a Music Department was established as part of the IPNGS to carry out research and establish an archive of such materials. IPNGS is presently a national cultural institution under the National Cultural Commission.

Music Archive collection

The Music Archive of the IPNGS's Music Department presently contains about 12,000 hours of recordings, mostly of Papua New Guinea music. These consist of original recordings made by IPNGS staff and other researchers, from 1974 to the present, as well as large collections of commercial recordings and materials obtained from other archives, primarily located overseas. This paper focuses on materials from the latter two categories, informed by the original recordings and research of its staff.

While many of these recordings concern traditional music, the Music Department is also interested in all other types of music performed by Papua New Guineans. As a result, there are also large collections of popular music (string bands, bamboo bands, power bands, etc.), hymns and other types of Christian music, and music of the military forces (brass bands, bagpipe and drum bands, etc.).

With such materials, the Music Department has tried to establish itself as the main centre for all materials concerning Papua New Guinea music and dance (Niles 1992a).[2] It was felt that all such materials should be together in one place in the country, rather than requiring researchers and other interested parties to visit numerous overseas archives as well. Consequently, in the process of collecting written materials about Papua New Guinea music, much was also learned about who made recordings of such music. Armed with such knowledge, it was possible to try to attempt to locate these recordings in overseas archives, and arrange for copies of recordings and documentation to be repatriated to IPNGS.

Beginning in the early 1980s and continuing to the present, locating and repatriating Papua New Guinea recordings has been very successful (see, e.g., Niles n.d., 1992a, 2002, 2004b, 2012; Moriguba 2010), and a number of published studies have made use of archival recordings (e.g., Webb and Niles 1986, 1990; Niles and Webb 1987; Niles 2000, 2011, To'Liman-Turalir 2002). These publications include academic studies as well as materials meant to assist teachers in schools. Many of the latter publications have been used for decades—an indication of their usefulness, but also of the lack of comparable publications. While the Music Department does not claim to document all but a fraction of the music traditions of the country, such efforts have been successful and in accordance with the intent of collection, preservation, and promotion.

Historical recordings of Kuman music

This paper focusses on three collections of music from Kuman speakers in Chimbu (Simbu) province in the Highlands of Papua New Guinea. It is estimated that Kuman is today spoken by about 115,000 people, making it the fourth largest language in the country, out of an estimated 836 living languages (Lewis et al. 2013). Although the first audio recordings were made in the coastal regions of Papua New Guinea in 1898, most of the central mountainous part of the country was believed to be uninhabited until the early 1930s when patrols by church, government, and commercial enterprises began to encounter large populations.

According to our best estimates (Niles 2012: 144-147), the first recordings made in the Highlands and, coincidentally of Kuman music, were made by Fr. Aloys Kaspruś (1900–1978) in 1936–37, during early missionization efforts by Catholics in this region (Kaspruś 1936–37). Copies of Kaspruś's wax-cylinder recordings were repatriated to Papua New Guinea along with many other historically significant recordings from the Berlin Phonogramm-Archiv (Ziegler 2006). Material recorded includes courting songs, yodeling following a death, and songs sung during feast preparations. A Kuman version of the Lord's Prayer reveals the progress of the work of local missionaries.

World War II meant closure of the Highlands to visitors, and no new recordings appear to have been made in the Kuman area until the region was reopened, allowing the visits of Swiss researcher Paul Wirz (1892–1955) individually and later with his son, Dadi Wirz (b. 1931), between 1949 and 1953, using a new medium for field researchers: reel-to-reel tape (Wirz and Wirz 1949–53; Niles 2012: 152-154).

Although more details about the Kaspruś and the Wirz collections have been published elsewhere (Niles 2012), the third collection of importance here has not received such attention. After initially being stationed in Papua New Guinea during the war, Australian Ray Sheridan (1916–2003) worked as an Education Officer for Music, 1947–49 (Sheridan 1972: 820) (Illustration 10.1).[3]

In 1947 he visited parts of the Highlands, although he was unable to make recordings at the time (Sheridan 1947). Returning to Australia, his interest in Papua New Guinea music continued. With the sponsorship of the Australian Broadcasting Commission and a number of other institutions, Sheridan was finally able to make tape recordings during a two-month visit in 1953. In 1954, he returned to Papua New Guinea and settled in Rabaul, on the island of New Britain, working in private enterprise, but conducting music research in his spare time wherever possible.

In 1955 and 1957, Sheridan privately released two 78s of music from the Sepik and Sio regions, and also visited the island of New Ireland for research. In 1958 he released the first commercial recording of Papua New Guinea music to be widely available: *Music of New Guinea: The Australian Trust Territory—an Introduction* (Illustration 10.2).

Actually, the first commercial recording containing Papua New Guinea music was the *Demonstrations-Sammlung* (Demonstration collection) (c. 1920), consisting of 120 cylinders from the Berlin Phonogramm-Archiv: fourteen were recorded in Papua New Guinea, between 1907 and 1911.[4] The next commercial recording consisted entirely of Papua New Guinea music recorded in 1949, but apparently not released until the following year: *New Guinea and Papuan Native Music*, comprising seven, 30 cm, 78 rpm discs. The original wire recordings were made by Australian Broadcasting Commission journalist Colin Simpson and technician John Cunningham. Although we consider them commercial because they were available for sale, neither of these recordings was widely available.

Illustration 10.1: Ray Sheridan discussing his activities concerning Papua New Guinea music (2003; photo by Don Niles)

Although Ray Sheridan was not involved in the recording itself, he wrote the accompanying notes for the 1950 release, most likely as a result of his post-war work as Education Officer for music in Papua New Guinea. Sheridan's choice of recordings on his own disc, issued eight years later, was perhaps meant to supplement what appeared on this recording. The majority of Simpson and Cunningham's recordings come from the southern region of the country, an area completely unrepresented on Sheridan's release. Sheridan also includes many examples from the New

Guinea Islands region, where he resided, but which is poorly represented by Simpson and Cunningham.

Illustration 10.2: *Music of New Guinea,* Ray Sheridan's LP released in 1958

Sheridan's 1958 disc was widely reviewed at the time (Pacific Islands Monthly 1958; Jones 1959; Meggitt 1959; Moyle 1959a, 1959b; Kaeppler 1963). For many libraries, this remained their only recording of Papua New Guinea music for decades.

Music of New Guinea was issued by an Australian company called Wattle Recordings.[5] Wattle existed from 1955 to 1963 and focused on the pioneer recording of Australian folk music. They also issued records of Australian Aboriginal songs and didjeridu playing, and political songs.

All Wattle publications were accompanied by booklets of notes on the music.[6]

Music of New Guinea has six tracks on side A and eight on side B, with each side lasting almost 24 minutes. Each track, however, contains between one and eight short items. In total there are seventy-five items on the LP, with some items lasting only a few seconds each. The accompanying four-page booklet gives brief information on each of the recordings.

Side A of his disc includes the provinces along the northern coast of the country that are today known as the Momase Region (Morobe, Madang, East Sepik, and West Sepik (Sandaun) Provinces); while side B includes islands in the Momase Region (Morobe Province) that link to the islands of what is now called the New Guinea Islands Region (Manus,[7] New Ireland, East New Britain, West New Britain Provinces, and the Autonomous Region of Bougainville), plus one track from the Highlands. This latter track contains seven items from what he calls the "Kundiawa–Goroka area" and one item from the "Kainantu area." The seven items from Kundiawa–Goroka are the first widely available commercial recordings of Kuman music,[8] illustrating communications with yodeling,[9] instruments (split rattle, end-blown flute with fingerholes, jew's harp, and paired side-blown flutes), and songs (courting and pig-killing).[10]

Although the geo-cultural diversity represented on the album is impressive, Sheridan was unable to visit all those regions. Rather, he often made recordings of people who were living and working in the Rabaul area, where he was based. Only in the case of some of the East New Britain and possibly New Ireland recordings was he actually able to visit the areas concerned. As a result, many of Sheridan's recordings are by single performers or very small groups. Nevertheless, the representation was an amazing accomplishment for someone who was self-supported in this music research.

Work with historical recordings of Kuman music

Gende has worked closely with the Kuman recordings in the Kaspruś, Wirz and Wirz, and Sheridan collections, particularly in attempting to provide further documentation of them by transcribing and translating song texts or expanding existing notes about what is heard on the recordings.

Between the mid-1930s and late 1950s, the technology for recording changed dramatically, from acoustic recordings made on wax cylinders to microphone-amplified recordings made on magnetic tape. It also saw the change from recordings made primarily for the purpose of documentation and meant for archival deposit, to those that were intended to expose such music to an international audience through commercial release.

It is now eighty years since the first recordings of Kuman music were made. Of what significance are these recordings made in the 1930s, 1940s, and 1950s to Kuman speakers today?

Certainly these recordings are quite readily recognizable as Kuman through the language used and the melodies. But there are also some notable differences between the recorded performances and present-day practice. In the discussion below, most of the examples are drawn from the Wirz collection, as that is by far the largest. Furthermore, since the most predominant song form presented in the recordings is of courting songs, comments focus on that genre.

Indoor courting between unmarried young women and unmarried or married men looking for an additional wife is common in many parts of the Papua New Guinea Highlands region. Although performance aspects vary considerably, they frequently involve dancing by the seated performers, and singing is performed by them and/or by onlookers (Niles 2011). Although no longer performed extensively, the Kuman area has a number of different forms or such courting, as described by Bergmann (1969, 1971), Gende (1998), and others.

Use of language. In contrast to the traditions found in some other parts of Papua New Guinea, Kuman songs today generally consist of text that is in the present-day language. While the musical and textual style is a continuation of ancestral traditions, songs are expected to have newly composed texts, rather than simply repeating previous ones. Even though the words of a recorded song are individually understood today, their overall meaning may be lost to people today because they have not been performed in context for quite some time. For example, consider this pig-killing song from a *bugla gende* performance:

> *Dua koiye simbukondi-i Nondkugl iroyeioae Kauglamugl iroyeioae* (3 times)
> *Aei-i-i-i-i aei-i*
>
> Break the wings of the rat and leave them at Nondkugl Kauglamugl
> *Aei-i-i-i-i aei-i* (Sheridan 1958:tr. B1e)

Here the words can be heard quite clearly, but the meaning of "wings of the rat," breaking them, and leaving them at the places mentioned are now lost to most listeners because *bugla gende* has not been performed for many decades. Or this might be an intentional playing with sounds, as observed below with other examples. Note also the use of the words Nondkugl and Kauglamugl. The actual name of the place concerned is Nondkugl; Kauglamugl is added as a type of poetic pairing or word play using similar sounds. Many additional examples of such poetic devices occur in the texts discussed here.

Some of the words in these historical recordings are difficult or impossible to understand today. For example, the old term *nogl* is used in song texts to indicate someone who is between a child and adult, someone who is attractive and ready to marry. *Nogl* is also the name of a colorful, attractive bird:

> *Kanamugl mitna enambro de-ende*
> *nogl kwiro kwiro de-ende*
>
> Are you two going up Kanamugl way, bright colours?
> bright male adolescent over there over there, bright colours (Wirz and Wirz 1949–53:It. B26)

Today, someone in the same stage of life would be called *mor*, but here there is no further link of *mor* to a beautiful bird.

In the following fragment, while *aiya* are line-ending vocables (a feature discussed below), *kuna* and *mba* might be the names of people, but the phrasing suggests this is not the case:

> *kuna kindo yomiwe aiya*
> *kuna kindo yomiwe mba kindo yoiwe aiya*
> *kuna kindo yomiwe aiya*
> *kuna kindo yomiwe mba kindo yoiwe aiya*
> *kuna kindo yomiwe aiya*

10 The Early Field

> *kuna* is there *aiya*
> *kuna* is there, *mba* is there *aiya*
> *kuna* is there *aiya*
> *kuna* is there, *mba* is there *aiya*
> *kuna* is there *aiya* (Wirz and Wirz 1949–53:It. A39)

The substitution of different words to indicate different kinds of animals or plants in successive lines is a common feature of Kuman song-poetry parallelism today. Such examples are found here as well. In this song, the *mogl* cuscus is paired with the *towa* cuscus:

> *mogl demne kwi praglendi*
> *towa demne kwi praglendi*

> just so that I can smell the nice fragrance of the *mogl* cuscus
> just so that I can smell the nice fragrance of the *towa* cuscus (Wirz and Wirz 1949–53:It. A32)

Sometimes the pairing may be of words that sound similar, such as *wiglki* and *kaglki*:

> *wiglki uro wanambrka paindume*
> *kaglki uro wanambrka paindume*
> *iya-a iya-a*
> *wiglki uro wanambrka paindume*
> *iya-a iya-a*

> Are they going to pick *wiglki* mushrooms and go about?
> Are they going to pick *kaglki* and go about?
> *iya-a iya-a*
> Are they going to pick *wiglki* mushrooms and go about?
> *iya-a iya-a* (Wirz and Wirz 1949–53:It. A38)

Although it is not known whether *kaglki* is also a type of mushroom or something else, such word play is typical of song texts in the region (cf. Niles 2011, 2015: xl-xlvii).

As another example of such paired word play, here *ima* follows *gaglma,* the name of a type of pine tree. However, *ima* is used just for its sound as a poetic pairing; it is not the name of another tree:

> *hme gaglma bro wagle ende ima bro gagle ende*
> *ima bro gagle ende gaglma bro wage ende*
>
> *hme* break the *gaglma* pine tree put it in the bag, break *ima* put it in the bag,
> break *ima* put it in the bag, break the *gaglma* pine tree put it in the bag
> (Wirz and Wirz 1949–53:It. A1)

In some cases old onomatopoeic expressions are used: *kigle kwi* and *kukumbeyo* (Wirz and Wirz 1949–53:It. A31, A36) are no longer used today.

Today's importance of Tok Pisin (Papua New Guinea Pidgin English) and increasingly English has also made some Kuman expressions surprisingly difficult for people today. For example, *kur tombuna muno* (Wirz and Wirz 1949–53:It. A37) for face or body tattoos, whereas today people often use Tok Pisin *mak* (mark) or *katim skin/pes* (to cut the skin/face), or the English *tattoo*, even when speaking Kuman. As another example, one song uses the word *bauwo* (Wirz and Wirz 1949–53:It. B22), referring to a relative on the mother's side, often the mother's brother. Today many people tend to simply say the English *uncle*. Present-day speakers would also have difficulty pronouncing some of the long words found in the songs, such as *uglkairowero* and *wanenambuglba* (Wirz and Wirz 1949–53:It. B27).

Although definitely recognizable as Kuman songs, such features of the song poetry involved challenge listeners today.

Changes in song structure. Differences are also found between the structure of these historical recordings and songs today. In courting songs today, the structure is often as follows. The melody for each verse is established by an initial statement sung only with vocables. The next verse then begins with a repeat of the final lines of these vocables and then a few lines of text are sung to the melody. The first lines of the subsequent verse repeat the concluding text from the previous verse and then new text is added to conclude it. This continues with new additions of text. The end of the song is marked by one last repeat of the melody with just vocables, as was done at the very beginning of the performance. Hence, if the first verse with vocables is indicated as XY and subsequent verses with text as A, B, etc., this chaining effect can be diagrammed as XY YA AB BC CD ... XY. Various modifications to this pattern are also possible, see, for example, the presentation in Gende [1998: 124-125];

for earlier discussions of Kuman song structure and poetry, see Bergmann [1969, 1971]).

In these historical recordings there are a number of notable variations from this form. From the Kaspruś collection, lines of vocables and lines of text are repeated over and over to two alternating melodies. For example, the opening line of vocables, "*Wai-i-i eiya hm hm*" is sung six times, with odd-numbered statements using one melody, and even-numbered statements a different one (Kaspruś 1936–37: reel 9, It. 2). Thus if numbered subscripts are used to represent melodies, the form of this first verse is: $X_1X_2X_1X_2X_1X_2$.

Another striking example uses the introductory vocable verse (X) in alternation with text verses (A, B, etc.) in a different kind of chaining or linking: XAB XCB XDBC (Wirz and Wirz 1949–53:It. B27). This seems to be a fragment of a complete song, so no final repeat of the vocable verse is sung.

Indeed, considered with an understanding of song structure as performed today, most of the recordings appear to be just fragments: often only including many repetitions of the vocable verse, which today only serves to establish the melody and conclude a song. For example, the following lines of vocables are repeated about thirty times:

> *pawaiya waiya-a waiya-a*
> *pawaiya pawaiya waiya-a waiya-a*
> *pawaiya waiya* (Wirz and Wirz 1949–53:It. B16)

No text follows. While it is possible that such a vocable-only structure existed in the past, it might be more likely to assume that the recordist did not try to record full songs: they would be lengthy and presumably tape would be at a premium. Additionally, the recordist may well have been unable to distinguish vocables from text, and the additional verses of text would really only be meaningful to someone familiar with the language, so he felt no need to include them. Even where some text verses are included, the number of them is fewer than in today's practice. Instead, the recordist probably wanted to record as many different songs and performers as possible, so songs were shortened and people came to perform whatever they wanted. At the conclusion of one performance, people can be heard saying "keep going, keep singing, don't stop, sing it again" (Wirz and Wirz 1949–53:It. A36), presumably because they felt that that is what was wanted for the recording. During another recording, someone says "sing one more time and let it flow" (Wirz and Wirz 1949–53:It. C5). Such a willingness to cooperate and the likely difficulties of communication may have resulted in the distortion of song structure for the sake of recording.

The recording of just the beginning vocables of a courting song is also found in the Sheridan LP:

> *welu wela*
> *welu welu wela-a, welu welu wela*
> *welu wela welu wela*
> *welu welu wela-a, welu welu wela*
> *welu wela welu wela*
> *welu welu wela-a, welu welu wela*
> *welu wela welu wela* (Sheridan 1958:tr. B1c)

In the notes accompanying this recording, Sheridan identifies the genre as *kuanade* and describes it as "a song to accompany a men's dance that is characterized by great leaps." The name of the genre should be *kuanand*, but the description of the song is entirely erroneous: *kuanand* are courting songs sung by seated dancers, not by leaping men.

Although there are similarities between such vocable-only performances on the recordings by Sheridan and by the Wirzes, Sheridan was producing an LP containing scores of short examples from around the country, so this may also be a factor influencing what is included and what was not.

Other differences from today's practice include the repetition of a vocable at the end of each line of text, such as the use of *aglke* here:

> *ambai Ndruagle ya aglke a-aglke*
> *ambai Ndre ya aglke*
>
> *Iawa suna undie a-aglke*
> *Kundi suna undie, Iawa suna undie a-aglke*
>
> *papa ndarua ndarua re a-aglke a-aglke*
> *pipi ndarua ndarua re a-aglke*
>
> hey girl Ndruagle *aglke, a-aglke*
> hey girl Ndre *aglke*

> I feel I am arriving in the centre of Iawa *a-aglke*
> I feel I am arriving in the centre of Kundi, I feel I am arriving in the centre of Iawa *a-aglke*
>
> *papa* brave the morning dew, morning dew *a-aglke, a-aglke*
> *pipi* brave the morning dew, morning dew *a-aglke* (Wirz and Wirz 1949–53:It. B19)

This feature also appears in an example discussed above. Although line-final vocables are common in performance traditions to the west (cf. Niles 2011; Niles and Rumsey 2011), they are not a feature of present-day Kuman performance practice.

Note also other examples of poetic sound play in other texts. One song concerns a girl called Ndre Ndraugle (also the name of an orchid), but her name is not sung as such. Instead it is broken up and sung in reverse order. She walks to Kundiawa, braving the morning dew. "Kundiawa" is also not sung as such, but is similarly split into two parts that are sung in reverse order: Iawa and Kundi. There is also word play on the vocables *papa* and *pipi* at the beginnings of the final pair of lines.

Another difference from present practice is having each line in a text as a question:

> *duglo sra duglo ine-e*
> *siune duglo duglo ino-o*
> *miugle duglo duglo ino*
> *duglo sra duglo ine-e*
>
> bird's skin, what bird's skin are you taking?
> *siune* bird-of-paradise skin, bird's skin are you taking or?
> *miugle* bird-of-paradise skin, bird's skin are you taking?
> bird's skin, what bird's skin are you taking? (Wirz and Wirz 1949–53:It. C5)

Duglo, the word translated here as 'bird's skin', is actually a stuffed bird skin with feathers used for decoration.

It is also interesting that the Kuman version of the Lord's Prayer recorded by Kaspruś differs significantly from that used today:

> *No neno ene kamn mitna motnga*
> *kangin manginagle wakai daraiglma*
> *ene kan yombuglo ere endno munmara unamba*

> *ene ka dinga ya nono kamn kuglo kwimbo primere*
> *mere maginagle kwi pra praiglma*
> *ene erme kaia mokna ninamnga pre ta noro* (Kaspruś x86-158, #10, It. 1)
> (Kaspruś 1936–37:reel 10, It. 1)

> Today:
> *No neno heven suna motnga*
> *ene kgin santu daraiglma*
> *ene kan yombuglo ere endno munmara unamba*
> *ene ka dinga heven suna primere*
> *mangnagle kwi pra praiglma*
> *no erme kaia mokna ninamunga pre erme ta norowa*

Such differences between the historical recordings and present practice stimulate discussion among Kuman speakers about what might have changed over time and what might simply have been alterations imposed by these past recording situations.

Threats to the future

The discussion above has been presented to give some idea of the type of work undertaken by the IPNGS with repatriated materials held in its Music Archives and the questions such work raises. However, the value of archives to the country is apparently not shared by everyone. Two recent examples are of great concern.

The National Broadcasting Commission (NBC) has established radio stations in all provinces. They provide an essential source of information, entertainment, and education for the people in these provinces. Attached to each station is a library or archive containing materials used for broadcast, in particular many programs and music recordings recorded at events within the province. These are important historical documents and are duplicated nowhere else in the country.

Since 1973, the station at Kundiawa, the capital of Chimbu Province, has been documenting news and music in the province. In 2010, it was reported that this building was removed for the construction of a regional treasury building. The building was demolished while various provincial Members of Parliament and the chairman of NBC looked on.

Before the demolition, staff collected what they wanted and left what they did not. Although staff had relocated to other offices three months ago, archival materials were not moved, leaving behind

> a rare collection of traditional Chimbu songs, string band music, legends and myths, and traditional bamboo flute sounds … By 6pm …, the public moved in and helped themselves, scattering the recordings … all over. (Per 2010; also see http://asopa.typepad.com/asopa_people/2010/05/chimbu-culture-trashed-while-bureaucrats-idle.html

No explanation was ever forthcoming from NBC regarding this apparent disregard for the heritage of the people of Chimbu.

Such apparent negligence of archival materials may be a one-off event, as there is no indication that other NBC archives are being similarly abandoned. While not directly concerned with archives at the moment, the next threat appears to be much more frightening and potentially destructive.

At the beginning of December 2013, newspaper reports revealed that the Speaker of Papua New Guinea's Parliament, Hon. Theo Zurenuoc, had removed and cut up the traditionally carved lintel that decorated the facade at the entrance to the National Parliament House on the night of 26 November (Evara 2013). Over the next few weeks, almost daily front-page stories on the matter in the *Post-Courier* newspaper, and hundreds of articles, editorials, letters to the editor, advertisements, and comments on Facebook and in blogs have gradually revealed various aspects of what was happening and reactions to it. Schram (2014) gives a good summary of events up until February 2014 and background to them.

Apparently, the Parliamentary House Committee, comprising the Speaker and other MPs, decided to undertake a program of "reformation, restoration, and modernization" of the Parliament House. As part of those efforts, they decided to remove the lintel and other carvings in Parliament that they felt were "ungodly" and adversely affecting the MPs and their work. Another target for removal and destruction was a wooden "totem pole" inside the building. In a four-page, full-color advertisement in a newspaper (Zurenuoc 2013), the Speaker explained his belief that parts of the carving represented gods of witchcraft, immorality, and idolatry. The pole was to be replaced with a "Pillar of National Identity and Unity," consisting of a four-layered base of the word of God, the Constitution, the People, and a covenant declared in 2007 between the then prime minister and the "God of Israel." This base would support the pillar itself, with the word "unity" translated into "all 840+ languages" of the country written on it, and topped with an electrically powered flame symbolizing direction in leadership.

It was also mentioned that references in the *Constitution* and the *National Pledge* to ancestral wisdom and traditions providing strength and influencing people today would be replaced with reference to the "God of the Holy Bible."

While the vast majority of Papua New Guineans today readily identify as Christian, ancestral traditions generally remain acknowledged and respected, and are still followed by some. This continuity with the past is illustrated in the preamble to the *Constitution* cited at the beginning of this paper. Furthermore, freedom of religion is guaranteed under section 45 of the *Constitution*, and there are certainly many different kinds of Christianity represented in the country, along with a smaller number of adherents to non-Christian religions.

Christian fundamentalist churches have been increasing in number since the end of World War II, and there appears to be growing interest by some people in Christian Zionism and prosperity theology. Certainly there have been numerous conflicts in the past between Christian attitudes and various customs. Nevertheless, tolerance and respect has generally been promoted as important elements in maintaining national unity. The actions by the Speaker and his followers, however, were against the National Parliament House, a structure that represents the nation as a whole, not just one group or belief system (Rosi 1991).

The Speaker's supporters claim that traditional beliefs have hindered Papua New Guinea's development. With the fortieth anniversary of independence to occur in 2015—and the supposed biblical numerological significance of the number forty—supporters observed that the present MPs have the opportunity to sever the country's ties with traditions, embrace "true" Christianity, and recognize the "God of Israel" as their God, thereby enabling prosperity to finally come to the people of this country.

But such attitudes do not just affect carvings in the National Parliament House. To obtain the desired prosperity, references to respect for ancestral knowledge and the importance of ancestors to people today in the *Constitution* must also be removed. They feel that Christianity alone will be a uniting force for Papua New Guinea, finally enabling to come the prosperity that it has long missed out on.

These attitudes jeopardize all collections of cultural materials and everyone working in cultural services. Museums and archives are particularly at risk since they contain much material that would certainly be considered "ungodly" and "demonic" by some and might be felt to be interfering with the country's longed-for progress and prosperity. While there is some vocal and eloquent opposition to these views, there also appears to be considerable support for them as well.

Yet, discrediting and disowning diverse ancestral traditions while embracing Christianity as a unifying factor essentially means the loss of Papua New Guinea's individuality through its diversity and an adoption of a mono-culture (cf. Simet and Iamo 1992). At the time, some comments sarcastically suggested that if such traditions are now considered demonic and unbefitting of the image of Papua New Guinea today, the 2014 Melanesian Festival of Arts should not be hosted; traditional dancers must not be used at functions for any MPs who support the removal of the carvings; no traditional dance, music, or decorations must be used during the planned hosting of the Pacific Games (2015) or Asia-Pacific Economic Cooperation summit (2018); no tourists should be allowed any glimpse of traditions; and all evidence of Papua New Guinea's "evil" past must be dumped into under-supported archives and museums, thereby erasing almost everything that makes the country and its people of interest to the world. These comments conclude:

> All the fundamentalist pastors and church leaders who put out that advertisement [supporting the removal of the carvings] … were right about one thing. The battle line is definitely being drawn, and it is our moment of truth. But not just between good and evil, also between knowledge and ignorance, understanding and disrespect, and wisdom and supreme arrogance.
> Papua New Guineans, where do you stand? Respecting your ancestors or disown[ing] them? (Nditing 2013)

As a further development, in April 2015, the Speaker and a contingent of MPs and church leaders traveled to an InterChurch Holiness Convention in Dayton, Ohio, USA. On 22 April, they received an original King James Version of the Bible, an English translation completed in 1611 for the Church of England. It was donated by Gene Hood, who had helped establish a religious radio station in the country some years ago. In spite of concerns over the possible use of public funds for this trip, the group returned to Port Moresby on 27 April to be met by the prime minister and a large crowd at the airport. They proclaimed the Bible a "national treasure." In August, a two-page advertisement asked Papua New Guineans to burn objects that do not glorify God and to contribute to an offering to give to Jews to return to Israel (National 2015). It does not appear that most people followed this advice. Nevertheless, the 1611 Bible was installed in Parliament on 16 September 2015, the fortieth anniversary of independence.

Institutions such as the IPNGS have made very significant attempts to locate Papua New Guinea materials overseas (considered by many people as "national treasures") and repatriate them, with the idea of making them available within the country for which they are most meaningful. Yet all these efforts are very much in jeopardy because of the attempts by some to deny Papua New Guinea's cultural heritage, force their beliefs on everyone, and tolerate no deviations from such beliefs because they impede progress.

This is by far the greatest challenge an archive of Papua New Guinea music has ever faced. As we write this article, it is clear that the battle is very far from being over. We sincerely hope that the recordings of traditional music held by our Institute and the performances still waiting to be documented will be as valued in the future as they have been in the past.

Notes
1 IPNGS was originally established under the *Cultural Development Act* 1974, but the wording in relation to its functions has basically remained unchanged in the most current legislation concerning it. Notably there is no mention of the necessity of maintaining an archive after its establishment.
2 Although dance is not explicitly mentioned in legislation concerning the functions of IPNGS, it has always been considered a part of the Music Department's activities. Nevertheless, it is only since 2001 that a full-time dance researcher has been employed.
3 Information about Sheridan primarily derives from a number of his publications (as cited above and elsewhere) and an interview conducted with him less than three weeks before his death (Niles 2003, 2004a; Sheridan 2003). Sheridan's original research on the development of popular music in the Rabaul area, as performed by the Tolai and "mixed-race" communities, has also greatly benefitted the work of Michael Webb (e.g., Webb 1995, 1997).

4 Some of these Papua New Guinea recordings appear on the LP version of selections from this collection (Reinhard and List 1963).
5 In collaboration with Wattle, the LP was also released *as An Introduction to Music of New Guinea: The Australian Trust Territory by Prestige International* (INT 25013) in the same year.
6 Valuable information on Wattle can be found at: http://www.abc.net.au/radionational/programs/hindsight/wattle-records-and-films/3416206 and http://nla.gov.au/nla.party-680076.
7 The Manus recordings were made by William E. Smythe; they are the only recordings on the LP not made by Sheridan.
8 Recordings of Kuman music by Australian anthropologist A. P. Elkin in 1955–56 were actually released commercially by the University of Sydney on a set of sixteen discs called New Guinea Musical Records (Elkin 1957). However, this release was aimed at researchers more than the general public, and apparently had a very limited distribution. Other Highlands recordings, although not from the Kuman area, were included on Simpson and Cunningham's *New Guinea and Papuan Native Music*. Note that some titles given for the Sheridan recordings are not in the Kuman language, but the texts of the songs are in that language. To account for such discrepancies, it is possible that errors were made in writing vernacular words, a different dialect is used, or the information is simply incorrect. At present, it is not possible to further resolve such issues.
9 For further information on the Kuman call language, see Gende (2010).
10 The front cover of the disc sleeve (figure 2) shows elaborately decorated male drummers/dancers from the Kuman area or somewhere nearby.

References

Beier, U. 2005. *Decolonising the Mind. The Impact of the University on Culture and Identity in Papua New Guinea, 1971–74*. Canberra: Pandanus Books.

Bergmann, H. F. W. 1969. *Die Kamanuku. Die Kultur der Chimbu Stämme. Eine Monographie*. 4 vols: Mimeographed.

— 1971. *The Kamanuku*. 4 vols. Harrisville, Australia.

Elkin, A. P. 1957. Australia and New Guinea Musical Records. *Oceania* 27 (4): 313–319.

Evara, R. A. 2013. Speaker "Cleans" House. Zurenuoc Banishes "Ungodly Images and Idols" from Parliament. *Post-Courier* (6 December): 1–2.

Gende, E. 1998. Highland Region of Papua New Guinea. Chimbu Province. Kuman. In *Australia and the Pacific Islands*, eds. A. L. Kaeppler and J. W. Love. *The Garland Encyclopedia of World Music*, vol. 9. New York: Garland Publishing, pp. 522–526.

— 2010. *Owa*. Bush Messages or Signs in the Form of Music. *Kulele* 4: 105–10.

Jones, T. A. 1959. Review of *Music of New Guinea* by Ray J. Sheridan. *Quarterly Bulletin of the South Pacific Commission* 9 (3): 49, 56.

Kaeppler, A. L. 1963. Review of *Music of New Guinea* by Ray Sheridan. *Ethnomusicology* 7 (1): 60–61.

Kaspruś, A. 1936–37. [Recordings made in Chimbu area]. Copies of wax cylinders from Berlin Phonogramm-Archive. Two 18 cm reel-to-reel tapes (contained in IPNGS x86-158, *9–10).

Lewis, M. P., G. F. Simons and C. D. Fennig (eds.) 2013. *Ethnologue. Languages of the World*. 17thed. Dallas: SIL International. Online version: http://www.ethnologue.com/.

Meggitt, M. J. 1959. Review of *Music of New Guinea* by Ray J. Sheridan. *Mankind* 5: 362.

Moriguba, B. 2010. Digitisation and Preservation of Papua New Guinea's Audio Heritage. *Kulele* 4: 165–171.

Moyle, A. M. 1959a. Island Music. *The Canon* 12: 352–55.

— 1959b. Review of *Music of New Guinea* by Ray J. Sheridan. *Oceania* 30 (1): 76–77.

National 2015. Tear Down the Idols. *The National* (14 August): 32, 41 (advertisement).

Nditing, Z. Y. 2013. Do Away Will [*sic*] All Cultural Expressions and Impressions. *Sunday Chronicle* (29 December): 11 (letter).

Niles, D. 1992a. Collection, Preservation, and Dissemination. The Institute of Papua New Guinea Studies as the Centre for the Study of All Papua New Guinea Music. In *Music and Dance of Aboriginal Australia and the South Pacific*, ed. A. M. Moyle. Oceania Monograph, 41. Sydney: University of Sydney, pp. 59–75.

— 1992b. *Konggap, Kap* and Tambaran. Music of the Yupno/Nankina Area in Relation to Neighbouring Groups. In *Abschied von der Vergangenheit. Ethnologische Berichte aus dem Finisterre-Gebirge, Papua New Guinea*, ed. J. Wassmann. Berlin: Dietrich Reimer, pp. 149–184.

— 2000. *Papua New Guinea (1904–1909). The Collections of Rudolf Pöch, Wilhelm Schmidt, and Josef Winthuis*. Book (223 pp.), five compact discs (OEAW PHA CD 9/1–5), and one CD-ROM (OEAW PHA CD-ROM/9). D. Schüller, series editor. G. Lechleitner, editor. E. Mack, music transcriptions. Tondokumente aus dem Phonogrammarchiv der Österreichischen Akademie der Wissenschaften. Gesamtausgabe der Historischen Bestände 1899–1950 / Sound Documents from the Phonogrammarchiv of the Austrian Academy of Sciences: The Complete Historical Collections 1899–1950, series 3. Wien: Verlag der Österreichischen Akademie der Wissenschaften.

— 2002. The Contribution of the Berlin Phonogramm-Archiv to the Study of Papua New Guinea Musics. In *Music Archiving in the World. Papers Presented at the Conference on the Occasion of the 100th Anniversary of the*

Berlin Phonogramm-Archiv, eds. G. Berlin and A. Simon. Berlin: Verlag für Wissenschaft und Bildung, pp. 189–200.
— 2003. Luksave long wanpela bikman bilong PNG musik. Ray Sheridan (1916–2003). *Wantok Niuspepa* (4 Desemba): 21.
— 2004a. Music Pioneer Passes Away. *Post-Courier* (2 January): 14.
— 2004b. Reclaiming the Past. The Value of Recordings to a National Cultural Heritage. In *Archives for the Future. Global Perspectives on Audiovisual Archives in the 21st Century*, eds. A. Seeger and S. Chaudhuri. New Delhi: American Institute of Indian Studies; Calcutta: Seagull Books, pp. 196–206.
— 2011. Structuring Sound and Movement. Music and Dance in the Mount Hagen Area." PhD dissertation, Anthropology and Sociology, University of Papua New Guinea.
— 2012. The National Repatriation of Papua New Guinea Recordings. Experiences Straddling World War II. *Ethnomusicology Forum: Journal of the British Forum for Ethnomusicology* 21 (2): 141–159.
— 2015. Introduction. Foi Songs and the Performance, Publication, and Poetry of Papua New Guinea Sung Traditions." In *Songs of the Empty Place. The Memorial Poetry of the Foi of the Southern Highlands Province of Papua New Guinea*, eds. J. F. Weiner and D. Niles. Canberra: ANU Press. http://press.anu.edu.au/titles/monographs-in-anthropology/songs-of-the-empty-place/ , pp. xv–xlix.
— n.d. Cylinders and Discs. The Early Recording of Papua New Guinea Music, 1898 to 1945 (73 pp). Unpublished Manuscript.
Niles, D., and A. Rumsey. 2011. Introducing Highlands Sung Tales. In *Sung Tales from the Papua New Guinea Highlands. Studies in Form, Meaning, and Sociocultural Context*, eds. A. Rumsey and D. Niles, 1–38. Canberra: ANU E Press. http://epress.anu.edu.au/sung_tales_citation.html.
Niles, D., and M. Webb 1987. *Papua New Guinea Music Collection.* Boroko: Institute of Papua New Guinea Studies. IPNGS 008. Eleven cassettes and book.
Pacific Islands Monthly 1958. A Recording of Weird New Guinea Noises. They're Looking for More Music from the South Pacific." *Pacific Islands Monthly* 29 (5): 63.
Per, Z. 2010. Sounds of Chimbu Destroyed. *The National* (18 May): 3. (also at http://islandculturearchivalsupport.wordpress.com/2010/08/02/sounds-of-chimbu-destroyed-in-kundiawa-png/).
Reinhard, K., and G. List. 1963. *The Demonstration Collection of E. M. von Hornbostel and the Berlin Phonogramm-Archiv.* Folkways 4175. Booklet and two 30 cm, 33 1/3 rpm discs.
Rosi, P. 1991. Papua New Guinea's New Parliament House. A Contested National Symbol. *The Contemporary Pacific* 3 (2): 289–323.

Schram, R. 2014. *A New Government Breaks with the Past in the Papua New Guinea Parliament's "Haus Tambaran"*. Material World, Properties and Social Imagination. Explorations and Experiments with Ethnography Collections, Occasional Paper, 4.
http://www.materialworldblog.com/2014/02/a-new-government-breaks-with-the-past-in-the-papua-new-guinea-parliaments-haus-tambaran/ [accessed May 28, 2017].

Sheridan, R. J. 1947. Report on Brief Survey of Music Made Between Mt. Hagen and Lae (30 pp). National Library of Papua New Guinea, PNG 780.995 SHE f vol. 1 & 2.

— 1958. *Music of New Guinea. The Australian Trust Territory – An Introduction*. Recordings by R. J. Sheridan and W. E. Smythe. Wattle Recordings D2. One 30 cm, 33 1/3 rpm disc (IPNGS c80-142).

— 1972. Music (2). In *Encyclopaedia of Papua and New Guinea*, ed. P. Ryan, 3 Volumes. Vol. 2. Clayton, Vic.: Melbourne University Press, pp. 817–821.

— 2003. *[Interview of R. J. Sheridan]*. Recorded by D. Niles and V. Palie. Two DAT tapes (IPNGS 03-062) and two video tapes (IPNGS 03-063).

Simet, J., and W. Iamo. 1992. *Cultural Diversity and the United Papua New Guinea*. Discussion Paper, 64. Boroko: National Research Institute.

To'Liman-Turalir, J. 2002. Why Historic Recordings Are of Value to the Tolai People Today. In *Music Archiving in the World. Papers Presented at the Conference on the Occasion of the 100th Anniversary of the Berlin Phonogramm-Archiv*, eds. G. Berlin and A. Simon. Berlin: Verlag für Wissenschaft und Bildung, pp. 54–58.

Wassmann, J. 1982. *Der Gesang an den fliegenden Hund. Untersuchungen zu den totemistischen Gesängen und geheimen Namen des Dorfes Kandingei am Mittelsepik (Papua New Guinea) anhand der kirugu-Knotenschnüre*. Basel: Ethnologisches Seminar der Universität und Museum für Völkerkunde. (Basler Beiträge zur Ethnologie Bd. 22).

— 1991. *The Song to the Flying Fox. The Public and Esoteric Knowledge of the Important Men of Kandingei about Totemic Songs, Names and Knotted Cords (Middle Sepik, Papua New Guinea)*. Trans. D. Q. Stephenson. Ed. D. Niles. Boroko: National Research Institute. (Apwitihire: Studies in Papua New Guinea Musics, 2).

Webb, M. 1995. *"Pipal bilong music tru" / "A Truly Musical People". Musical Culture, Colonialism, and Identity in Northeastern New Britain, Papua New Guinea, after 1875*. PhD dissertation, Wesleyan University.

— 1997. A Long Way from Tipperary. Performance Culture in Early Colonial Rabaul, New Guinea, and the Genesis of a Melanesian Popular Music Scene. *Perfect Beat* 3 (2): 32–59.

Webb, M., and D. Niles. 1986. *Riwain! Papua New Guinea Pop Songs*. Institute of Papua New Guinea Studies IPNGS 007. Two cassettes and book.

Webb, M., and D. Niles. 1990. *Ol Singsing bilong Ples.* Boroko: Institute of Papua New Guinea Studies IPNGS 010. Two cassettes and book.

Wirz, P., and D. Wirz. 1949–53. [Recordings made in Chimbu area]. Three, 13 cm reel-to-reel tapes (IPNGS x05-675).

Ziegler, S. 2006. *Die Wachszylinder des Berliner Phonogramm-Archivs.* Veröffentlichungen des Ethnographischen Museums Berlin, 73. Berlin: Ethnologisches Museum Staatliche Museen zu Berlin.

Zurenuoc, T. 2013. Removal and Replacement of the Carved Images in the Grand Hall of the Parliament. *The National* (18 December): 33–36 (advertisement).

Angella Meinerzag

11 Foreign Confidants. A Field Diary Narrative

Introduction

At first the Hinihon people whom I encountered during my fieldwork felt foreign to me, but over time and accompanied by a lot of ups and downs, they became more familiar. My selected diary notes, which will be presented here, clearly depict this process. In the end I realized that I myself had become such a foreign confidant.

Before starting my first fieldwork I often asked myself how I would mentally and emotionally adapt. I knew about participant observation but had no idea what it would do to me, the observer. Especially the reports of Bowen (1954), Powdermaker (1966) and a personal friend's diary offered a glimpse into what it means to conduct anthropological fieldwork. Real insights were offered at the monthly working session "Oceania" held at Jürg Wassmann and Verena Keck's place in Heidelberg, where personal aspects of fieldwork could be discussed. Still, I kept thinking that I could only adequately encounter the others when I myself was more or less free from presumptions, anger, desperation and all other emotions that influence perception. From experience I knew that reflecting on myself through writing was always a good option to clear off knots and to calm me. Thus, writing about the feelings I had in the field was for me a method of reflection. It was a sort of externalization of my inner emotions and it was always a possibility to create distance. Davies pointed out that

> (...) immersion, as we know, often evokes powerful subjective reactions which can either enable or inhibit the understanding that it aims to generate. Insofar as this is true, charting these reactions can contribute to the task of further understanding the processes of anthropological knowledge construction (Davies 2010: 94).

Reactions such as strain, dissonance or disorientation, but also agreeable ones, such as wideness, lightness and the opening and sensitization of the senses can be experienced to different degrees. To observe and understand these processes is a possibility to adjust the "human instrument" (Davies 2010: 80) of being a fieldworker. When I returned to the Hinihon three years later, I no longer had the impulse to write about my inner state of mind.

The Hinihon and the Adelbert Range

During my trip in 2000, I was first accompanied by Jürg Wassmann and Verena Keck, my doctoral advisor and his colleague/wife. We visited several villages in the Adelbert Range and presented the project of my fieldwork.

The Hinihon live in the Adelbert Range that towers above the lowlands of the Madang Province and physically isolates the people from the coast. There is no access by road, only by paths. By car and on foot it took me two or three days, with an overnight stay in Sevan, to reach the Hinihon coming from Madang. The village of Aton lies 896 m above sea level and is surrounded by mountains. Aton consisted of fourteen bamboo houses situated on poles surrounding a square. I lived with the family of Andobulu and his wife Andobifoa in a house where I had a room to myself. The Hinihon, however, live mainly in their gardens and not in the village (see A. von Poser, this volume) as I gradually became aware of over the course of my anthropological fieldwork (Meinerzag 2015).

The following text is an English translation of my field diary covering the years 2000 and 2001 when I stayed with the Hinihon for nine months. It accounts for my feelings in the field and offers an insight, just like a documentary. Analyzing my notes, I can distinguish three main topics: the huge number of ambivalent feelings, the process of learning and immersion and the constant social, bodily, and emotional reorientation.

Feeling ambivalent in the field

The greatest discrepancy was to be and feel alone amidst a community where everyone has their own social network. I longed to see friends, people to chat and share my thoughts with, but was confronted with a very different situation. It took some time until I learned about people's lives and could share their interests. On the other hand, I wanted to be alone in order to sort out the intensive inputs; I was left exhausted by all the new things to assimilate.

In order to keep my identity, I had to develop a working relationship with the Hinihon. This saw me remaining a foreigner and a familiar person who is part of their life, for example by walking with them while simultaneously recording their conversations, a constant oscillation between the two extremes of proximity and distance. My new identity felt strange and powerful but also gave me a sense of freedom. I wondered how I would feel when returned to Germany.

Aton, 04th of September 2000
For the first time I am completely alone. Not only for a few minutes, but for hours. The village is quite empty; except for some elders, chicken and pigs, there is nobody. It is a wonderful sunny day and I profited from the good light to take some pictures. Impressions encroach on me and I am glad to sort them in peace. There is so much information, so many faces and smells that are new. There are constant discoveries and I try hard to bring them in order. My system of orientation gets into gear: to bring people in some order - who is whose brother or sister, who is first-born, second-born, who are the parents, the true ones?

Aton, 06th of September 2000
The first low is here. I do not care for anything. Dissatisfied and agitated. I dreamt strange things. I think I would like to chat again in German. Tears come to my eyes. I miss them all. I feel like I am at an impasse. I cannot move forward or backward. A lot of contradictions. I feel alone, but happy to have my peace. Would like to have company, but do not want to have a conversation.

Aton, 18th of October 2000

Foreign Confidants could be a good term for my relationship with the people here. They are so strange and unfamiliar for me, just as I am for them. I understand why I am suffering so much. I am alone, surrounded by people who have their own social network. This is the contradiction I am confronted with every day. They have their friends and their family whereas I am alone, without roots.

Aton, 29th of December 2000

During a walk people tell me a lot. I often noticed it. They are in their element. I should take the tape recorder with me, because taking notes while walking is not really comfortable. I already know a lot of names and I only have to memorize the new ones. I was frisky. They were very happy to have the opportunity to show me everything.

Aton, 01st January 2001

Now I feel good here. All the inner struggles come to an end. I can see people, but can also work and read alone in tranquillity. I have a good relationship with the people - we respect each other. With some I feel close and it is good to know them. I developed a new kind of relationship, one I had not experienced yet. It is a mixture of being one of them and being in a working relationship. Sometimes I notice that I have to keep my distance, that I need it for myself to see me like this. I assimilated and adapted so much that I need time for myself to keep my identity.

Madang, 20th of January 2001

I don't know what has happened. I just wrote a very short email, feeling disconnected from everything. I do not have access to the world out there. I am in my own sphere in between: between Madang, Aton and Germany. To immerse myself in the world up there with the Hinihon I had to engage with them. I learned to live in a new way and gave up quite a lot. It is like being new-born. I can't really describe to people in Germany what I experienced up there but my task is to do exactly this. This will be my challenge but not now - for now I am *meri bilong bush*[1], a "bushwoman."

Aton, 01st February 2001
There is a lot going on in my head, distance and proximity during the trip to Madang. My wish was fulfilled by a miracle, but I could not enjoy it, because the others did not come along. We were walking the whole day as a group, a walking community. However, this communal feeling was suddenly broken when I alone left to finish the last part of the trip by car, a privilege granted for being white.

Aton, 21th of February 2001
My feelings and thoughts are so ambivalent. It was like this during my whole stay. I enjoyed the experienced freedom, it is an explosive feeling. But I am afraid of my inner disruption and I don't want that a part of me remains here. I want to be full of enthusiasm and not to get stuck in-between the worlds. I can't guess how I will react once I am back home, because of the changed, new me that came into existence here. The term "Foreign Confidants" refers not only to me being with the Hinihon, but also to myself, because I no longer am familiar with myself.

Learning and immersion

The process of learning went step by step. Yet, sometimes I got flooded by information and had difficulties sorting it all out, sometimes I had to wait for new impressions. Slowly I could recognize everyone and relate them to their families, by understanding and interpreting the structures of interrelationship. Consequentially emotive reactions and statements became comprehensible and I could respond appropriately. As a result, relationships became easier for me.

Recognizing plants, paths, gardens and being able to distinguish between bush and garden was a further step on the way of understanding. My perception channels were open for new smells, noises and I learned their meaning: sounds transported information such as the coming rain, birds that cry only at certain time of the day, or small earthquakes signaling the change of weather.

I appreciated some customs previously unknown to me, such as washing at the source or waterfall and diving in the floats, walking with a torch at night, sitting close to the fire in the colder evenings, esteem food that was disgusting for me in the beginning. My sense of time adapted, too. Once I used to think about minutes, now I thought about days and I learned how to recognize signs for departure instead of relying on a certain date and time.

I had to develop my new skills fast and I struggled with most due to a lack of personal communication and a possibility to reflect on things. The lack of known references and communication partners left me in a desperate search for answers and solutions. In addition, I often had to overcome my limitations, dealing with situations I had to accept as I could not change them, such as pains during long walks. This was the point at which I tried to find inner resources. The solitude I felt transformed into embeddedness and I felt stable and secure standing within my environment. Physically, I also felt the shift.

Aton, 01st September 2000
It is incredible. They show me so much. I learn several Hinihon terms. A few sentences for everyday life, kitchen utensils, weapons, plants. Kinship terms and how they count: they bend their fingers and count with their feet [see Wassmann 2016]!

Aton, 09th of September 2000
Today is a good day. Why the days are good or bad is hard to say. I'll try: it is easier with the family. We can assess each other and I feel free. We make jokes and have good moments. This morning, a lot of people were here, we sorted out kinship terminology and it is becoming clearer to me; this is a good feeling. Andobifoa tried to braid my hair. Other kids and adults came and touched my hair. The caresses felt good. Crossing these boundaries was good and necessary - for me and for them.

I am aware of how wonderful nature is around me, the moon, the birds and plants - it is divine.

Aton, 02nd of October 2000
I want to get away from here. Perhaps it will be better once I am back from Madang. I just waited too long here. I have nobody to talk to. No one to share my feelings with. My sorrows and anguishes consume me from the inside. Tomorrow I will be saved when I can start walking. I will go crazy if it rains and we therefore cannot leave.

Now, I go for a walk.

11 Foreign Confidants 179

Sevan, 05th of October 2000
I am stuck in Sevan and there is no way to get out. The pickup left yesterday already. Tomorrow there might be one, but who knows? We waited this morning for the bus, assuming it would leave. I can't walk to Bunabun, my knees hurt too much. Nobody would come with me. But tomorrow, I will leave with or without somebody to accompany me. Then my knees will also be better.

Slowly, I'm getting an idea of why there are so few reports about personal experiences during fieldwork. It's quite demanding and nobody gets to look good. Still, I'm determined to keep going and come back stronger.

Aton, 28th of October 2000
Tomorrow, we will leave for Madang. Probably. I am looking forward to it. But I could also stay here. However, it is different from last time when I planned to go to Madang.

I notice the simplicity of the people, the authenticity in their movements, glances and gestures and I try to absorb all this. Often I have tears in my eyes because of feeling lucky and because of my emotions. The vacuum I had felt before has been filled.

Aton, 16th of December 2000
It was great yesterday when we bathed in the waterfall. Both Andobifoa, Andobipuhak and the little Andobembam. Initially I washed only the upper part of my body in order to refresh from the long walk, then I dressed again. I would have liked to bathe, but did as usual: wait and see. And then the older Andobifoa went rapidly to the waterfall - it looked great. I just followed her. The two others came along. We stood in the flow, washing our backs mutually. It was deep enough to plunge in. I could dip into the fresh water, like a baptism. It was great, after walking barefoot through the mud, uphill and downhill.

Aton, 15th of January 2001
The atmosphere is easy-going, we laugh a lot and are in a good mood. I played volleyball with them - it was nice not to be the worst player.

Today, the whole village went to Ululu to pay our last respects to a dead man. Sumeakom told me, the man had died because of unsettled anger. Here are the oppressing problems I know from the book [see Keck 2005].

Aton, 09th of February 2001
I made progress and became quiet again. The main knot is untied, it is loose. Some small and some bigger ones still remain and will always remain. The last few days, I walked around this knot; for weeks, I observed it. I looked for a spot, trying to pull it open, then suddenly it falls apart. I think it calms me to no longer have this knot in front of me.

Aton, 27th of February 2001
Yesterday I went to the garden Kapung Mene. I quickly packed my little bag and off I went with Andobifoa and her kids into the bush. We slept in the garden house. It was so windy, cold and hard at night that I hardly slept. I kept on fanning the flame and warming my feet in a sitting position.

In the morning we, around 30 men and seven women, went to hunt tree kangaroos. We, the women beat the ground and the leaves with sticks, while the men waited with bow and arrow for the game. I also spent time with the men. Walking in the bush and crouching down was like a bath in the greenery. I am fully imprinted by the trees and smell from the contact with leaves and branches.

Reorientation

With time, I wondered how many things became normal. Comparing the Hinihon with neighbouring groups I became aware of their unique cultural life-world. Over time I noticed the changes I had undergone and I was happy to see the progress of acclimatization and how it helped me with my work. At the end of my stay, I attended a meeting in the same house as at the beginning. All participants were familiar, I could understand what they were talking about and comprehend what was happening. I then noticed my transformation from a puzzled observer to a contributing participant.

Aton, 16th of October 2000
I constantly revise my opinion. Today, I realized people are most of the time in the bush, they sleep and work there. They have a small house and sleep on the ground on a palm mattress close to the fireplace. The gardens are spread all around the village. It was a real discovery for me:

their life does not take place in the village, but in the bush. They live just like nomads walking from garden to garden. No wonder I felt strange and alone. Life is in the bush - not in the village where I was staying.

Aton, 15th of December 2000
What a feast! Village life appears so luxurious in comparison with garden life. It is strange to write in a clean book without dirt. I stayed for two days in the garden Pihom and I experienced incredible things. First the Mesekor, a neighbouring group, who arrived in the village shouting loudly, with torches in their hands. They had carved sticks and had decorated themselves with fern and leaves. We sat until midnight in the house of old Akom. And at 4 o'clock in the morning I packed my overnight bag and we started walking. The mountain up, up and then down. And I was in the middle of this shouting crowd. All walking in line, the smell of the leaves, torches and kerosene lamps. The way was a perpendicular, muddy path. At sunset we arrived at the garden. The crowd stood there with their sticks, they looked like trees. They started to dig out the ground, loud shouting and dancing.

Sevan, 18th of January 2001
I am knocked out from a twelve hour walk but have no pain in my knees. Walking is fun, especially the way from Kumbu to Sevan. The first time I struggled downhill, this time I just ran down. I left my escorts behind and arrived first. I smell terrible, have bites all over and I have an allergy were my socks were. Once again I missed the bus. However, I am not as desperate as the last times, because now I know the surroundings and I know the drivers.

Aton, 08th of February 2001
I am back from two days in the gardens of Kapung Mene. They are all up there, and I miss them. I had a great time. We, nine adults and seven kids, were all in one big room with six fireplaces, we ate together, talked, played cards and slept close to the fire. In the bush we danced and sang with Andobifoa in the moonlight. In the morning we woke up together and kindled the fire. The fog was coming up, clouds were at the coast. One can see very far, we had a great view.

Now, I am sad to be alone in the village, find my feelings bewildering. I just want to lay next to them, to be with them. And simultaneously, it is good to have my own time. I now see village life differently.

Aton, 03rd March 2001
The circle is closed: just as I sat in the beginning with Jürg and Verena in the big house presenting our project, I sat this evening in the middle and we prepared the party for my departure. Now I know all the people, their families and relations and share a part of my life with them. Yet, it is not a circle, it is a spiral.

Conclusion

With my field diary narrative, I hope to have conveyed the idea that "[f]ield work is a deeply human as well as a scientific experience and [that] a detailed knowledge of both aspects is an important source of data in itself, and necessary for any comparative study of methodology" (Powdermaker 1966: 9). While in the field, a constant and critical examination of my own complex and sometimes quite ambivalent feelings became crucial for discerning local ways of being and becoming a person within the Hinihon socialscape (Meinerzag 2015). From the present perspective, walking, that is moving and immersing myself with all my senses, takes quite a central place in my field notes. To adapt and learn was in fact like walking along a spiral, thus following a Hinihon statement: being automatically means walking.

Note
1 *Meri bilong bush* is a Tok Pisin (Melanesian Pidgin-English) term often used by people themselves who live in the rural and more remote parts of Papua New Guinea.

References
Bowen, E. S. 1954. *Return to Laughter*. New York: Harper and Brothers.
Davies, J. 2010. Disorientation, Dissonance, and Altered Perception in the Field. In *Emotions in the Field. The Psychology and Anthropology of Fieldwork Experience*, eds. J. Davies and D. Spencer. Stanford: Stanford University Press, pp. 79–97.

Keck, V. 2005. *Social Discord and Bodily Disorders. Healing Among the Yupno of Papua New Guinea*. Durham: North Carolina Academic Press.

Meinerzag, A. 2015. *Being* Mande. *Person, Land and Names among the Hinihon in the Adelbert Range, Papua New Guinea*. Heidelberg: Universitätsverlag Winter. (Heidelberg Studies in Pacific Anthropology, Vol. 3).

Powdermaker, H. 1966. *Stranger and Friend. The Way of an Anthropologist*. New York: Norton.

Wassmann, J. 2016. *The Gently Bowing Person. An Ideal among the Yupno in Papua New Guinea*. Heidelberg: Universitätsverlag Winter. (Heidelberg Studies in Pacific Anthropology, Vol. 4).

Shahnaz R. Nadjmabadi

12 Endangered Fields.
Experiencing Anthropological Research in Iran

Introduction

Anthropological knowledge is not only shaped by the identity of the researcher, his or her background, but also depends on the circumstances in the field which impact data collection as well as its interpretation. To take the example of research in border areas: many factors and components come into play, impeding and circumventing the flow and progress of research. In the following I would like to illustrate some of the methodological and theoretical challenges anthropologists encounter when researching in border areas, drawing on my own experience during my various anthropological investigations in Iranian border areas since the seventies: the first field research was conducted in 1970-1971 on nomadic people in Lorestan, western Iran, at the Iran-Iraq border, 1975-76 and later in 2011-2015 I was doing research on transborder relations in the eastern province of Khorasan at the Iran-Afghanistan border and, finally, on transmigration and economic exchange between the Iranian population and their Arab neighbors in the coastal areas of the Persian Gulf in southern Iran (1985-2009). I will particularly point out one specific event during my very first field experience in Lorestan which strongly altered the direction of my later anthropological research in Iran; this illustrates how anthropologists' own experiences of, and reactions to, uncertainty, change, risk and unexpected events may disrupt well-organized field research and consequently change perceptions and interpretations. These events, while hindering access to certain domains of fieldwork, nevertheless offer the opportunity to gain different anthropological insights (Howell 1990).

Many of the issues I raise in this paper are known and familiar to any anthropologist who has carried out research in remote and endangered areas which are subjected to particular security measures. Howell (1990), for example, indicates in his research on safety in the field that at least 42 percent of anthropologists reported experiencing "criminal inter-personal hazards" (robbery, assault, rape, murder), 9 percent reported "arrests in the field," 22 percent reported "living through political turmoil" (revolution, war, rioting), 15 percent reported that they were under "suspicion of spying," 12 percent reported experiencing "factional conflict" (acute hostilities within the group under study). Yet, these experiences and consequences are hardly ever mentioned and analyzed in the anthropological texts and publications that originate from their research. There are different reasons for this: concerns about the manner our research results may be perceived, worry about political consequences and bureaucratic complications.[1]

Border research

Border areas are mainly characterized by the presence of police and military forces, and border management always pursues the goal of securing and facilitating interaction across borders, while simultaneously developing and implementing policies to prevent any negative externalities of these interactions. Thus, constraints for interaction are put in place, while on the other hand a specific form of interaction that allows for positive externalities is encouraged and fostered through policies of cooperation. The tension between these two conflicting goals of border management shapes the character and dynamics of cross-border relations and interactions and molds the local attitudes of the borderland populations. As guarantor and representative of a state authority, the tactics of security forces include strategies for surveillance. Being aware of this, populations inhabiting border areas often hesitate to talk freely, for doing so might bring them and others trouble. Some subjects may be taboo or too risky, while others, though sensitive, may be addressed indirectly. Therefore, any level of discussion in border areas is related to or demands political sensitivity. Hence ethnographers working in border areas and contested fields are advised not to attract unwelcome attention to their research subject, to constantly monitor the security situation, to analyze risks and in particular to listen to the advice of local informants. Additionally, and more than in other anthropological field situations, there is a great need for confidentiality.

Very often and in different situations when collecting data in Iranian border areas, I had to realize that anthropology as a discipline does not provide its researchers with a practical and critical methodology for conducting research in endangered and jeopardized areas. The traditional methodologies that anthropologists have been using are based on rigid frameworks and fixed assumptions about social systems which are explored and analyzed through formalized approaches to acquiring data. These research methods try to organize the findings on social systems in a way that presents a fairly accurate emic understanding of the society under consideration and presuppose field circumstances / conditions which are harmonious, stable and peaceful. They are based on the idea that the anthropologist is in command of the field situation. However, in the context of research in remote and endangered fields one has to admit that circumstances are quite different, compelling the researcher to use creativity and flexibility, to apply strategies and techniques to gather information and collect data, simultaneously keeping in check / limiting his or her risk exposure.

Anthropological research in Iran: Staying with nomadic groups in Western Lorestan

Anthropological research in rural and remote border areas in Iran always touches on state policy and is never a neutral / non-political topic. When I began my anthropological research in Iran, I did not have the intention of specifically investigating border areas. But the topics and subjects I was interested in, especially processes of social change and development in rural areas, led me to conduct research in border areas, which in turn presupposed mobility and adaptability to the ever changing research context. In each new research site, I had to constantly reassess the risks and vulnerabilities of all persons affected by my research to provide for their and my own safety.

My personal living conditions during my various research projects were all very similar: I was hosted by a family as a guest, and although the bond between my hosts and me always grew very close, this did not mean that I was part of them. As a guest, the limit of participation is determined by the host. Simultaneously, my hosts had to carry the heavy burden of taking responsibility for me, my safety and well-being.[2] My

Iranian nationality notwithstanding, I was always dependent on letters of support by some government or scientific institution, university and the like. In addition, the support of local partners and their backing advisors was imperative and indispensable in order to navigate the complex web of security considerations and political constraints. I was always accompanied and introduced to the community by a member of the community. For the people themselves, it usually was and still is difficult to understand the motives and objectives of my research in and on the border areas. In most of the cases they approached me kindly, with a mélange of curiosity, reluctance, and suspicion. There were instances when I found it necessary to identify myself as an historian rather than as an anthropologist. Especially when I thought it was too complicated or confusing to explain what anthropologists do.

The case I would like to recount in the following is an event which dates back to my very first anthropological field research in 1970. Since it immensely influenced my later anthropological research in other parts of Iran, it is worth being presented here in full. Back then, I was staying with nomadic groups in Lorestan, Western Iran, approximately 200 km from the Iran-Iraq border. There, the aim of my research was to collect empirical data for my PhD thesis on the kinship system among nomadic groups. I was trying to find out how this system was defined by the cultural context of the nomadic groups, who in that particular period of the 70s had come under strong state pressure to be sedentarized. The intermediary who introduced me to one of the tribal groups in Lorestan was the then director of the cultural heritage center in Khorramabad, the center of Lorestan province. He himself was a member of a small tribal group, the Shirawand, whom I was going to live with during the following 10 months. It was only through his mediation, influence and support that I was given permission by government authorities and security services to stay in these remote areas.

The Shirawand were semi-nomadic groups who lived in the mountainous region of western Lorestan, in the district of Teshkan, at a distance of about 70 km from Khorramabad, the center of Lorestan Province. The region's infrastructure was weak; the only means of transportation available to get there were off-road vehicles, in those days American Jeeps and British Range Rovers. The early 70s were a difficult period for nomadic groups all over Iran. There was a strong sedentarization movement by the Iranian government to get nomads to settle down, to subordinate them to state control, to abolish their traditional social organizations and to integrate them into the national political and economic system. Gendarmerie positions were established all over the remote areas, young tribesmen were coerced into military service, and security services always had some local middlemen at their command who kept them informed about events among the tribal groups. Previously, intra-tribal conflicts had been dealt with by tribe members and their headmen themselves, but now government officials started to interfere heavily, and any kind of conflict had to be reported to the next Gendarmerie office. The nomadic population largely opposed this new kind of government intervention and was not willing to acquiesce into the new system of "law and order." Consequently, the conflict between government authorities and nomadic people became a permanent one.

Before joining the settlements of the Shirawand up the mountains, a great many warnings had been issued to me by townspeople and city dwellers to be careful with those "wild, uncivilized" tribesmen, while the nomadic people in turn advised me to be particularly careful with government representatives, security and military services, whom they accused / suspected of telling lies about the nomads and misrepresenting their culture. Shortly after my arrival in Teshkan I became aware of the high tensions and the existence of bitter and grave conflicts among the various tribal groups. Though most of the clans and lineages were related to each other through kinship and genealogies, this did not prevent mutual acts of hostility and aggression. Disputes were occurring nearly on a daily basis, and in frequent armed raids and robberies many tribesmen got killed. Since murder demanded revenge, a vicious cycle of escalating hostility and violence ensued.

Every now and then, government authorities showed up either to recruit conscripts or to persecute individuals who had committed illegal acts. However, I realized that very often, government officials and military agents were rather helpless and desperate when faced with the mountainous and often inaccessible physical conditions of the region on the one hand, and the nomadic groups permanently moving between summer grazing sites and winter settlements on the other.

My various initial attempts to approach members (both men and women) of different lineages and to elaborate questions about kinship terminology and classifications along with my theoretical assumptions in most cases ended up in heated accusations against government institutions, blaming them for delimitating the grazing rights, taking away productive and valuable manpower through compulsory military service, interfering with their traditional tribal rights, inducing conflicts by implementing new legislation etc. All in all, the nomadic populations presented themselves as victims of state authorities, oppressed and deprived of their rights without any support or backing to defend and secure their claims. Under these external conditions, it was difficult to advance my investigations on the social structure and the kinship system and I faced serious limitations in gaining insight into a highly complex web of lineages, clans and tribal confederations which were permanently in flux, splitting and fissioning, to be reconfigured and newly composed soon after.

At quite an early stage of my research I had been told by some Shirawand members that many years ago, a number of Shirawand lineages had split up and had moved out of the region as a consequence of internal conflicts. Apparently, they had become sedentarized and were living today at a significant distance on "the other side of the mountains" in the district of Tarhan (approx. 120 km from Teshkan) closer to the Iran-Iraq border. The conflicts between the two groups had been settled in the meantime, so relations were now peaceful and harmonious.

After having spent about three months in Teshkan, my curiosity drove me to seek contact with the Tarhan group: on the one hand, I wanted to learn more about whether and how those out-moving and sedentarized groups, had undergone processes of change. On the other hand, I was hoping to get more insights into the complex web of kinship ties, so I started to look for an occasion to move to Tarhan. One day, by pure chance, I overheard a conversation among some people who were planning to go to see their parents "on the other side of the mountain," so I immediately seized the opportunity and decided to join them, without either informing my intermediary in Khorramabad nor consulting my host family.

My sudden arrival in Tarhan without any previous planning and a mediator to present me and the reason and aim of my visit there led to some confusion: I struggled to find a host family similar to the one I had in Teshkan, and I was not received with warmth and kindness but, on the contrary, faced mistrust and suspicion. In addition to the human coldness and distance, I had to deal with terribly cold weather conditions: the rainy season had started and the roads were muddy and difficult to pass. The clay huts and houses lacked heating facilities, so I was shivering with cold all day. I was in a gloomy mood and lacked the motivation to approach people who treated me with a luke-warm and reluctant politeness anyway. As for the topic of my research, the general assumption in Tarhan was that, in one way or the other, I must be related to government authorities, hence they believed that I could support them on their claims and requirements and contribute to a resolution of their conflicts with the state administration. Thus my vague sketchy attempts to question them about the relations to their Teshkan relatives, here again, led people to level accusations and complaints against government agencies, portraying themselves as subordinated and disenfranchised victims of state authorities.

In the middle of my reflections about how to come to grips with the new situation and pondering on how to return to Teshkan, an event beyond my control set an abrupt end to my time in Tarhan: One very early morning, before sunrise, a government Jeep stopped in front of my host's small house. Two young Gendarmerie soldiers got out of the car and told my scared hosts that they had been sent by the chief officer from the central Gendarmerie in Kuhdasht, the center of Tarhan district, with the order to come and pick up the young woman who was staying with them. In no time, the Jeep was surrounded by neighbors and some villagers, who had been informed in the meantime, and everybody was trying to identify the cause and the rationale behind this order which the authorities had given the Gendarmerie. However, there was no way to get any information. Up until then, I had not had any encounter either with the Gendarmerie or with any government authority. I was not really worried nor troubled and I was convinced that I had to accompany the soldiers and that probably I would be back later during the day. Without taking anything with me, leaving behind personal belongings, photos, notes etc., I joined the soldiers and we traveled the road through a landscape I had no knowledge about, nor any orientation where and at which distance the district center Kuhdasht was located.

After more than two hours of driving, crisscrossing on muddy roads through what seemed to me a land of a thousand hills, with the sun slowly climbing up the sky, and with the two soldiers and the driver unwilling to reply to my kindly forwarded questions about landscape and locality, I started to lose my temper and remembered the stories my interlocutors had told me about the arbitrariness of the Gendarmerie, their tyranny and their despotic and discriminatory ways. Up to that moment, my interlocutors' complaints and accusations had remained quite abstract to me and at times I had even grown tired of listening to their constantly recurring stories, which I had found boring and exaggerated. Faced myself with a similar situation, not knowing where I was going, not having the possibility to address myself to anybody, I started to comprehend and develop a concrete understanding of what I had been told about the relationship between government agencies and the population. For the first time (and fortunately for the last time) during my various field research trips, I felt threatened, helpless and in danger. In such a difficult situation, there are moments you lose – as an anthropologist – your illusions about text book methodologies in the field.

I was lucky this feeling did not persist for a long time, as finally, it must have been around noon, I recognized from far away the shapes and outlines of some buildings which I supposed must be the district center Kuhdasht. Tired, exhausted, and covered with mud and dirt, I was led directly to the Gendarmerie office, where the courtyard and the building were crowded over and over with men, mainly nomadic people, waiting for their case to be dealt with. When I entered the office of the chief officer, he welcomed me politely, I was offered warm tea and sweets, accompanied by general, non-committal conversation. About 20 minutes later, one of the soldiers got the order to accompany me to the private house of the chief officer, where his wife and his little daughter were already waiting for me. Here again I was welcomed cordially, with great kindness I was offered sweets, fruits, and an excellent meal and even a comfortable bath was suggested to me (things I had missed since my arrival in Teshkan and Tarhan).

It was late in the afternoon when the chief officer accompanied me back into his office where another colleague was present and they explained to me the reason why they had sent for me to come to Kuhdasht: They had been informed by one of their informants in Tarhan about my arrival there, I had entered a border area, which had been placed under high security restrictions and permanent military surveillance. No outsider had the right to travel into this area without official order and without informing the Gendarmerie and district administration. I tried to explain the reason for my stay in Tarhan, mentioned that I had official permission for research in the district of Teshkan and named the intermediary person in Khorramabad who had introduced me into the region. All my explanations were useless, they had to be verified, particularly as I had no papers with me. The verification would take time; in those days there were no mobile, internet or other communication facilities. Even a phone connection was extremely difficult to establish. So I had to wait in Kuhdasht until clarity was provided. For nearly a week I stayed in Kuhdasht and there was no question of residing anywhere else than with the family of the chief officer.

This put me in an extremely precarious situation: on the one hand I enjoyed and appreciated the hospitality in the chief officer's house, and was happy to live in a kind of luxurious surrounding after having spent three months in almost spartan simplicity. I found myself sleeping in a warm and comfortable room, enjoying good meals and having the company of the officer's wife who had lived in this area for over three years and was happy to tell me all kinds of stories about the region, the population and the relationship between settled and nomadic people. On the other hand, I was aware that I was losing time and benefiting from the hospitality of those who, in the perception of the tribal groups with whom I was doing my research, were considered enemies and oppressors. I was concerned that the Shirawand might perceive this as betrayal, and I was frightened by the idea that by now probably everybody knew about my actual residence. How were they going to encounter me upon my return in Tarhan or Teshkan?

Simultaneously, I experienced something different during my "forced" absence from my actual field, passing my time with the chief officer himself and other colleagues who came to see him in his house and during some evening invitations in the company of other people. Whenever the discussion turned towards the relationship between nomads and government institutions as well as urban people, they – for their part – came up with stories about the everlasting quarrels among the nomadic groups themselves and particularly with their settled neighbors: for exceeding grazing and water rights, for claims to inheritance but also for leadership, power and influence, with most of these conflicts ending up in violent confrontations and armed hostilities. To give more importance to their stories and to prove that they were telling me the truth I was shown evidence, where all these conflicts had been documented in written forms. On several occasions I was also shown photos from those young Gendarmerie soldiers who, just for having fulfilled their duty and for having looked after law and order, had been attacked and put to death by the nomads.

Getting back

When after a week I was accompanied back to Tarhan, though I did not stay there for long. I was yearning to get back to Teshkan, where I needed some time to "tune in:" nothing could be taken for granted any more. I was painfully aware that I had been perceiving a very particular and partial version of events and opinions and how they were being interpreted, and that I had in turn interpreted these perceptions on the basis of information that had been available to me up to my arrival. I needed to reconsider my perception of dominant dynamics, question my own assumptions and my interpretations of interpretations, even if the answer at the end of this process turned out to be the same as before.[3]

Also, some of my interlocutors became more cautious in dealing with me; they provided politically correct answers and in many circumstances deliberately obscured them, an understandable measure of self-protection. Through my own experience with authority I could now better understand their complaints: This illustrates how shared experiences can create an intersubjectivity which enables the ethnographer to understand the other (Tedlock 1991: 70-1).

My newly attained awareness and the fact that, during my research, the working hypothesis had to be revised and renewed again and again on the basis of field observation and contradictory information, led me to realize that my theoretical framework about kinship classifications and genealogies would edit out many of the processes and interlinkages actually occurring and that my theoretical approach resulted in a selective interpretation of events, in particular with respect to narratives regarding security. I was struggling with theory and methodology and understood that my theoretical constructs had to be critically interrogated and problematized rather than operationalized. Theory should not take precedence at all. I should better concentrate on how people related security questions to their lives, identities, communities and care about theory later. The knowledge I gained at this point was that research should remain flexible and adjustable to crucial local circumstances, currents and frameworks. Instead of trying to track down only a narrow range of assured, already expected knowledge, one's own individual experiences should be valued and explored creatively.

Conclusion

During my research in Lorestan, I did not realize the extent to which I had been put under surveillance nor did I have any preconceptions of what was or was not possible. Although this experience illustrates the disadvantages and even dangers of entering a setting naïvely and unprepared for unexpected events, discussions with colleagues nevertheless supported the notion that it is hardly possible to prepare oneself fully for what will happen during fieldwork. There are a great number of anthropologists who experienced similar situations and they have at their disposal plenty of documents and depictions that reflect the insight that insecurity and hostility are common dimensions of life in remote, endangered and border areas. Writing about these conditions must not be avoided, bypassed, or obscured, but encountered with creativity and inventiveness.

As anthropologists, we actively and deliberately censor our work to keep it acceptable for the people concerned. In conducting my research in border areas I was (and still am) particularly concerned about how I would keep my publications from jeopardizing local population. Not anticipating what the government officials will find offensive, sensitive, or problematic in my writing could always get people into trouble. My doubts and concerns about what can be written down and what cannot in order not to create threats to the personal safety of the people I work with led to the fact that, although I gathered ethnographic data on a number of contemporary topics, I could not succeed in resolving this dilemma, so that an important part of my ethnographic material still remains unpublished.[4]

To sum up the result of my very first anthropological field experience, which strongly impacted my further anthropological research in and on Iran, I have to admit that in the Lorestan case, my forced absence from the field, and my encounter with security agencies completely altered my initially designed research program. Nevertheless, I think the knowledge I produced, knowing that I was under surveillance, has perhaps more validity than it might have without this experience.

In this encounter which involved real fear, the experience of helplessness and a considerable amount of discomfort, I did not only learn more about the Shirawand and their relationship with government authorities, but also highlighted one specific tension of fieldwork: it brought me closer to the people's lifeworld. At the same time, the unexpected event challenged my theoretical assumptions, altered my methodology and also rechanneled my research and possibly improved its truthfulness.

Notes

1 A few anthropologists have presented some perspectives referring to violence, terror and supervision by security forces: Daniel (1996); Mahmood (1996); Pollard (2009); Tambiah (1992); see Sökefeld and Strasser 2016.
2 In the article "From "Alien" to "Own" and back: Field experiences in Iran," I talk extensively on the conditions of conducting field research as an Iranian "at home" (Nadjmabadi 2004).
3 Hastrup (1998) suggests, during fieldwork more attention should be given to control, power relations and knowledge.
4 I was not the only anthropologist to be caught in such dilemmas. Several other scholars did not publish their material as well; see Nadjmabadi (2009).

References

Daniel, E. V. 1996. *Charred Lullabies. Chapters in an Anthropology of Violence*. Princeton: Princeton University Press.

Hastrup, K. 1998. *A Place Apart. An Anthropological Study of the Icelandic World*. Oxford: Clarendon Press.

Howell, N. (ed.) 1990. *Surviving Fieldwork. A Report of the Advisory Panel on Health and Safety in Fieldwork*. Washington, DC: American Anthropological Association.

Mahmood, C. K. 1996. *Fighting for Faith and Nation*. Philadelphia: University of Pennsylvania Press.

Nadjmabadi, S. R. 1975. *Die Shirawand in West-Lorestan. Mit besonderer Berücksichtigung des Verwandtschaftssystems*. Unpubl. Dissertation. Heidelberg.

— 2004. From "Alien" to "Own" and Back. Field Experiences in Iran. *Iranian Studies* 37 (4): 603–612.

— 2009. *Conceptualizing Iranian Anthropology. Past and Present Perspectives*. New York and Oxford: Berghahn.

Pollard, A. 2009. Field of Screams. Difficulty and Ethnographic Fieldwork. *Anthropology Matters* 11 (2): 1–24.

Sökefeld, M., and S. Strasser (eds.) 2016. Under Suspicious Eyes – Surveillance States, Security Zones, and Ethnographic Fieldwork. *Zeitschrift für Ethnologie* 141 (2).

Tambiah, S. J. 1992. *Buddhism Betrayed? Religion, Politics, and Violence in Sri Lanka*. Chicago: University of Chicago Press.

Tedlock, B. 1991. From Participant Observation to the Observation of Participation. The Emergence of Narrative Ethnography. *Journal of Anthropological Research* 47 (1): 69–94.

VERENA KECK

13 Exchanging Anthropological Knowledge. A University Partnership Program between Madang and Heidelberg

Introduction

Important and much debated current topics in Pacific anthropology are the various forms and different levels of a reciprocal exchange of anthropological material with the people we study, the imparting of knowledge for the civil society, both in the host and in our own country, and the new responsibilities and roles of anthropologists.

Anthropologists in the Pacific today are faced with diverse tasks and demands that require taking on different roles. As someone who values indigenous knowledge, as a documentarist and local historian, he or she actively supports the reawakened interest in cultural traditions which are appreciated by the peoples of the Pacific as an expression of their distinct cultural identities and can be taken as their response to the experienced levelling process in a globalized world (Keck 2014). Other new challenges include working as a consultant or lawyer regarding copyright and land issues or the role of the anthropologist as a teacher in Oceanic educational institutions, which is the topic of this contribution. One of the more recent tasks of anthropologists concerns the reciprocal exchange of knowledge and more specifically of anthropological knowledge. The question of how we can give back ethnographic material or knowledge to people we lived with for some time, we worked with, people who might have adopted us into their kinship group, this question has become more and more important during the last ten years. On a more general level, we have to reflect on how we can develop reciprocal forms of communication. This was also the topic of the 8th Conference of the European Society for Oceanists (ESfO) in St Andrews, Scotland, in

2010: "Exchanging Knowledge in Oceania". In the, at the time, internal description of the conference topic, it was written:

> "Oceanic peoples and Oceanist academics share a contemporary dilemma: how to re-describe and transfer knowledge and so make their cultural resources useful, effective and resilient in the contemporary world. But what kinds of 'knowledge' are at stake? ... What kinds of new social relations might we create between Oceania and European-based universities in the twenty-first century?" (Crook 2010).

One of the rare studies on the theme of reciprocity of ethnographic material is Sjoerd Jaarsma's edited volume *Handle with Care: Ownership and Control of Ethnographic Material* (2002), where a number of well-known scholars working in the Pacific address the complex questions of property and the returning of field material and publications. Despite all the different positions, the authors agree that this process of returning knowledge has to be handled in a well thought-out way, and that the chances and risks inherent in it have to be carefully balanced. A more recent contribution *Relations and Products: Dilemmas of Reciprocity in Fieldwork* has been compiled by Glowczewski et al. (2013), wherein the authors, anthropologists, historians and linguists reflect on the "products" of their field research and the consequences of this exchange. It takes place on different levels, between the researcher, the local host community, the civil society and academia and, accordingly, differing demands are raised and various evaluations are made.

In this contribution I focus on yet another, related form of reciprocity – not the returning of tangible field data such as publications or photographs to the local community ("the village"), but a university partnership exchange program in anthropology between the Divine Word University in Madang, Papua New Guinea, and the Institute of Anthropology at Heidelberg University. It represented a different way of "giving back" anthropological knowledge and insights that have been shared with the anthropologists Jürg Wassmann and myself, by two Papua New Guinean societies, the Nyaura (West Iatmul) people in the Sepik region, East Sepik Province, where Jürg Wassmann has been doing field research since the 1970s, and the Yupno people in the Finisterre Range, Madang and Morobe Provinces (where Jürg and I have repeatedly done fieldwork since 1986). This fieldwork material from the Sepik and the Yupno (cf. Keck 2005; Wassmann 2016) was decisive for our academic anthropological career, and to now train Papua New Guinean students in Pacific anthropology seemed to be a logical step and a viable way of demonstrating reciprocity and exchange of knowledge.

Background

The beginnings of this partnership project lay with a number of research traditions, facts, and fortunate circumstances and go back a number of years. Being trained in anthropology in the 1970s and 1980s at the Institute of Anthropology at Basel University under the auspices of Meinhard Schuster had meant a fieldwork-oriented, ethnographic education with a regional focus on Oceania and, more precisely, Papua New Guinea. In addition, at the Institute at this time, a number of colleagues were working on a long-term project, *the Historical Atlas of Ethnic and Linguistic Groups in Papua New Guinea*. The aim was to establish an overview of the increase of knowledge about ethnic and linguistic groups in the various regions of Papua New Guinea, such as Madang, Sepik and Highlands, islands such as New Britain, New Ireland and Bougainville and other regions. On a temporal scale, the Atlas was structured into five periods, beginning in 1873 (the year of Captain John Moresby's landing) and ending in 1975 with Papua New Guinea's independence. All published sources and information were compiled according to the five temporal periods (cf. Keck 1995; Schuster 1995; Wassmann 1995).

I was working on the Madang section, and through this work of compiling sources and data I became quite familiar with the research situation, the enormous cultural and linguistic diversity and the anthropological knowledge available on these local societies in the Madang region. It became evident that, compared to Sepik river cultures ("over-researched", as a senior anthropologist in Port Moresby remarked) or Highland societies, anthropological research about the Adelbert Range and the Ramu River societies were rather scarce.

Added to this is the historic situation: At or around the time of the German colonial occupation of New Guinea in 1884, the first German missionaries arrived, and since these years, volumes of historical and anthropological studies were written in German containing rich historical descriptions. A larger collection of these manuscripts, written by missionaries from the Society of the Divine Word who worked along the North-East Coast of New Guinea, are preserved in the Noser Library of the Divine Word University in Madang but, because they are written in German, they are inaccessible to non-German speaking students and researchers. (It should become an important part of the students' internship in our project to catalogue these sources).

Since the beginning of the then-founded Institute of Anthropology at Heidelberg University in 1995 under the directorship of Jürg Wassmann, the regional focus was Oceania and, more precisely, Papua New Guinea. All these facts, the regional Oceania focus, scarcity of anthropological knowledge about parts of the Madang province together with scientific curiosity, the desire to learn more about these societies and interesting historical sources led to a research project in 2003 called "Person, Space and Memory in the Contemporary Pacific"[1], that was generously sponsored by the Volkswagen Foundation and provided grants for eight doctoral students; three of whom conducted fieldwork in three different Ramu-River societies (A.T. von Poser (2014) among the Kayan, A. von Poser (2013) among the Bosmun, Herbst (2016) among the Giri people, see also Meinerzag (2015), who did research among the Hinihon).

Because of its location and size, Madang was an ideal "base camp" for our own field research among the Yupno people in the late 1980s, our "outside world", a place for getting away from the village, a place with shops and a pharmacy, an ideal location for buying supplies, for relaxing for few days and enjoying a cold beer by the sea, for scrutinizing data and rethinking topics, and, in the following years, a place with access to the internet. The infrastructure and local knowledge kindly provided and shared by Divine Word University colleagues in Madang and the hospitality of Diane Cassell of the Madang Lodge made Madang a very pleasant base station for Heidelberg anthropologists working in the rural regions of the north-east coast.

Repeated visits for fieldwork among the Yupno as well as exploration trips within the Madang province to find suitable fieldwork locations for the doctoral students led to an increasing intensification of contacts with colleagues from the Divine Word University (DWU)[2] in Madang. Mark Solon, then Dean of the Faculty of Arts, and Pat Gesch, Head of the Papua New Guinea Studies Department were very open-minded towards anthropology and invited us to give lectures.

13 Exchanging Anthropological Knowledge

In 1996 the Catholic Divine Word University was granted university status and, with Australian support, in the following years new buildings, the "Friendship Library," many computer labs and lecture halls were built. During the last twenty years the university expanded rapidly. Today, with its five faculties (arts, business, health, education, theology) and approx. 3000 students, it is one of the leading academic institutions of Papua New Guinea.

Closer contact was also established with the University of Papua New Guinea Branch in Madang and its Head Greg Murphy[3] and, thanks to and together with him, numerous joint exploratory trips to Mikarew, Giri, Kayan, Bosmun and to other regions became possible.

Illustration 13.1: Entrance gate of the Divine Word University (2008)

As the first step in a planned closer cooperation between the DWU and Heidelberg, in 2005 the DWU and the Heidelberg Institute entered into a Memorandum of Agreement "to share educational, cultural, human resource and research expertise" between the institutions (Solon 2006: 2). Building on this Memorandum of Agreement, a concrete joint project was established and funded by the German Academic Exchange Service (DAAD). The DAAD offered an exchange program between German universities and universities in developing countries[4], a program that was really customized for this purpose, and the project was funded from 2008 to 2011. In these four years, a curriculum for anthropology was jointly developed and implemented as a Bachelor strand at the Papua New Guinea Studies Department at the Divine Word University. Another ambitious subsequent goal, the introduction of a Master of Arts in Anthropology and the establishment of a department of anthropology, however, could not be realized. In these four years, lecturers from Heidelberg regularly taught courses in Madang, and vice versa, lecturers from DWU came and taught in Heidelberg.

Illustration 13.2: DWU students under the banyan tree (2008)

Why anthropology?

Forty years after independence, Papua New Guinea today is confronted with a variety of problems. They include the turning of the societies traditionally characterized by a subsistence economy into a globalized monetary economy, the slow dissolution of traditional communities of solidarity into, under "Western" influence, increasingly individualized two-class societies with many "losers" who, in some cases violently, express their dissatisfaction, the migration of large parts of the population into towns, and the difficult approach of the political elite to power and money. Another factor is a kind of health transition with new health issues. All these problems and their possible solutions confront the education system with major challenges. Papua New Guinea is also subject to rapid cultural change. In past decades, many Papua New Guineans – also under the influence of missionary work but, even more, under the influence of Christian fundamentalist denominations – have turned away from their own cultural past. Yet, at the same time, against the background of global processes and as a consequence of the general insecurity regarding goals in life and job opportunities, a return to identity-establishing traditions is taking place and there was and is associated with this a stronger interest in social or cultural anthropology. "Anthropology presents a chance to local people to understand and appreciate the cultural diversities of their country and apply them to social development strategies" (Solon 2006: 1).

In our opinion, however, anthropology should not only investigate and document the uniqueness of the extremely different local cultures and, through teaching and learning, thus create awareness of the richness of indigenous knowledge systems in the Pacific but, by comparing them, also include other, Pacific and non-Pacific cultures. Topics such as globalization and migration, legal and medical pluralism, environmental pollution (climate change and the rising sea level, a threat to viability on numerous islands in the Pacific), mining and logging should also be considered. As a result, one's own positioning in an increasingly more interconnected world should become easier. To quote Mark Solon (2006: 4):

> Students entering DWU come from various parts of PNG [Papua New Guinea]; they will, after graduation, become intellectual leaders, research initiators, change agents in nation building. Their abilities to design, implement change and lead research projects will raise awareness and confidence for the nation and its leaders when taking decisions and designing policies.

Anthropological training, the first goal alongside the academic education with its theoretical concepts, should promote appreciation of one's own cultural identity and traditions – with its over 800 different cultures and languages, Papua New Guinea possesses an enormous cultural diversity and many different world views. A number of languages are about to disappear and many cultures today face rapid transformations and many aspects of indigenous knowledge are going to be lost – forgotten, no longer shared, no longer regarded as a valuable resource, or abandoned in favour of modern, "Western" knowledge. At the same time, a process that is known as *kastom*[5] can be observed in today's Pacific region. This reorientation towards *kastom* can, as the recently awaked interest in one's own language (see, for example Hawaiian, Maori or Chamorro people) shows, be seen as a clear attempt toward heterogeneity in a world that is becoming more and more globalized and homogenized. This *kastom* practice also allows a more conscious realization or strengthening of one's own cultural identity. Examples of such a *kastom* or of a revival of a form of knowledge that had almost been forgotten and that, especially when confronted with modern knowledge, has been regarded as inferior, are the knowledge of traditional healers and their herbal medicine, and traditional navigation as it occurs in Micronesia and other parts of the Pacific (Keck 2014). The two most recent examples of the latter are the Hōkūleʻa, a replica of a traditional Hawaiian voyaging canoe that embarked on a three-year circumnavigation of the globe (Parker 2015) and the revival of large-scale outrigger canoes in Lihir, New Ireland documented in the film *Kabelbel* (Batty 2015).

Rates of local transformation have increased tremendously under post-colonial regimes: the forces of globalization, which rapidly distribute commodities, images, political and moral concepts across the region, have presented Pacific populations with an unprecedented need and opportunity to fashion new and expanded understanding of their cultural and individual identities. Although much important research on these processes has been done already and philosophies of building bridges between cultural traditions and modern ways of life have been conceptualized by various Pacific scholars such as – just to mention two prominent Papua New Guinean writers and scholars – the late Bernard Narokobi (and his "Melanesian Way") or Steven Winduo (in his numerous essays and poems), crucial questions have remained unanswered, questions that should be reflected on and responded to by Pacific scholars themselves. Local voices and reflections on these ongoing transformations and the place of cultural traditions within these global changes should be heard and acknowledged.

Anthropological training should empower people to appreciate and pass on this local, indigenous knowledge. Many Papua New Guineans, old and young, villagers, urban dwellers, educated and uneducated people, are aware of and express their unease regarding the loss of their own cultural identity. This identity has albeit never been a static or homogeneous entity, has been profoundly shaped by one's own cultural traditions and practices, values, language and knowledge, and has given orientation in life and a sense of belonging.[6]

Connected with this, a further goal is the development of tolerance towards other, alien or unfamiliar traditions, i.e. the promotion of transcultural competence and cultural sensitivity to alternative worldviews. The frequently characteristic local ethno-centrism should be eliminated: "Anthropological understanding will reduce prevalent cultural stereotypes by creating a sensibility for ethnic and cultural values and diversities" (Solon 2006: 4).

Globalization and standardization have not only resulted in a certain uniformity but – and to the surprise of many – also in heterogeneity and new forms of cultural difference. "Ethnic and cultural fragmentation and modernist homogenization are not two arguments, two opposing views of what is happening in the world today, but two constitutive trends of global reality" (Friedman 1994: 102). Anthropology has much to offer here, since it not only concentrates on and documents the richness and diversity of traditional cultures, but engages itself in the contemporary changes as well. In short: anthropology is not limited at all to *tumbuna samting*, to "things of our ancestors" – an often heard assumption – but, as a dynamic, broad discipline, is especially suited for interdisciplinary work, and for addressing many issues that are relevant worldwide, for Pacific and other societies alike.

Indigenous anthropology and Divine Word University students' comments

Over the last decades, anthropologists have become more sensitive concerning their role as researchers and the expectations regarding the research results, their exchanges and the practical relevance for the people that they studied. Today, the voices of many indigenous Pacific scholars are becoming louder in their demand that western anthropologists should acknowledge the obligations and responsibilities arising from research-specific relations with people in Oceania. Indigenous people observe that the anthropological material collected over many years by anthropologists is rarely returned to them, and they postulate the right to gain access to the recorded descriptions and analyses (Glowczewski 2005: 145).

Linda Tuhiwai Smith, herself a Maori and a professor in education as well as the director of the International Research Institute for Maori and Indigenous Education at the University of Auckland, very clearly expresses this in her book *Decolonizing methodologies: Research and indigenous people* (1999). Critical and sceptical vis-á-vis the participation, the usefulness and the benefit of many "Western" projects and as a way to keep control over indigenous knowledge, many indigenous people today want to actively participate in defining research topics and conditions – a fact anthropologists have to acknowledge and to deal with.

To train young Papua New Guinea students to become "indigenous anthropologists" was therefore seen as a valuable way of reciprocity and a way towards sustainability. It is, too, a longstanding demand made decades ago by Louise Morauta, who was teaching at the University of Papua New Guinea at the time (Morauta 1979, see the comments by Sullivan 2014).

In many statements by the students, their actual situation of "finding themselves between two worlds" becomes plainly apparent. Tradition is seen as a "backbone", culture as something one can be proud of, but a strongly developed national identity as young Papua New Guineans is also expressed (Becker 2010a).

Gaius, a DWU student, states:

> I think culture are the social norms, rules and laws, it brings about the conduct of you in the society, and traditions, I call them basically the (…) physical practice of culture, that is like singing, dancing, the *bilas*, the attire they use during dances or songs, meetings. I believe it is very important because (…) as a proud Papua New Guinean I would say it is (…) our backbone. Without culture, there would not be any partnership within a society, all societies are bound together because of culture, it is a belief, tradition, practice, that has been passed on, and so I would say it is very important. Of course I will pass it on. But it will depend on how much of the changes that are coming about, the westernized changes and other changes that are going on. We have to change in order to live. If we

are not changing, we won't go anywhere. So I believe as I pass my culture and traditions on to my children, it will not be the original one, but it will be a bit changed, modified (…).

And asked: "Are you proud of your culture?", he answered, "Yes of course, I am proud to be an Eastern Highlander," and Jimmy, another DWU student, adds: "I am very proud of my culture, it makes me identify myself as an individual and makes me into an element of what this society, the overall Melanesian society, demands!"

Illustration 13.3: Cultural Day at the Divine Word University, a student in her traditional *bilas* (decoration) (2009)

Sarah remarked (Becker 2010a):

> For me tradition means a lot of things, it could mean the way of life, or the way we are here, the way we have grown up doing things, our traditional dresses and the way, you know, social activities we take part in, things like marriage ceremonies and mourning sessions, and a lot of social activities in our village could mean my tradition. It could mean the

> type of food that I eat, or the kind of attitude that I have, it could also mean my traditions, something that has been part of me, and it is installed in me, it has been passed on from generation to generation, the way of life!

Ruth shared this opinion:

> Culture gives me a place of belonging because I grew up in the city, it is like people identify you not by who you are but where you are from, like they see me and think "Oh, she is from the islands." So for me to maintain my culture is a very important thing. So if I don't know my culture, I am (…) how would I say, I am [in Tok Pisin] *mipela tok olsem em i man nating o em i meri nating*. I am just someone, I do not have a background or anything like that. So yeah, my culture is very important, not only for myself but like for me to pass on and to teach like to my nieces or my nephews or my own children. For me personally, my tradition and culture, it shapes me, it shapes my attitude or my personality, so like wherever I go, I conduct myself, it goes back to my cultural roots or how my parents have told me according to cultural values.

As these statements make clear, culture is understood by the students more as a "stable package" and definitely "territorialized" and not as "fluid or unbounded" and thus in no way corresponds to a contemporary anthropological concept of culture. A concept discussed by the students and held to be positive is the "Melanesian Way" developed by Papua New Guinean philosopher, writer and politician Bernard Narokobi, a philosophy that invites one to build a bridge between indigenous, cultural traditions and modern ways of life.

University training is critically reflected, together with the wish for a qualified education; a good professional position is also expected by the parents as a "return on investment." But the value of one's own culture is also discussed, as is the missed chance of getting to know the local "traditional" village life, which parents often judge in a derogative manner.

The difficult balance between modernization and global influences as well as the preservation of autonomous cultural traditions which are definitely seen as valuable, meaningful and identity-constructing, is described by Lawinia, who describes her situation as follows (in Becker 2010a):

> We are caught between two worlds and I think it had a lot of influence on our traditions that we seem to be forgetting our traditions, which some traditions are very good and we should uphold, and soon we realize that it is too late (…).

The Divine Word University students had their own opinion on anthropology and its value for them.[7] When asked which topic the students would like to learn more about, an often heard answer was "Cultural or Social Anthropology".

> I would like to learn more about Social Anthropology especially in regard to changes that are taking place – cultural shifts.

> I like to learn more about indigenous anthropology and how it is influenced by Western academics.

> I am from a village in a rural area, therefore I feel that learning anthropology is very important to me. I would like to suggest that anthropology must be a field of its own! DWU should have a department of anthropology in the future.

> Any topics of anthropology that are of relevance to the contemporary PNG and Pacific societies should be taught to students, and should be given enough time because the pool of knowledge about our society is [more] present in anthropology than any other discipline.

> Personally I would like to learn more about methods of decolonizing and the recovery of many traditions. In addition, to learn how indigenous people can represent and talk about their own culture rather than having Western representation.

> Because I come from a country which consists of diverse cultures, languages, beliefs etc., I'd rather want to learn more about Cultural Anthropology.

And, referring to the "Interpreting cultures"-seminar, a course with a strong cross-cultural focus:

> By studying this course "Interpreting cultures" I realized how important a culture is to a society.

Or:

> That was an interesting course, we did enjoy the classes – it can help us to write books on our own cultures and preserve it for our future generations because our culture is changing every day.

And:

> I liked this course, it helped me a lot in reflecting my own culture and traditions back home (…).

> I would like to learn more about the different cultures and how they influence our politics/politics of the world.

> I learned about many different views on the ways of living in different societies all around the world. It is very interesting to learn about different cultures and compare them with my own.

Or, very short:

> "All in all, this course was the BOMB!!!"

And on the "Globalization in the Pacific"-course students commented:

> I enjoyed studying this unit. (…) I've learned that culture is a process and that there is constant change. I see that globalization may be helping in some way but in the end, it will take away our culture and traditions and destroy the link we have with our ancestors, our way of life and our sole identities as indigenous people and as Papua New Guineans.

> This unit "Globalization in the Pacific," I believe will be useful in decision-making on socio-economic developments because if the understanding of a people, culture and society is clearer, then better choices and decisions can be made to benefit all.

The program: topics and experiences

The first aim of this academic exchange has been the implementation of an anthropology curriculum within the already existing Bachelor of Arts

(BA) program of the Papua New Guinea Studies Department, Faculty of Arts. It was addressed to all students, from year one to year four, and integrated or complemented already existing courses such as "Gender Issues," "Comparative History of Indigenous People" and "Melanesian Religion."

Illustration 13.4: Reading Malinowski's Argonauts with students at Divine Word University (2008)

The course topics, the system of assessment and practicalities such as visa, accommodation, office space, literature, technical infrastructure (photocopies, access to Internet, Moodle – an open-source learning platform –, data projector and so on) had been discussed in Madang during previous visits, and following these talks and also based on our own teaching experiences, we developed teaching courses with topics such as "Introduction to Cultural Anthropology," "History and Theories of Anthropology," "Interpreting Cultures," "Research Methods in Anthropology," reading courses of classical and contemporary ethnographies, scientific report writing, "Globalization in the Pacific," a medical anthropological lecture series about aspects of the ongoing "Health Transition" in the Pacific, and a film series with the topic "People and Land." The teaching material and the movies were given to colleagues in Madang. The teaching language was English, sometimes Tok Pisin.

Illustration 13.5: "Interpreting Cultures"-course, Divine Word University 2008 (with Pat Gesch as guest auditor)

Teaching experiences by Madang colleagues in Heidelberg and vice versa were central aspects of this exchange program in these four years, 2008 to 2011. Mark Solon was the first Papua New Guinean lecturer in this reciprocal exchange and taught a course in Heidelberg with the title "Melanesian World View of Land and Development," a central theme in understanding the very close social, spiritual and cosmological relationship of people with their land and their place of living. Anastasia Sai from DWU offered a course on gender constructs in the contemporary Pacific. Heidelberg students therefore had the chance to learn about Papua New Guinea, the Pacific and its current issues from Pacific scholars who presented based on first-hand subjective experiences and with insights that were different from those non-Pacific scholars could give. The Pacific scholars looked at how sex and gender shaped gender relations between women and men in the different Pacific societies. Anastasia Sai commented on this exchange and on broadening perspectives: "Having a different perspective contributes to quality. The Papua New Guinea way is not the only way, we have to learn there is a bigger world out there and we are in this big world" (Becker 2010b).

Illustration 13.6: Staff meeting, Divine Word University 2008. From left to right: Anastasia Sai, Mark Solon, Anita von Poser, Pat Gesch, Jürg Wassmann, Samuel Roth and Alexis von Poser (from behind).

In addition, a number of Heidelberg students[8] were involved in this program. In the form of internships, they had different tasks and gained as diverse experiences as being tutors, working in the archives of the Noser library, cataloguing German manuscripts, designing an inventory file and establishing an inventory in the local museum, *haus tumbuna*, in Madang as well as participating in film projects. The time in Madang also gave students the chance to conduct their own research for their MA theses and eventually to return to Papua New Guinea for a doctoral thesis. What could not be accomplished was sending Papua New Guinean BA students to Heidelberg – the exchange of students was, on the one hand, not sponsored by this program, and even if we had found the means for this, on the other hand, due to language barriers (since almost all courses on a BA level in Heidelberg were and are taught in German) postgraduate (MA) students would benefit considerably more from such a study trip to Heidelberg. They would more likely then possess the qualifications required for admission to begin studying at a German university.

For the Heidelberg anthropologists taking part in this exchange program, the teaching at Divine Word University was a challenging experience that really questioned their own professional self-conception. It was a great chance to try to inspire the students coming from so many different regions with differing biographies and to make them enthusiastic about anthropological topics. And we learned that what seems for us here in Europe an important part of anthropological teaching – reading books by the famous Bronislaw Malinowski, the founder of British social anthropology, or discussing important texts such as Clifford Geertz's seminal article about the Balinese cockfight, are for Papua New Guinea students of medium interest at best. We tried to include material that they could identify with – work by Pacific scholars, texts or modern Pacific ethnographies and many films that turned out to be very good and popular didactic tools. Among these films, the 12 twenty-minute episodes of *Elsewhere* (2002), directed by Nikolaus Geyrhalter, presented people from very different cultural and geographical backgrounds, Sami, Tuareg, Himba, Korowai, Rei Matau (from Woleai in the Central Caroline Islands), Ladakhis, Sardinians and others. Recent productions were the Marshallese movie *Morning Comes So Soon* (Condon and Cruz 2008), a story about a Marshallese boy and a Chinese girl who fell in love and became outsiders – the story ending with a suicide; the movie *Sun Come Up* (directed by Jennifer Redfearn 2010) about the relocation of Carteret Islanders, or *Crater Mountain Story* (2008), directed by Papua New Guinea filmmaker Martin Maden.

Given Papua New Guinea's rapid socio-cultural transformation and confronted with a number of social, ecological, and medical problems, some of these topics should be addressed in the respective Master units. The topics include the high rate of crime and violence especially in towns, or (locally often connected to *sanguma* [sorcery] accusations) the increasing number of HIV/AIDS infections, and new and large mining and fishery projects with long-lasting, huge socio-ecological impacts, such as Ramu Nickel, the planned Frieda River mine, the Nuigini liquid gas project or the Pacific Marine Industrial Zone. These Master units had been developed in 2010, but to date an MA in anthropology could not be realized, and the units exist only on paper. These MA units have close ties to indigenous knowledge systems and, at the same time, most of them are strongly oriented towards applying the knowledge, i.e. allowing the students to find jobs. They cover topics that colleagues in Madang think are relevant and important for Papua New Guinea today. The topics included "Global Processes and Local Identities in the Pacific," "Issues of Indigeneity: a Comparative Perspective," "Selected Readings in Anthropology," "Anthropology of Museum and Tourism," "Medical Anthropology," and the following three that should be presented in somewhat more detail.

Media Anthropology

Media anthropology is a recent and growing sub-discipline of anthropology, and its emergence is closely related to the on-going global expansions of the media and the processes in which flows of new technologies such as mobile phones, telecommunication, information technology, and the Internet distribute and propel news, images, new values and meanings around the globe at high speed and intensity. The field of media anthropology covers a broad range of topics: media participation, the cultural and social aspects of mass media, its usage and its active reception by various audiences, the representation of others and selves, culture and gender in the context of the media (questions of the perpetuation of stereotypes, of indigenous ways of presenting selves etc.), and the manifold influences that film and media have on cultural worlds.

Besides the critical understanding and knowledge of media (the side oriented towards theory), the unit aims to provide students with practical knowledge of visual and media anthropology. Especially in the Pacific region with its traditionally oral cultures, documentary and ethnographic film and other visual and auditory means are useful, creative tools for documenting traditional and new cultural forms in contexts undergoing transformation. They are also tools that allow for an active indigenous, local participation and the development of a community-based production of documentaries ("indigenous filmmaking"). As we realized in the Bachelor courses, where we used a number of films to delve into various topics we discussed, they provoked most interesting discussions among the students. For example, Martin Maden's movie *Kantri Bilong Yumi* (2002) is a film about his own family in New Britain and their very different approaches to life, a portrait of three generations and the impact of historic events such as the white colonial world and the country's independence. This screening resulted in discussions that were much more engaged and lively than reading a text could provoke.

Another example to illustrate the relevance of media anthropology is a project that creatively uses new media. Barbara Glowczewski developed a CD-Rom with an interactive multimedia program, *Dream Trackers: Yapa Art and Knowledge of the Australian Desert* (2000/2001) for the Warlpiri in Central Australia. She writes: "Today, multimedia technology and the internet offer a fantastic way to promote and transmit oral cultures both for the benefit of the Indigenous peoples concerned, as well as to demonstrate the importance of local knowledge in the global system" (Glowczewski 2005: 145). On this CD she compiles a network of "dreamings" that are especially meaningful for Warlpiri people and arranges them as autonomous modules, containing texts, sounds and images that could be connected to each other and that transpose the cognitive map of this society (the way that people organize their relation to space and knowledge). Her aim was twofold: The project should allow an intergenerational transfer of indigenous knowledge as part of a bilingual, Warlpiri-English school program, and it should introduce non-Aboriginal people to the cultural and spiritual richness of local knowledge and the complexity of Warlpiri society (Glowczewski 2005: 146-148).

Anthropology of mining

Over the last decades, the mining sector and other forms of resource extraction have been the dominating economic force in Papua New Guinea and have influenced the politics in many ways. With huge new mining projects being started (such as the Ramu Nickel) or planned (Frieda River) and two of the country's largest mining projects, Porgera and Ok Tedi, the lives of many people in the vicinity of these mining sites have changed dramatically. While, on the one hand, local landowners have benefitted from the economic development related to the resource extraction, on the other hand the social, cultural and ecological risks and impacts of mining on local communities are tremendous and generally not what these communities or planners had expected; community responses to mining are accordingly highly diverse. Traditional indigenous cosmologies and cultural Melanesian identities have often been anchored in landscapes that were destroyed in the mining process. Many ideas about "promises of modernity" in often remote rural regions include access to medical care, education, jobs, roads and commodities such as store goods (Filer and Macintyre 2008); these perceptions of development and various local hopes and images for a bright future are entangled in this mining discourse. The issue of minerals extraction in other Pacific countries (New Caledonia, Australia) and similarities and differences will provide a broader perspective. The perspective of the local people and others such as mining companies, developers, the government, environmentalists, groups which claim a stake in mining issues, and the role of anthropologists as consultants and advocates will be discussed.

Fieldwork and linguistic anthropology

The on-going loss of various cultural traditions and indigenous world views is accompanied by a loss of the diversity of languages in the Pacific, which is especially noticeable in Papua New Guinea, probably the most linguistically diverse nation in the modern world. The shift to the dominant languages English and Tok Pisin is underway and many local languages are severely endangered. Although Sapir-Whorf's famous hypothesis about the correlation of language and thought has been debated and modified in the last decade, it still holds that cultural world views are expressed in indigenous languages, and when a language dies, a part of the cultural diversity of our world dies as well.

The scholar Steven Winduo (2010a) writes:

> "The world of the indigenous people is viewed through their language. (...) Our language diversity is closely linked to our biodiversity that without attending to the specific demands for protection, development, and sustainability we can lose cultures, knowledge, and people in this tide of modern changes (...)."

He continues with the observation by linguist Tove Skutnabb-Kangas (2004: 2) that "linguistic diversity and biodiversity are correlational" (...) and that knowledge about "how to maintain biodiversity is encoded in small local languages. Their speakers live in the world's biologically and often also linguistically most diverse areas. Through killing these languages (or letting them die), we thus kill many of the prerequisites for maintaining biodiversity" (Skutnabb-Kangas 2004: 2). With this unit we wanted to train students in doing fieldwork, the central empirical method of anthropology, in order to document aspects of their (or another) local culture, and to conduct a linguistic survey (collecting word lists, creating an indigenous language dictionary, recording and preserving oral traditions and histories), and therefore help to promote and revive traditional knowledge and skills for the benefit of future generations. This echoes Winduo's (2010b) plea to encourage the documentation of cultural knowledge systems in any form. In a similar effort, he had asked students from the University of Papua New Guinea to write down stories and cultural knowledge from their area. Lyne Kuraiba, one of these students, whose father comes from the East Coast of New Ireland, writes about the culture-specific practice of tying up a *tanget*. "When a *tanget* leaf [cordyline terminalis] is being tied up by someone, then this normally means danger or that something has gone wrong", and she gave the example of a son who had left home after a dispute with this father. "After some time the father discovers that a *tanget* near the house is tied up. This is read as a message that the son has vowed never to return to his family. (…) To reconcile the differences and unite the father and son, the father must kill a pig and have a feast to bring his son back into the family" (Winduo 2010b: 5)

Concluding remark

Peter, a Divine Word University student, should have the last word:

> I came here, and I was starting some of the courses offered by Papua New Guinea studies, and I realized that culture was so important in our societies, and when I looked around the campus I usually see students expressing themselves in different ways, mostly the westernized ways. And I really see that we are moving so fast and we are adopting new cultures where we shouldn't be, because for my case, I see that it is a danger without really knowing what that culture is bringing to our society. We then tend to adopt this culture. One clear example that I would give is that when I came to this university I realized people hugging. When I go to my society, I would not do that because my society does not allow like just hugging with women or women hugging with men.
> And if you do that, then you are going to violate the customs, the tradition of a society, and you might come into conflict with the society's values. That is why I thought that it is very important that you know your

culture. And some of the studies we are taking in these three years I tend to neglect what I used to do when I was in the village. I did not take notice of some of the traditions practiced and some people died and for myself I neglected that. I would have adopted some of the things what my elders were doing in the society. For me, they would have knowledge of wisdom from a perspective that I was studying, because I realized that those traditions which were practiced by my elders had some meaning in life.

Notes

1. The same name had been chosen for an anthropological book series, originally started in 2004 and published by Berghahn Publishers, see A. von Poser (2013) and Herbst (2016).
2. It developed from the Divine Word Institute founded in 1980.
3. The intended partnership with the state University of Papua New Guinea (UPNG) in Port Moresby was made difficult by the unstable security situation in Port Moresby; with the change of the Open Campus of the UPNG Branch in Madang into a distance-learning university, more intense cooperation and an academic exchange with this institution became impossible as well.
4. An additional form of a mutual exchange of research results is represented by the Tandem Research Program initiated by J. Schlehe together with students of Gadjah Mada University in Indonesia. Anthropology students of both universities jointly conduct training fieldwork while annually alternating between Indonesia and Germany (Schlehe 2013).
5. In some Melanesian societies, today the concept of *kalja* (or *kalsa*, "culture"), is preferred with a significance differing from *kastom*. *Kalja* practices are seen as a resource to which each individual of the respective group has access and as a chance of earning money (e.g. in tourism) (Dalsgaard and Otto 2011: 142-144). On the occasion of performing a dance imported from a different region of Papua New Guinea in 2007 in the Yupno village of Gua, the performers, some of them from other regions and working as teachers in the Yupno region, also talked about *kalja* and were hoping for advice how to market their dance on a national and an international level – an example of how the concepts *kastom* and now *kalja* are spreading and now being given a new local significance. What is clear is that the two concepts *kastom* and *kalja* can be understood in different ways not only in the anthropological discussion but in the respective local context.
6. While, in current anthropology, the "preservation of identity" is criticized as an out-dated, static concept, whereas anthropologists are talking about a person's multiple identities and see identity as constructed, as a constantly

changing cultural process, many Divine Word University students understand cultural identity as something clearly more fixed, static and permanent.

7   These and the following statements were given when the different anthropology courses were evaluated.
8   These Heidelberg students, although participating actively in the exchange program, were funded separately by individual grants provided by the DAAD. The University Partnership program supplied the means for the exchange of lecturers, but not for students.

Sincere thanks go to all who have contributed, participated and assisted in many ways and during a number of years so that this partnership could be realized, namely Mark Solon, Pat Gesch, Anastasia Sai, Jerry Semos, Anita and Alexis von Poser, Franziska Herbst, Michèle Ducommun, Christiane Falck, Fabienne Becker, Frauke Meeuw, Lea Stephan, Karin Hermes, Lena Borlinghaus and Paul Bruch. To them and to all others who are not mentioned by name here: *Bigpela tenkyu tru.*

References

Batty, D. 2015. *Kabelbel.* Film. http://www.kabelbel.com/index.php [Accessed November 4, 2015].

Becker, F. 2010a. Cultural Shifts in Papua New Guinea. A Discussion among Students of the Divine Word University. Unpubl. M.A. Thesis and Film, Institute of Ethnology, Heidelberg University.

— 2010b. *The Heidelberg-Madang Academic Partnership.* Film.

Condon, A., and M. Cruz 2008. *Morning Comes So Soon.* Film.

Crook, T. 2010. *Re-describing and Transferring Knowledge in Oceania.* European Society for Oceanists, Eighth ESFO conference, 5th – 8th July 2010. Centre for Pacific Studies, University of St. Andrews. http://www.st-andrews.ac.uk/esfo2010/ [accessed October 15, 2015].

Dalsgaard, St., and T. Otto 2011. From *kastam* to *kalsa*? Leadership, Cultural Heritage and Modernization in Manus Province, Papua New Guinea. In *Made in Oceania*, eds. E. Hviding and K. Rio. Wantage: Sean Kingston, pp. 141–160.

Filer, C., and M. Macintyre. 2006. Grass Roots and Deep Holes. Community Responses to Mining in Melanesia. *The Contemporary* Pacific 18 (2): 215–231.

Friedman, J. 1994. *Cultural Identity and Global Processes.* London et al.: Sage.

Geyrhalter, N. 2002. *Elsewhere.* Film.

Glowczewski, B. 2000/2001. *Dream Trackers – Yapa Art and Knowledge of the Australian Desert.* Paris: UNESCO Publishing. CD-Rom.

— 2005. Returning Indigenous Knowledge in Central Australia. "This CD-ROM brings everybody to mind." In *The Power of Knowledge, the Resonance of*

Tradition, eds. G.K. Ward and A. Muckle. Canberra: AIATSIS Research Program (Papers from AIATSIS Indigenous Studies Conference, September 2001), pp. 145–160.

Glowczewski, B., R. Henry, and T. Otto 2013. Relations and Products. Dilemmas of Reciprocity in Fieldwork. *The Asia Pacific Journal of Anthropology* 14 (2):113–125.

Herbst, F. 2016. *Biomedical Entanglements. Conceptions of Personhood in a Papua New Guinea Society.* New York and Oxford: Berghahn. (Person, Space and Memory in the Contemporary Pacific, Vol. 5).

Jaarsma, S. R. (ed.) 2002. *Handle with Care. Ownership and Control of Ethnographic Material.* Pittsburgh: University of Pittsburgh Press.

Keck, V. 1995. *Historical Atlas of Ethnic and Linguistic Groups in Papua New Guinea* (Volume 1, Part 3: Madang). Basel: Wepf.

— 2005. *Social Discord and Bodily Disorders. Healing among the Yupno in Papua New Guinea.* Durham, NC: Carolina Academic Press.

— 2014. "Handle with Care." Reziproker Wissenstransfer in Ozeanien und die Verantwortung des Ethnologen im 21. Jahrhundert. *Paideuma* 60: 67–88.

Maden, M. 2002. *Kantri Bilong Yumi.* Film.

— 2008. *Crater Mountain Story.* Film.

Meinerzag, A. 2015. *Being Mande. Person, Land and Names among the Hinihon in the Adelberg Range, Papua New Guinea.* Heidelberg: Universitätsverlag Winter. (Heidelberg Studies in Pacific Anthropology, Vol. 3).

Morauta, L. 1979. Indigenous Anthropology in Papua New Guinea. *Current Anthropology* 20 (3): 561–567.

Parker, L. 2015. A Hawaiian Canoe Crosses the Oceans, Guided by Sun and Stars. *New York Times* (Science), November 2, 2015.
http://www.nytimes.com/2015/11/03/science/a-hawaiian-canoe-crosses-the-oceans-guided-by-sun-and-stars.html?emc=eta1&_r=1
[Accessed November 4, 2015].

von Poser, A. 2013. *Foodways and Empathy. Relatedness in a Ramu River Society, Papua New Guinea.* New York and Oxford: Berghahn. (Person, Space and Memory in the Contemporary Pacific, Vol. 4).

von Poser, A. T. 2014. *The Accounts of Jong. A Discussion of Time, Space, and Person in Kayan, Papua New Guinea.* Heidelberg: Universitätsverlag Winter. (Heidelberg Studies in Pacific Anthropology, Vol. 2).

Redfearn, J. 2010. *Sun Come Up.* Film.

Schlehe, J. 2013. Wechselseitige Übersetzungen. Methodologische Neuerungen in transkulturellen Forschungskooperationen. In *Ethnologie im 21. Jahrhundert*, eds. T. Bierschenk, M. Krings and C. Lentz. Berlin: Reimer, pp. 97–100.

Schuster, M. 1995. Preface. In *Historical Atlas of Ethnic and Linguistic Groups in Papua New Guinea*, Volume 1, Part 3: Madang, ed. V. Keck. Basel: Wepf, pp. vii–ix.

Skutnabb-Kangas, T. 2004. On Biolinguistic Diversity – Linking Language, Culture and (Traditional) Ecological Knowledge. Invited Plenary Lecture at the Interdisciplinary Seminar "At the Limits of Language", organized by the Department of Biology and Department of Linguistics and Philosophy, Universidad Autónoma de Madrid and Cosmocaixa (March 2004). http://www.helsinki.fi/hyy/skv/v/Sk-Kangas_Madrid_March_2004_paper.doc. [Accessed October 27, 2015].

Solon, M. 2006. Proposal: Fostering Ties, Building Human Capacity and Strengthening Cultural Partnerships between Heidelberg and Divine World Universities. Unpubl. Document.

Sullivan, N. 2014. Blog. http://nancysullivan.typepad.com/my_weblog/2014/06/anthropology-inside-out-applied-indigenous-ethnography-for-papua-new-guinea.html. [Accessed October 27, 2015].

Tuhiwai Smith, L. 1999. *Decolonizing Methodologies. Research and Indigenous Peoples.* London et al.: Zed Books.

Wassmann, J. 1995. *Historical Atlas of Ethnic and Linguistic Groups in Papua New Guinea* (Volume 3, Part 4: New Britain, Part 5: New Ireland, Part 6: Bougainville). Basel: Wepf.

— 2016. *The Gently Bowing Person. An Ideal among the Yupno in Papua New Guinea.* Heidelberg: Universitätsverlag Winter. (Heidelberg Studies in Pacific Anthropology, Vol. 4).

Winduo, St. 2010a. Language is a Living Museum. http://stevenswindow.blogspot.de/2010/10/language-is-living-museum.html. [Accessed September 28, 2015].

— 2010b. Our Knowledge System. *The National, National Weekender* Friday March 10, 2010, p. 5.

ALEXIS TH. VON POSER

14 The Restitution of a Carving Pattern to Kayan, Papua New Guinea[1]

Introduction

One important task, which also provides the opportunity to return to the field, is the restitution of what one has achieved with the help of the local people. This is part of the basic ethical rules of behavior for every ethnographer. Returning the results of previous fieldwork and thus paving the way to discuss them again with one's interlocutors opens new doors, enabling the ethnographer to make important changes or to adjust the material to the actual concerns of the people, which sometimes went out of focus once the ethnographer was back at home at the desk, compiling and editing the material gathered to create a coherent whole (see Feld 1990: 239-268).

I returned my dissertation in 2010 on a very short trip back to Papua New Guinea,[2] but so far there has been no chance to return again and question the people about their impression of the contents of the book, which by now they have had enough time to read. Together with my thesis, however, I returned something else and this is what I want to write about here. It concerns the story of a spirit woman that left Kayan village approximately a century ago in a special container, which was stored in the collection of the Reiss-Engelhorn-Museums in Mannheim and which only recently was recognized for what it is (Illustration 14.1). The only information available was that it is obviously a slit drum from New Guinea's north coast. As such, the slit drum has remained without an individual identity for more than a century. This was to change, but let me first say a few words about slit drums, before coming to that special drum in the collection of the Reiss-Engelhorn-Museums.

Illustration 14.1: The slit drum from Mannheim (copyright: Reiss-Engelhorn-Museums Mannheim)

Slit drums

Slit drums can be found in many parts of the world, from Africa via Asia to Oceania. This group of instruments can be traced back to the Neolithic (Collaer 1965: 110) and includes some of the largest and heaviest instruments on earth. Among the Naga in India, for example, slit drums can reach a size of up to twelve meters (Reck 2000: 86). Regardless of their name, slit drums are not really drums, since they lack a stretched membrane. They are nevertheless counted among the instrumental family of drums because of the percussive way of playing the instruments with drumsticks. These *idiophones* ("self-sounders," Fischer 1986: 18-38) may consist of segments of bamboo or pieces of wooden trunks in which a slit has been carved. Wooden instruments are furthermore hollowed to amplify the sound. Slit drums can be trampled upon with feet, hit with hands or beaten with drum-sticks to accompany dances or ceremonial contexts. They can also be used to transfer messages. In some places, people invented actual drum-languages: In Africa (Reck 2000: 195) and Oceania (Neuhauss 1911: 314-318; Gardi 1956: 92-94; Leach 2002: 718-719; Zemp and Kaufmann 2010), for example, people can communicate more or less complex messages over wide distances using rhythmical patterns.

14 The Restitution of a Carving Pattern to Kayan 225

In Papua New Guinea, slit drums are scattered along the North Coast and on several islands (Kunst 1967: 40-41; Gourlay 1979; Niles 1983; Swadling et.al. 1988: 66-67; McLean 1994: 52). In the lingua franca of the country, the Neo-Melanesian Pidgin-English Tok Pisin, they are called *garamut* and in most cases they are carved from the very hard and insect-resistant wood of the *vitex confossus* tree, which is also called *garamut*. In most places in Papua New Guinea, where social organisation is marked by a separation into female and male gender, the slit drums are considered part of the male social sphere and the production is subject to strict taboos. The technique of hollowing the trunks belongs to the realm of secret knowledge; therefore the carving of a drum has to take place in secrecy, hidden from the eyes of women and children.

Prior to the introduction of iron tools, the production of a slit drum was extremely time-consuming and arduous: only by means of controlled fire, stone- and bone-tools, could the body of the drum be hollowed out. Sometimes, complex decorative patterns were carved into the sides and the handles of the drums with sharks' teeth, the surface ground with ray-skin. Even with iron tools, the carving of a slit drum is still laborious, if not as time consuming as before. In former times it could take several months to complete one of these prestigious instruments. Today, the work may be done in weeks, or even in a few days.

In Papua New Guinea, some centres of slit drum manufacture are of very long standing. From these areas, instruments were traded to neighboring groups. One of these old centres is the Lower Ramu area (Graebner 1902). Several villages near the mouth of the Ramu River specialised in the production of slit drums. From there, many of these expensive instruments reached other coastal villages, nearby islands and, eventually, different museum collections in Australia, Asia, Europe, and America. Since the area had been part of the former colony of German New Guinea before the First World War, many instruments from that region can be found in German museum collections today.

One slit drum from the collection of the Reiss-Engelhorn-Museums in Mannheim (ID III SÜ 4301/64717) comes from exactly that area, from the village of Kayan (formerly spelled Kajan) to be precise. It was collected before 1914 by a colonial officer by the name of Carl Leidecker who later published his memories of his time in Papua New Guinea in a book (Leidecker 1916). There are several iconographic hints that support the fact that the drum was not only collected in Kayan but was also produced there. The decoration of the drum includes elements that are specific to the carvings of this village: the handle is executed in a typical way with an anthropomorphic figure that is supported on the back by a stylized animal that protrudes over the head of the figure, looking over its cone-shaped head-decoration. Also, the decorative bands at each end of the carved sides of the drum show a pattern that can still be found on drums from Kayan.

The tradition of producing slit drums can be traced back by the villagers to mythical times. Because of the durability of the drums, which in this region are not destroyed when the owner dies as is the case in other regions (Leach 2002: 727), and because of the formerly very limited number of drums allowed in each group, workshops for the production of new drums were probably not set up more than once or twice in each generation up to the 19th century.

Only village chiefs[3] were allowed to commission new drums and each men's house had no more than five of these instruments. Commoners could neither commission a new drum nor were they allowed to privately own such a prestigious object. Since the arrival of colonial officers and collectors from overseas in the 19th century however, drums were traded or sold more often, sometimes they were also stolen or destroyed. As a result, replacements were needed more regularly (Meiser n.d.: 12). For this reason specimens from the time just before the First World War are comparatively common. Gradually, after the Second World War, the restrictions on the production of slit drums were loosened, but private persons have only been allowed to own slit drums since the 1990s although not without having to ask the formal consent of a member of the chiefs' families first.

Even though not everyone was allowed to own a slit drum, every adult male member of the village community was associated with his own rhythmic pattern with which one could be called by the others. There were also drum signals to call a meeting, to transmit the news of a death in the village, to announce foreigners in a neighboring village or to order the necessary prerequisites for a feast: betelnut, tobacco, coconut and banana. People had signals to influence the weather, to end the rain on festive days or to call the rain in times of drought. All slit drums had personal names, and in each men's house a set of names available for these instruments is still kept. Should one named drum get lost through destruction or trade, it will be replaced as quickly as time allows.

The very first slit drum is said to be Ruknai, which is supposed to have been brought by a spiritual woman from the hinterland to the coast in mythical times. The older version of this drum unfortunately was destroyed by a German punitive expedition in 1901 (Vormann 1901/02), but it was replaced afterwards. The version which was carved at that time can still be seen in Kayan. During the Second World War, all but a few of the other large drums were destroyed. Thus, in an unprecedented and spectacular event, over 25 of these instruments were produced at once in the mid-1950s to fill the gaps. Whenever a new drum is brought to the village after having been produced in one of the secret workshops in the bush, a ceremony is held that serves as a reminder of the myth of how the slit drum came into being, identifying the instrument as originating from the large cassowary bird (whereas hourglass drums are seen in connection with the bird of paradise). The following is my recounting of this myth.

The myth of the slit drum sound

Once there were two orphans, a boy and his sister. They lived with the family of their uncle who raised them like his own children. One day, they had an argument with their uncle's real son and in the evening, their uncle filled their plates with water instead of sago – a strong gesture of admonition. In anger, the two siblings fled the village and ran into the forest, where the boy became a bird of paradise, flying easily to the tops of the highest trees and feeding from the sweet fruits up there. His sister turned into a large flightless bird, a cassowary.

She tried hard to follow her brother but could not get up the tree. Saddened, she called up to her brother to throw some of the fruits down to her so that she could eat them (see also Feld [1990: 20] on a similar myth among the Kaluli of Papua New Guinea). The Kayan say, that her mournful calls sound out in each beat pounded on a slit drum. Whenever a new drum is brought into the village, a song is sung in which this story is remembered:

> ac-na ndange godub amte ac mbo ‚raba' yor in peka irik-o
> my brother, when you are eating, throw a "raba"-fruit down to me
> (the name of the fruit changes in every verse)

Many of the carving patterns used on the drums were subject to strict copyrights. Each of the three main social units in Kayan has its own carving pattern that the respective members were to use to decorate their slit drums. Unauthorized use of a carving pattern from another group could cause a lot of trouble and even lead to inter-group war. Only members of the Samngae group, for example, were allowed to carve handles with one male and one female figurine. Their drums were adorned with the *bair warup* pattern on the sides.

The Nongdagan had the privilege of using the *raing* pattern. The carving patterns called *daugui ndamot* and *rangrang nimung* underlied no restrictions and could be used freely by all groups.

Especially the former is therefore widespread and it can be found on many slit drums in museum collections (Antwerpen, Chicago, Hiltrup, Leipzig, Prag, Zürich, etc.; see also Meyer 1995: 176). All of the patterns named were still present on drums in Kayan village in 2005. Only the pattern called *yor mbermber* that was associated with the Warngemb group was considered lost.

The village's oldest man, Blasius Jong, who was a member of the Warngemb and was respected as a cultural expert in the whole region (von Poser 2010, 2014: 14-17), knew this carving pattern only through the stories of his father and uncles. He was uncertain about how this pattern could have disappeared from the village completely. Normally, every loss was replaced quickly, thus making sure that nothing could be erased from the communal memory. The disappearance must have happened at a time when a replacement was either not possible or not desired. I would like to propose a possible historical scenario based on my discussions with Jong:

Apa I. was the grand-uncle of Jong and he became the first *luluai* (village headman) appointed by the German colonial administration. On mainland New Guinea, these appointments were not made before 1911. In many cases, candidates who already had some experience with colonial administration or other Europeans, for example through work on plantations or through contact with the mission, were chosen for these jobs. So it is likely that Apa I. had some contact experience when he was chosen to become the village leader. He was also, by birthright, the head of the very branch of the Warngemb group that was responsible for controlling the communal sacred objects. Thus, he also had authority over the sacred spiritual drum Garum that was thought to harbor the female guardian spirit of the group; this made it of the highest importance to the pre-Christian religious system. It can be taken for granted that this drum was decorated with the specific carving pattern of the group, being one of the core objects of religious and social life. Certainly, Apa I. had contact with the new religion in the area – Christianity – very early, since, as a *luluai,* he was the first contact person for outsiders. Maybe he had already been influenced by Christianity before – a mission station opened a few miles away in Monumbo in 1901. The idea spread that everything that stood in connection to the old religion, especially the practice of headhunting that was central to pre-Christian times, was sinful and demonic. To give away the drum without replacing it, thus erasing one part of the tradition that was considered "heathen" and "uncivilized," would fit into that time of societal transformation in Papua New Guinea in which so many radical changes happened on the village level. This could explain the complete disappearance of the important *yor mbermber* pattern.

The slit drum in Mannheim shows no signs of having been played on the sides, as a normal use of such a drum would show. Normally, these slit drums are beaten with a long stick on one side and therefore quickly show traces of wear at the relevant spots of the playing area. The Mannheim drum only shows signs of use at the sides of the slit. This points to a way of playing that is only practiced with spirit drums: pulling a jagged stick from the inside of the drum out along the edge of the slit. The resulting noise is thought to represent the rising of the spirit from the drum. The spirit drums were played in this way mainly before and after headhunting expeditions and on other special occasions in connection with the secret cult.

The Mannheim drum is clearly from Kayan, as the above-mentioned details illustrate, but it is decorated with a carving pattern that is not known in Kayan (any more?). It was collected at exactly the time when Apa I. was village headman, simultaneously presiding over the group responsible for the religious objects. Finally, the drum is most likely a spirit drum that was central to pre-Christian religious practices. All these points substantiate the supposition that the Mannheim drum is the only surviving copy of a spirit drum of the Warngemb group, bearing the *yor mbermber* pattern that was believed to be lost.

In 2010, I brought a poster-sized copy of the carving pattern taken from the Mannheim drum to Kayan and showed it to Jong. From the memory of what he had heard about *yor mbermber*, pondering on all available pieces of information about the drum, Jong identified the

Mannheim drum clearly and without a doubt as the spirit drum Garum with the lost carving pattern (Illustration 14.2). In a public ceremony, I handed the poster over to Apa II., the direct descendant of Apa I., who promised to carve a new drum with this design to revive the broken tradition. During the ceremony, Apa stated:

> *Em olsem baksait bun bilong mipela Kayan nau [...]*
> *olsem ol pikinini bihain long dispela bung ol bai bihainim [...]*
> *mipela olgeta bai idai*
> *em bun bilong yu, ples Kayan, nau mipela kamapim pinis.*

("This is the backbone of us Kayan now [...]
after this meeting, all children are going to follow this [...]
eventually, we are all going to die
but your backbone, Kayan village, we have created")

Illustration 14.2: Blasius Jong identifies the *yor mbermber* pattern

Even if some voices were heard that requested the original slit drum to be returned to Kayan village, most of the people present were content with the return of the carving pattern. The general agreement was that the original slit drum was most probably sold and therefore rightfully in a German museum. It was considered positive that the museum cared for the drum so that it was still in existence and in good condition. The return of the carving pattern was considered important support for the identity of the Warngemb group in particular and all Kayan in general.

Conclusion

Sadly, Jong died only a few weeks after this happy day, but his knowledge and memory made it possible for a new drum to take its place in Kayan: in 2014 I received an email from a fellow researcher who worked on slit drum manufacturing in the Lower Ramu area (email communication with Alphonse Yambisang). He sent me a picture of a new large drum, showing the *yor mbermber* pattern (Illustration 14.3). So, a circle that spans one century has been closed, enabling young Kayan to choose from the whole set of carving patterns again, should they decide to maintain the tradition of slit drum manufacture in the future.

Illustration 14.3: Finally: the *yor mbermber* pattern appears on a new drum (photo by A. Yambisang)

This example shows an interesting by-product of an ongoing interaction with the field. The returned carving pattern was just a coincidentally conceived side effect, but it may help contemporary Kayan to gain new confidence in their material heritage as envisaged by Apa II and Jong.

Notes

1. This article is a translation of a German contribution to an exhibition catalogue (von Poser 2011) that is expanded by more recent material.
2. My stay in Papua New Guinea in 2010 was financed by the German Academic Exchange Service.
3. Indeed, in Kayan there was a chieftain system in existence that mirrored a similar system from Manam Island (see Lutkehaus 1995: 26-30).

References

Collaer, P. 1965. *Ozeanien. Musikgeschichte in Bildern (Band 1: Musikethnologie)*. Leipzig: VEB Deutscher Verlag für Musik.

Feld, S. 1990 [1982]. *Sound and Sentiment. Birds, Weeping, Poetics, and Song in Kaluli Expression*. Philadelphia: University of Pennsylvania.

Fischer, H. 1986. *Sound-Producing Instruments in Oceania*. Boroko: Institute of Papua New Guinea Studies.

Gardi, R. 1956. *Tambaran. Begegnung mit untergehenden Kulturen auf Neuguinea*. Zürich: Orell Füssli Verlag.

Gourlay, K. 1979. *An Approach to the Traditional Music of Papua New Guinea*. Goroka: Goroka Teachers College.

Graebner, F. 1902. Holztrommeln des Ramudistriktes auf Neu-Guinea. *Globus* 82 (19): 299–305.

Kunst, J. 1967. *Music in New Guinea. Three Studies*. S'Gravenhage: Martinus Nijhoff.

Leach, J. 2002. Drum and Voice. Aesthetics and Social Process on the Rai Coast of Papua New Guinea. *Journal of the Royal Anthropological Institute* (N.S.) 8: 713–734.

Leidecker, C. 1916. *Im Lande des Paradiesvogels. Ernste und Heitere Erzählungen aus Deutsch Neu-Guinea*. Leipzig: E. Haberland.

Lutkehaus, N. 1995. *Zaria's Fire. Engendered Moments in Manam Ethnography*. Durham: Carolina Academic Press.

McLean, M. 1994. *Diffusion of Musical Instruments and Their Relation to Language Migration in New Guinea* . Boroko: National Research Institute. (*Kulele 1*).

Meiser, L. n.d. *Compilation of Matter for a Description of the Tribe of the Kaean*. Unpublished Typescript, Madang.

Meyer, A. 1995. *Oceanic Art. Ozeanische Kunst. Art Océanien*. Köln: Könemann.

Neuhauss, N. 1911. *Deutsch-Neuguinea* (Three Volumes). Berlin: Reimer.

Niles, D. 1983. Why are there no Garamuts in Papua? *Bikmaus* IV (3): 90–104.

von Poser, A. Th. 2010. Blasius Jong – Ein ethnografischer Nachruf auf einen allwissenden Informanten aus Papua-Neuguinea. *Baessler Archiv* 58: 131–138.

— 2011.Die Rückkehr der Geisterfrau. Die Geistertrommel der Kayan (Papua-Neuguinea) in den Sammlungen der Reiss-Engelhorn-Museen. In *Musik-Welten*, eds. H. Wiegand, A. Wieczorek, C. Braun and M. Tellenbach. Mannheim: Verlag Regionalkultur, pp. 83–90.

— 2014. *The Accounts of Jong. A Discussion of Time, Space, and Person in Kayan, Papua New Guinea*. Heidelberg: Universitätsverlag Winter. (Heidelberg Studies in Pacific Anthropology, Vol. 2).

Reck, D. 2000. *Musik der Welt*. Hamburg: Rogner und Bernhard.

Swadling, P. et al. 1988. *The Sepik-Ramu*. Boroko: National Museum.

Vormann, F. 1901/02. Monumbo. *Steyler Missionsbote* XXIX: 55–56, 70–72, 90–91.

Zemp, H., and C. Kaufmann. 2010. Towards an Automatic Transcription of Melanesian "Drum Languages" (a Kwoma Example, Papua New Guinea). *Kulele* 4: 51–102.

SVENJA VÖLKEL

15 Challenges and Profits of Interdisciplinary Fieldwork in Linguistic and Cognitive Anthropology

Introduction

In the past 20 years interdisciplinarity has become a trendy keyword of academia, primarily in research (e.g. various Max Planck Institutes, collaborative research centres and the centre for interdisciplinary research at the University of Bielefeld) but also in teaching. However, interdisciplinary work is not at all a new invention – it had been practiced long before by various scientists – but it has recently been particularly emphasized on a broader scale (Frodeman et al. 2010). From this development one expects a gain of new, interlinked knowledge and scientific enrichment for each single discipline and science as a whole. However, this expectation is only met if one is able to cope with the challenges of interdisciplinary projects. This article will approach these issues with a focus on fieldwork in linguistic anthropology and cognitive anthropology, two interdisciplinary areas of research to which I can contribute my own empirical experiences (Völkel 2010; Tietz and Völkel 2013; Völkel 2016).[1]

Cultural anthropology – An interdisciplinary discipline?

Cultural anthropology studies the life of peoples in all kinds of settings around the world. It is a discipline with a wide scope of topics, including all kinds of aspects of the ways of life in a specific community (i.e. culture-specific behavior, ideas, concepts, practices, artefacts, developments, etc.). Hence there are various anthropological subfields, such as ethnobotany, ethnomusicology, anthropology of religion, economic anthropology, political anthropology, medical anthropology, etc. This demonstrates that, all in all, cultural anthropology can be regarded as a very interdisciplinary-friendly discipline offering interfaces with various other disciplines.

The interdisciplinary field of linguistic anthropology, which is concerned with the relationship of language and culture, is also called anthropological linguistics or ethnolinguistics. While German researchers prefer to use the term ethnolinguistics, the other two variants are more common in the English-speaking area. The denotation of linguistic anthropology versus anthropological linguistics is often associated with different perspectives. While linguistic anthropology describes this interdisciplinary field as a subdiscipline of cultural anthropology, it is regarded as subdiscipline of linguistics if described as anthropological linguistics. This terminological distinction might come along with different perspectives and research traditions, including typical research questions and focuses, methodological techniques, etc. However, they all share the same thematic interest: the relationship between culture and language (Duranti 1997: 1-5; Foley 1997: 3-5). Therefore, I will use the terms interchangeably. Compared to Europe, where the few ethnolinguists are located either at linguistic faculties or at faculties of cultural anthropology (apart from Max Planck Institutes, research centres, etc.), some American universities have faculties of linguistic anthropology or anthropological linguistics. This has an impact on the interdisciplinary training, the job situation of interdisciplinary academics, etc.

In cognitive anthropology, a subdiscipline of cultural anthropology, the topic of interest is the relationship of cognition and culture. Another discipline which is concerned with this topic is cross-cultural psychology, a subfield of psychology. Again, these are two different perspectives and research traditions which work on the same interdisciplinary field (Senft 2003) and which are also only represented by single scientists at German universities. Moreover, among others, cultural anthropology, psychology and linguistics are part of the cognitive sciences, a complex interdisciplinary network of sciences with a focus on cognition. In the few last years, however, cultural anthropology is less present in this group (Bender 2013: 289-290; Cohen and Lefebvre 2005).

As culture, language and cognition are finally all interrelated (e.g. language is a tool to memorize and think about experiences as well as to express cultural concepts and issues)[2], the two interdisciplinary fields of cognitive and linguistic anthropology are interlinked and partly overlap (Senft 2013: 273-282; Bender 2013: 287-290). There are further subdisciplines which should be considered as they contribute to the study of this complex topic too, such as cognitive linguistics (Evans and Green 2006) and cultural linguistics (Sharifian 2011).

Interdisciplinary versus multidisciplinary research

Interdisciplinarity has to be distinguished from multidisciplinarity. While the former describes the collaboration or co-operation of different disciplines,[3] including a joint research process, the latter means that different disciplines only meet to bring together their respective findings concerning a special topic (Keck 2008: 256). Thus, for interdisciplinary research, it is necessary not only to have a shared research topic or question and united research findings but also to cope with the research methods, procedures, approaches and ideas of both disciplines.

Interdisciplinary research topics or questions can generally not be answered by single disciplines. Two aspects are characteristic for different interdisciplinary studies, including cultural anthropology. First, they are concerned with the relationship between cultural aspects and another issue, such as language in linguistic anthropology. Second, the anthropological approach contributes to a broader and less "Western"-centric perspective of the knowledge in most disciplines. Cognitive anthropology or cross-cultural psychology, for instance, investigate cognitive and psychological issues not only in "Western" contexts but also with a focus on so-called non-Western small-scale societies in the local and global context. This reveals the scope of cultural particularities as well as cross-cultural commonalities.

What makes interdisciplinary research comparatively laborious is the joint research process. This is exactly the period in which the majority of the challenges evolve that have to be faced in interdisciplinary projects. It requires methodological and basic content knowledge in both disciplines (see Dasen, this volume), either *in persona* (i.e. an academic with competences in both disciplines) or in small teams or bigger research groups (i.e. collaborating academics from different disciplines) (Keck 2008: 258-270). While interdisciplinarity *in persona* requires an education in both disciplines which is very time-consuming and comes with a lot of effort, researchers in interdisciplinary groups need to interlink their knowledge. Therefore, interest in mutual understanding, flexibility, creativity and endurance are necessary or even mandatory. The main reason for the failure of interdisciplinary projects is actually a too strong adherence to or even insistence on the procedures, ideas and academic traditions of one's own discipline. In this case, at best multidisciplinary findings can be gained, i.e. each discipline works on its own until the merging of the single results. However, if the team succeeds in real interdisciplinary collaboration, each discipline can profit from the other (methodologically as well as content-wise) and generally new perspectives and a more networked comprehension are gained for a more holistic understanding.

To achieve this objective, at best not only the research methods are developed and applied in shared work, but also the analysis, evaluation and interpretation of the data are a joint process. This generally involves a lot of effort, including long discussions on different points of view, the in-depth analysis of reasons for divergent viewpoints and the development of a shared understanding of technical terms and scholarly concepts (see note 2 and note 11). Frequently, the final challenge is a collaborative publication of the interdisciplinary project. It needs to fulfil the formal and content-related requirements of each discipline, and it needs to be published in a way accessible to the academics of each discipline respectively.

If one aims at a university career in cultural anthropology, linguistics or psychology, a focus on interdisciplinary research at an early- or mid-stage of the career might be problematic and risky for the following reason, especially if interdisciplinarity is carried out *in persona*: First, it is very labour-intensive and time-consuming. Second, as long as one cannot prove experience and skills in core domains of one discipline, one is not regarded as a serious academic of either discipline. Interdisciplinary work might even be attacked by both disciplines for reasons of flaws in the different approaches, as I will discuss later. Therefore, a lot of academics only develop an interdisciplinary focus at a later stage of career, that is, when they hold a permanent position. This also means that one can acquire interdisciplinary skills or skills in a second discipline while already having higher competence in the other discipline.

Cultural anthropology and fieldwork

Without a doubt, fieldwork is the crucial research method of cultural anthropology to study cultural communities from an emic perspective. It can be carried out in various ways. However, the main characteristics of this empirical method are:

1. *data collection in the field*, i.e. in the "natural" living environment of the informants and not in the laboratory, at the researcher's desk, at home or in the library,
2. *the combination of different techniques and survey procedures* (suitable for the research question); such a methodological combination contributes to the obtainment of complementary and reconsidered data,
3. *a targeted but also holistic approach*, i.e. a well-prepared, consciously planned, theory-based and conceptually reasoned procedure with a focus on a specific research aspect, yet taking the general cultural context into account (Beer 2008: 11-13).

Anthropological fieldwork generally consists of different stages. While it comprises practical as well as content-related preparations at a stage prior to the field stay, the fieldwork period itself generally consists of an orientation stage, an explorative and descriptive stage, and subsequently, a more topic-oriented or hypothesis-testing stage. Afterwards, the data is processed, analysed and interpreted – partly still in the field but mainly after the field stay. Finally the data is published, generally in the form of articles or monographs for an academic readership and/or in the form of lectures for such an audience (Beer 2008: 17-29).

Based on the characteristics described above, anthropological fieldwork varies depending on the time and place of research (e.g. ranging from rural places to urban centres, international organisations and even companies), the research topic, the specific methodological techniques and procedures, the researcher's personal characteristics and qualities, his/her informants (their characteristics and qualities, their knowledge and their expectations) and other factors. From an interdisciplinary perspective, this includes the crucial distinction of *in persona* interdisciplinarity vs. collaborative teamwork (including a joint fieldwork period vs. temporally non-overlapping stays), and the often challenging combination of fieldwork techniques or field-adjusted methods of both disciplines.

Despite all this variation of methodological techniques and procedures, participant observation is the core technique of anthropological fieldwork. Participant observation means that the researcher is observing while not only being present but participating in the life of the people to be studied with the aim of learning their cultural practices and values, their language, etc. from an emic perspective. Therefore, participation ideally involves a steady life within the community and the interaction with the people in all kinds of situations of daily life. Of course, this can be more or less profound including, for example, not only physical participation but also social, emotional and mental engagement, and more or less active attendance. However, taking the role of a leader or initiator would be inappropriate. Moreover, participation is always limited by the capability or willingness of the researcher as well as by the permission of the community. In each community, there are restrictions due to age, gender and other personal characteristics or qualities and ideas of privacy or taboo. Further distinctions that can be made are systematic vs. unsystematic and open vs. hidden participant observation.[4] All in all, participant observation is a balancing act between proximity (participation) and distance (simultaneous observation). It is a fundamental and unique part of the methodological procedure of cultural anthropological fieldwork (Fischer 2002: 11; Hauser-Schäublin 2008: 37-38, 41-45; Beer 2008: 169-173).

While participant observation is generally the crucial technique of the exploration stage of fieldwork to gain a holistic understanding of practices, values, items and other particularities that exist in the community to be studied, it is by and by supplemented by various other methodological procedures and techniques, such as interviews, questionnaires, systematic observations and even tasks or field experiments. These are of central importance at the topic-oriented or hypothesis-testing stage of fieldwork to systematically collect data about specific research topics. However, the weighing of the different stages and their techniques may differ strongly depending on the research issue (Fischer 2002: 13, 18, 20; Beer 2008: 17-18). Furthermore, once explorative pre-work exists (either in the form of previous fieldwork of the researcher him-/herself or of other researchers who conducted fieldwork in the same field), the exploration stage may be much shorter. Yet altogether, it is common practice that anthropological fieldwork lasts at least twelve months. This time is generally necessary to learn the local language and culturally appropriate behavior to become an integrated, "natural" part of the community that is no longer given special attention or treatment (Fischer 2002: 14-15). This has to be considered if the fieldwork period is severely shortened.

Empiric research in general shows a strong tendency towards explorative techniques aiming at a holistic overview, such as participant observation and open interviews. These are to be applied before more topic-focused techniques which contain a conscious reduction of aspects, such as experiments or systematic questionnaires with standardized questions and limited response options. The crucial reason for this sequence is that a reasonable reduction of aspects requires holistic knowledge.

For interdisciplinary anthropological fieldwork, this results in the following consequences: First, the methods to be applied have to be suitable for use in the field, which particularly poses a challenge for laboratory methods. Second, for the adaptation to the field context in terms of a reasonable reduction of aspects, prior explorative work is necessary. Therefore, the "other disciplines" have to be open to the necessity of the comparatively time-consuming technique of participant observation, and cultural anthropology has to be open to subsequent, more operationalising techniques creating "unnatural" yet culturally adequate situations.[5] In interdisciplinary teams, this work might be partly split, i.e. one can fall back on the cultural knowledge, experiences and infrastructure of the cultural anthropologist. However, this requires intensive exchange of information and numerous discussions within the team.

Linguistic anthropology and interdisciplinary fieldwork

The collaboration or even merger of linguists and cultural anthropologists is not a recent interdisciplinary phenomenon (Malinowski 1920; Silverstein 1973; Keesing 1979). However, only quite recently Foley (1997) and Duranti (1997) published the first monographs on linguistic anthropology or anthropological linguistics as an interdiscipline. Subsequently, interdisciplinary book series and journals have evolved which provide a basis for interdisciplinary research to be visible or even prominent in both disciplines.

Language has always been an issue in anthropological fieldwork, although often not in terms of linguistics (i.e. with a research focus on language structures) but at least in terms of language practice. In order to study the local cultural practices, items, and issues from an emic perspective, cultural anthropologists are aware of the importance of the local language(s). The question is whether knowledge of a lingua franca is sufficient to participate in a community's life and to capture their values and practices if these are not encoded or differently conceptualized in the lingua franca (Völkel 2010).[6] Thus, the acquisition of the local language should ideally be part of the anthropological field research process (Fischer 2002: 14; Senft 2008). If publications on the local language or particular aspects are available, this acquisition of language skills can and should be started during the preparation stage prior to the actual fieldwork. Should nothing be published about the local language, it is recommendable to search for information about languages of the same language (sub)family. If this is done during the preparation stage of the fieldwork, one could collaborate with linguists who do not necessarily have to join the fieldwork. Altogether, linguistic expertise in terms of structural knowledge and methodological knowledge for language descriptions generally supports faster language acquisition. As these languages are often not or only insufficiently documented, cultural anthropologists often also contribute to the linguistic subdiscipline of language documentation by generating word lists or by collecting texts of different genres. Sometimes they even write manuals for language acquisition or even grammatical notes which are generally not comparable to linguistic reference grammars. They do however contain valuable information which provides a basis for further research in this field.

Just as cultural linguistics has an interest in language, linguistics makes use of fieldwork as a central research method, at least in various subdisciplines, such as language documentation and descriptive linguistics, anthropological linguistics, dialectology, sociolinguistics, studies in semantics, pragmatics, language contact and language socialisation (Thieberger 2011; Senft 2002: 353-354; Senft 2003). However, the emphasis and length of the different fieldwork stages as well as major techniques vary according to the main focus of thematic interest. Documentary and descriptive linguists (as well as dialectologists) use this method primarily for collecting language data in the field which provides "unlimited" access to native speakers. They primarily use interviewing and elicitation techniques to compile text collections of different genres, dictionaries and/or grammars.[7] Anthropological linguists (as well as sociolinguists) study linguistic forms and practices regarding their context of use and their socio-cultural meaning (Duranti 1997; Foley 1997).[8] This requires, of course, a more anthropologically oriented fieldwork, including participant observation and tape or video recordings of language in specific natural contexts of use. Altogether, linguistic fieldwork does not fundamentally differ from anthropological fieldwork. It also consists of an orientation and exploration phase, followed by a more systematic data-capturing phase (Senft 2002: 357-362; Beer 2008: 29). However, the weighting is generally slightly different. While the explorative phase plays a crucial role in anthropological fieldwork, linguistic fieldwork rather comprises a shorter exploration phase and lays emphasis on the systematic data-capturing phase, including specific linguistic techniques such as elicitation (i.e. the structured questioning to gain language data) and transcription (i.e. the processing of raw language data in terms of structured linguistic conventions, particularly phonetic transcription using the International Phonetic Alphabet). The collection of data by elicitation and interview techniques as well as linguistic tasks and experiments goes hand in hand with the data processing and data analysis by creating phonological, orthographic and morphemic-interlinear transcriptions (Senft 2002: 359-362). Thus, just like anthropological fieldwork, linguistic fieldwork also combines different techniques (in a sequence from more descriptive to more topic-oriented ones) as well as work with main informants and with a broader group of community members.

Hence, due to the great similarities of the crucial fieldwork method and the combinability of the various techniques as well as the thematic overlaps and the same crucial field sites, anthropological linguistic interdisciplinarity should not involve major challenges regarding these aspects of the research process. Consequently, there is already a longer shared tradition between linguistics and cultural anthropology. All of this might also explain why most interdisciplinary research in linguistic anthropology or anthropological linguistics is carried out *in persona*, i.e. the researchers are trained in both disciplines, being able to write an ethnography as well as a linguistic grammar. However, it is a comparatively small group of linguists as well as cultural anthropologists who work in this subdiscipline. From a linguistic perspective, a reason for this might be the comparatively time-consuming empiric procedure to capture languages that the researcher generally does not know prior to research in their socio-cultural context compared to research procedures applied in other linguistic subdisciplines. Furthermore, only a few cultural anthropologists gain profound enough overall knowledge in linguistics to be able to describe not only semantic or some pragmatic issues (such as metaphors, terminology of semantic fields, speech acts) but also more formal issues, such as phonology, morphology and syntax (at best even with typological skills).[9] Likewise, Evans (2011) mentions that only few linguists reach the point where they have deeper knowledge in all spheres of human life. Therefore, he stresses the alternative of interdisciplinary fieldwork in teams, for instance, to study the language of disease and illness together with a medical anthropologist and medical experts or to study the linguistic encoding of person together with a social anthropologist (for more examples, see Thieberger 2011).

Cognitive anthropology and interdisciplinary fieldwork

The collaboration of cultural anthropologists and psychologists on an established interdisciplinary basis has evolved in the last decades, among others within the cognitive science framework. Since then, several monographs have been published on the relationship between culture and cognition (e.g. D'Andrade 1995; Cole 1996; Shore 1996; Ross 2004; see Dasen, this volume). Moreover, there are by now several journal and book series.

Still, the collaboration of cultural anthropologists and psychologists seems to be slightly more problematic. Ross (2004: vii) mentions in the introductory notes of his book on culture and cognition that there will be many opponents on both sides, experimental psychologists as well as anthropologists, mainly for methodological reasons.[10] While fieldwork is the crucial method of cultural anthropology, experimental psychologists primarily work with experimental designs in the laboratory (see Funke, this volume). These are two methods which could hardly be more different, particularly in terms of natural vs. artificial setting (Hauser-Schäublin 2008: 38). However, in order to study the relationship between culture and cognition and to reveal cross-cultural commonalities or universals[11] as well as the scope of the cultural diversity of cognitive processes, including community-internal variations (e.g. ideas of causality, theory of mind, emotions, decision-making, patterns of categorization and memory), interdisciplinary research is necessary (Heine 2010). To achieve this, it is advisable to be aware of the strengths and weaknesses of each approach and to combine their potentials.

In their experiments, psychologists have paid little attention to certain characteristics of the people being analysed. For reasons of easy accessibility, students from "Western" countries (mainly the United States) are by far overrepresented (Heine 2010: 1425). This means that the impact of culture as an important factor is not considered, and consequently, the universal validity of such acquired findings is questionable. Thus, further systematic studies in different cultural settings are needed. This is, of course, an aspect to which cultural anthropology can provide a valuable contribution. The pure transfer of laboratory experiments to different fields leads to inappropriate situations, questionable responses of the test persons and debatable results.[12] Consequently, the experiments have to be appropriately adapted to the field, i.e. as far as possible, the experimental tasks have to represent natural and familiar situations (Ross 2004: 81). Furthermore, it is crucial to know the interfering variables which are sometimes difficult to control in the field. These must at least be considered. All this is only possible on the basis of holistic emic knowledge of the cultural context (Tietz and Völkel 2013: 51-54; Wassmann and Funke 2013: 247-248). Thus, anthropological fieldwork, including participant observation, is needed at a prior stage. Therefore, psychologists have to be aware of the importance of this time-consuming, explorative pre-work and they have to be open to necessary adaptations despite concerns about methodological vulnerability according to standards in laboratory experiments. Likewise, cultural anthropologists have to realize that for a systematic study of cognitive processes which cannot be captured by direct observation (but only indirectly through actions, language, etc.), more analytical aspect-reducing/-controlling methods are needed, including experimental designs and more sophisticated statistical procedures. Despite the necessity for adaptations of experiments to the respective field situation, they are problematic in terms of cross-cultural comparison as each field requires other modifications. Hence, the only possibility for an appropriate experimental design is to be creative and to find a compromise or solution based on the evaluation of the respective advantages and disadvantages.

Apart from psychological experiments (e.g. reasoning tasks, such as the change of location task and the deceptive container task; see Tietz and Völkel 2013: 52-54), further techniques that are used in cognitive anthropology and cross-cultural psychology are free-listing, pile-sorting, triad tests, ranking scales, paired comparison, allocation and mapping tasks or frame techniques (Ross 2004: 86-117; Antweiler 2008: 238-245; Bender 2013: 290-293). These include componential analysis and analysis of hierarchical structures of semantic fields (originally methods of linguistics),[13] network analysis, etc. All these are tasks that are generally feasible in the field as they do not require much equipment. However, the way informants deal with the different tasks may vary according to cultural customs. Thus, the appropriateness of each task has to be considered, taking into account the cultural setting and the research topic. Generally, several techniques complementing one another are combined in fieldwork. Of course, their sequential order has to be considered too (e.g. free-listing prior to pile-sorting or ranking scales). Further influencing factors are the language being used (local variety vs. lingua franca), the persons carrying out or attending the task (locals vs. foreign researchers, familiar vs. unfamiliar), the test persons (education, gender, age, social status), the social relationship between test person and task leader or other people who are present, the location of the task, objects being used in the tasks or topics of discussion.

The cognitive anthropological techniques come along with statistical evaluation methods, such as multi-dimensional scaling (to determine the degree of distance between items measured in pile-sorting or triad tests) or cultural consensus analysis (to determine the degree of cultural consensus between the members of a community; see Gatewood 1999). Finally, the holistic cultural understanding acquired in the explorative stage is again of central importance: For the appropriate interpretation of the data, the cultural context has to be taken into account from an emic perspective (Tietz and Völkel 2013: 65-73; Wassmann and Funke 2013: 248-249).

Thus, for successful interdisciplinary research in cognitive anthropology, the researcher conducting the study *in persona* needs to be trained in explorative field techniques, particularly participant observation, as well as in more analytical techniques, particularly experimental techniques and more sophisticated statistics. In interdisciplinary teams, each researcher needs a deeper methodological understanding of the other discipline as well. As fieldwork can only to a certain degree be planned in advance and there are always unexpected things which might happen, at best the team of cultural anthropologist(s) and psychologist(s) would conduct the fieldwork simultaneously, at least the middle part towards the end of the anthropologist's explorative stage and at the beginning of the psychologist's experimental stage. This is the crucial period in which the team has to combine their knowledge for the creative development of an appropriate, feasible continuing procedure. Anthropological knowledge is primarily necessary for the development of appropriate field experiments in terms of familiar experimental objects and tasks in a cultural setting and for the interpretation of the data on the basis of emic ideas and practices. So, it is not unusual that unexpected factors become apparent only during or after the experimentation phase. Further modifications which have to be developed in teamwork might then be necessary.

Conclusion

Interdisciplinary fieldwork in linguistic and cognitive anthropology consists of two major parts: First, an explorative and descriptive stage including the crucial technique of participant observation, and second, a more topic-oriented or hypothesis-testing stage comprising more operationalising and aspect-controlling techniques. These include elicitation, systematic interviews and language tasks in linguistic anthropology and primarily conceptualisation tasks or field experiments in cognitive anthropology. The holistic emic cultural understanding that is gained in the first stage is mandatory to adjust the techniques that are used subsequently to the cultural context. Otherwise, inadequate questions and tasks will result in questionable responses and debatable data. Of course, these two stages do overlap and participant observation at best accompanies tasks in the second stage.

Furthermore, these systematic techniques are accompanied by specific data-processing methods such as transcriptions and annotations according to linguistic conventions and statistical evaluation methods. The combination of these extremely different techniques in fieldwork requires a broad range of methodological skills, training in participant observation as well as profound knowledge of these analytical tools. As only few scientists have the qualifications to conduct such interdisciplinary fieldwork *in persona*, others work in interdisciplinary groups or teams. This teamwork often means that there is more specialized knowledge but the researchers of the different disciplines have to interlink them in order to develop joint research questions and procedures. This is generally the most challenging part and the more diverse the disciplines are, the more problematic this might be. However, as anthropological fieldwork generally comprises a combination of different techniques, it provides a good framework for interdisciplinary studies in which techniques of other disciplines can be integrated as long as they are feasible in the field.

Consequently, cultural anthropologists do not have to fear that their crucial method of fieldwork which includes participant observation has be given up in interdisciplinarity, but they should be open to complementary aspect-reducing techniques from other disciplines. These are necessary in order to analyse specific aspects more systematically, particularly those which are not observable. Although these techniques might involve a less natural setting, cultural anthropologists can contribute to appropriate familiar experimental setups and procedures through adaptation to the cultural ideas and practices. Finally, the different techniques provide complementary and reconsidered data. Likewise, linguists and psychologists should be aware of the complex cultural contexts and thus not avoid the time-consuming explorative technique of participant observation. Otherwise, it would be impossible to draw conclusions on the relationship between cognition or language and culture. As no methodological technique or approach is usable with all kinds of research questions or aspects, the combination of techniques, their sequential order and the detailed procedures (i.e. the options within a technique) have to be chosen in consideration of the strengths and weaknesses.

Finally, the systematically acquired and evaluated data has to be interpreted in its cultural context. This again requires the close collaboration of both disciplines. Altogether, such interdisciplinary research is very time-consuming and involves mutual interest and understanding, endurance, flexibility, creativity and humour. If it is successful, however, valuable insights into the complex relationship between language, culture and cognition from a more holistic and less

"Western"-centric perspective can be gained which no discipline can achieve by itself. Yet, cross-cultural comparison is extremely challenging as individual methodological adaptations to the respective field counteract each other. Creative solutions have to be developed in each fieldwork project.

All in all, "[t]his kind of research [i.e. interdisciplinary projects] takes its time, and it may be strenuous, but it pays off at the end" because each researcher gains valuable experience and a broader understanding, as Wassmann and Funke (2013: 250) aptly conclude.

Notes

1 Since 2002, I have conducted several periods of fieldwork in the island kingdom of Tonga, Polynesia, mainly with a focus on ethnolinguistic topics (honorifics, the encoding of kinship, space and possession) but also studies in cognitive anthropology (theory of mind) and cognitive linguistics (categorisation of kinship and word classes).

2 Of course, language and mental knowledge are part of a cultural world. This also becomes apparent in the subject-matter descriptions of linguistic and cognitive anthropology: "language [i]s a social tool and speaking [...] cultural practice" (Duranti 1997: 1), "language in its wider social and cultural context, its role in forging and sustaining cultural practices and social structures" (Foley 1997: 3) and "culture shapes people's thoughts and behaviours [... and it] refers to any kind of information that is acquired from members of one's species through social learning" (Heine 2010: 1423). However, it is extremely difficult if not impossible to describe the relationship between language or cognition and culture without using the term "culture" as differentiated from language and cognition. This does not imply a static or homogenous understanding of culture. In contrast, studies on culture and language change point out that language and culture are in a constant process of transition. Furthermore, numerous studies on language communities as well as cultural communities have shown that these are neither necessarily congruent nor are they homogenous in the sense that all members share the same ideas, beliefs, emotions, language skills and practices, etc. However, despite all heterogeneity, a community is characterized by a certain consensus on these aspects, as emphasized elsewhere in this essay. Culture, language and cognition do not form relationships of unilateral mandatory impact – the various studies of linguistic and cognitive anthropology rather suggest that it is a complex system of mutual impact.

3 The delimitation of academic disciplines is generally rooted in their historical development. Depending on the disciplinary traditions, interdisciplinarity can

also occur between different subdisciplines with distinct academic approaches. However, if the subdisciplines share long traditions and have similar approaches, there is no longer any reference to interdisciplinarity.

4   The distinction open vs. hidden relates to the knowledge of observed people about the presence of the observer, the motifs and/or the topics of the observation. While the revelation of all aspects prior to the observation might provoke "unnatural" behavior, the entirely hidden observation is problematic for ethical reasons.

5   This problematic becomes apparent, for instance, in Fischer (2002: 14, translated by the author, S.V.) who first says that "Feldforschung ist weder Fragebogenaktion noch Experiment. Sie wird geradezu definiert als Forschung in einer 'natürlichen Situation'. [Fieldwork is neither a questionnaire campaign nor an experiment. It is literally defined as research in a 'natural situation']". However, later in his article on anthropological fieldwork he mentions the feature of methodological diversity, i.e. the combination of different supplementary techniques including, in addition to participant observation, even field experiments (Fischer 2002: 19-20). And this might be a challenge since these techniques are extremely contrasting (Hauser-Schäublin 2008: 38).

6   The study of Tongan reveals that, compared to English, Tongan has no language of respect to encode the societal hierarchy of kingly, chiefly and common rank. Likewise, English does not make a formal distinction between different kinds of possessive relationships according to the idea of control (A- vs. O-possession), nor does English categorize kin along the same parameters as Tongan does – the distinctive parameters of categorization in Tongan kinship terminology even coincide with the features determining status inequalities within the kindred (Völkel 2010). For further examples see Duranti (1997), Foley (1997) or Senft (2013: 273-282).

7   Text collections can subsequently be used in corpus linguistics, and referential grammars provide the database for numerous studies in language typology.

8   Based on the different traditions, the subdisciplines of dialectology and sociolinguistics work more in "Western" fields, while documentary and descriptive linguists as well as anthropological linguists or linguistic anthropologists generally work in "non-Western" fields. These correspond to the traditional field sites of social anthropologists.

9   Most studies in linguistic anthropology or anthropological linguistics focus on semantic and pragmatic aspects of language, not only due to a lack of skills in describing and analysing more formal aspects, but primarily because cultural ideas, beliefs and practices are most obviously encoded in these linguistic fields (e.g. the conceptualisation of meaning in the lexicon or rather semantic subfields such as kinship, color or spatial terms, and classifiers,

conversational patterns and speech acts, including the encoding of politeness, gender, social inequalities, genres, the processes of language socialisation and culture and language change; see Duranti 1997; Foley 1997; Thieberger 2011; Senft 2013; Sharifian 2015). To reveal relationships between language and culture, the linguistic subdiscipline of language typology provides a good point of departure. It is an inductive approach that compares the languages of the world to reveal in which aspects they are all alike, in which aspects they differ and what the range of variation is. Proceeding from the information on language-specific particularities, linguistic anthropology could follow with the question of whether there are culturally specific aspects that contribute to the development or maintenance of these linguistic forms or practices (Völkel 2010). Furthermore, language typology provides linguistic terminology not only to describe features that exist in Indo-European languages but the whole range of linguistic phenomena that occur in the languages of the world.

10 This again demonstrates that interdisciplinarity is often not a recommendable field for an easy academic career in terms of acknowledgement within the major disciplines.

11 "Universals" is one of the terms that have proven to be controversial in cultural anthropology. As anthropological research generally provides detailed descriptions of specific cultural communities, the sum of ethnographies results in an overall picture of diversity which is often emphasized in cultural anthropology. This extreme interest in one end of the scale often results in a lack of interest or even refusal of the other end of the scale, in this case cross-cultural commonalities or universals. Therefore, most cultural anthropologists refuse to talk about universals. However, this idea of universals is not at all deterministic but developed on the foundation of empirical data, i.e. comparable to the approach of language typology which is inductive compared to Chomsky's deductive approach of a universal grammar (Comrie 1989: 1-5; see also note 9). Furthermore, research in language typology has shown that most universals are not absolute but statistical, i.e. by far most languages have or have not certain features but not all. If the anthropological knowledge of cultural diversity is structurally brought together in terms of cross-cultural comparison, cultural anthropology has a lot to contribute on the cross-cultural commonalities or universals and the scope of cultural diversity.

12 Even more problems arise if the test persons would be taken out of their natural settings to a laboratory in a place outside their country or region. In this case, even more unwanted interferences from the surrounding are to be expected.

13 Semantics is one central field of interrelation between cognitive anthropology and linguistic anthropology. The world is encoded and conceptualized in linguistic terms on the basis of cultural ideas, which also becomes evident in

studies of cultural linguistics (Sharifian 2011) and cognitive linguistics (Evans and Green 2006).

References

Antweiler, C. 2008. Kognitive Methoden. In *Methoden ethnologischer Feldforschung*, ed. B. Beer. Berlin: Reimer, pp. 233–254.
Beer, B. 2008. Einleitung. Feldforschungsmethoden. In *Methoden ethnologischer Feldforschung*, ed. B. Beer. Berlin: Reimer, pp. 9–36.
Bender, A. 2013. Kognitionsethnologie. In *Ethnologie. Einführung und Überblick*, eds. B. Beer and H. Fischer. Berlin: Reimer, pp. 287–307.
Cohen, H., and C. Lefebvre (eds). 2005. *Handbook of Categorization in Cognitive Sciences*. Amsterdam: Elsevier.
Cole, M. 1996. *Cultural Psychology. A Once and Future Discipline*. Cambridge, MA: Belknap Press.
Comrie, B. 1989. *Language Universals and Linguistic Typology. Syntax and Morphology*. 2nd edition. Oxford: Blackwell.
D'Andrade, R. 1995. *The Development of Cognitive Anthropology*. Cambridge: Cambridge University Press.
Duranti, A. 1997. *Linguistic Anthropology*. Cambridge: Cambridge University Press.
Evans, N. 2011. Anything Can Happen. The Verb Lexicon and Interdisciplinary Fieldwork. In *The Oxford Handbook of Linguistic Fieldwork*, ed. N. Thieberger. Oxford: Oxford University Press, pp. 183–208.
Evans, V., and M. Green. 2006. *Cognitive Linguistics. An Introduction*. Edinburgh: Edinburgh University Press.
Fischer, H. 2002. Einleitung. Über Feldforschungen. In *Feldforschungen. Erfahrungsberichte zur Einführung*, ed. Hans Fischer. Berlin: Reimer, pp. 9–24.
Foley, W. 1997. *Anthropological Linguistics. An Introduction*. Oxford: Blackwell. (Language in Society, Vol. 24).
Frodeman, R., J. Thompson Klein, and C. Mitcham (eds.) 2010. *The Oxford Handbook of Interdisciplinarity*. Oxford: Oxford University Press.
Gatewood, J. 1999. Culture … One Step at a Time. *The Behavioral Measurement Letter* 6 (2): 5–10.
Hauser-Schäublin, B. 2008. Teilnehmende Beobachtung. In *Methoden ethnologischer Feldforschung*, ed. B. Beer. Berlin: Reimer, pp. 37–58.
Heine, S. 2010. Cultural Psychology. In *Handbook of Social Psychology*, eds. S. Fiske, D. Gilbert, and G. Lindzey. Berlin: Reimer, pp. 1423–1464.
Keck, V. 2008. Interdisziplinäre Projekte und Teamarbeit. In *Methoden ethnologischer Feldforschung*, ed. B. Beer. Berlin: Reimer, pp. 255–275.

Keesing, R. 1979. Linguistic Knowledge and Cultural Knowledge. Some Doubts and Speculations. *American Anthropologist* 81: 14–36.
Malinowski, B. 1920. Classificatory Particles in the Language of Kiriwina. *Bulletin of the School of Oriental Studies, London* 1 (4): 33–78.
Ross, N. 2004. *Culture and Cognition. Implications for Theory and Method.* Thousand Oaks, CA: Sage Publications.
Senft, G. 2002. Linguistische Feldforschung. In *Arbeitsbuch Linguistik*, ed. H. Müller. Paderborn: Schöningh UTB, pp. 353–363.
— 2003. Ethnographic Methods. In *Psycholinguistik. Ein internationales Handbuch*, eds. W. Deutsch, T. Herrmann, and G. Rickheit. Berlin: Walter de Gruyter, pp. 106–114.
— 2008. Zur Bedeutung der Sprache für die Feldforschung. In *Methoden ethnologischer Feldforschung*, ed. B. Beer. Berlin: Reimer, pp. 103-118.
— 2013. Ethnolinguistik. In *Ethnologie. Einführung und Überblick*, eds. B. Beer and H. Fischer. Berlin: Reimer, pp. 271–286.
Sharifian, F. 2011. *Cultural Conceptualisations and Language.* Amsterdam: Benjamins. (Cognitive Linguistic Studies in Cultural Contexts, Vol. 1).
Sharifian, F. (ed.) 2015. *The Routledge Handbook of Language and Culture.* London: Routledge.
Shore, B. 1996. *Culture in Mind.* New York: Oxford University Press.
Silverstein, M. 1973. Linguistik und Anthropologie. In *Linguistik und Nachbarwissenschaften*, eds. R. Bartsch, and T. Vennemann. Kronberg: Scriptor Verlag, pp. 193–210.
Thieberger, N. (ed.) 2011. *The Oxford Handbook of Linguistic Fieldwork.* Oxford: Oxford University Press.
Tietz, A., and S. Völkel. 2013. Theory of Mind in Tonga. The Onset of Representational Change and False Belief Understanding in Tongan Children. In *Theory of Mind in the Pacific. Reasoning Across Cultures*, eds. J. Wassmann, B. Träuble, and J. Funke. Heidelberg: Universitätsverlag Winter, pp. 39–78. (Heidelberg Studies in Pacific Anthropology, Vol. 1).
Völkel, S. 2010. *Social Structure, Space and Possession in Tongan Culture and Language. An Ethnolinguistic Study.* Amsterdam: Benjamins. (Culture and Language Use, Vol. 2).
— 2016. Tongan-English Language Contact and Kinship Terminology. *World Englishes* 35 (2): 242–258.
Wassmann, J., and J. Funke. 2013. Epilogue. Reflections on Personhood and the Theory of Mind. In *Theory of Mind in the Pacific. Reasoning Across Cultures* eds. J. Wassmann, B. Träuble, and J. Funke. Heidelberg: Universitätsverlag Winter, pp. 233–256. (Heidelberg Studies in Pacific Anthropology, Vol. 1).

Pierre R. Dasen

16 The Trouble of Having a Psychologist Sharing Fieldwork

Introduction

Jürg Wassmann has always had an interest in multi-disciplinary research and has not hesitated to ask colleagues from various fields to join him in fieldwork. As a developmental psychologist, I have worked with him in Papua New Guinea and twice in Bali, each time for two or three months. In this chapter, I propose to give a personal account of our interaction during these periods of fieldwork.

I will first recall briefly the reasons for working together, outlining how this collaboration was beneficial for both of us and led to studies neither of us could have done alone, at least not as well. Among these reasons, there are some practical issues (Jürg spending lengthy periods on fieldwork as an anthropologist, I having to steal time during university breaks) but also many methodological ones, some of which will be detailed in another chapter of the volume (see Völkel, this volume). Among these, I might mention:

– How important is it to have a theoretical background before starting research? Do we even need a hypothesis to be tested?
– Who are our informants? Is the expert knowledge of one or two key informants enough, or should we have large samples? How do we define "large"? How is a particular knowledge base shared in different population strata?
– Once the data have been collected, how are they analyzed? What is the use of descriptive statistics? How about some inferential statistics?
– How important are individual thought processes? Can we study these through observation of daily activities, or do we need to introduce unfamiliar situations that need individual problem solving? If we do use tasks or tests, how do we insure their ecological validity?

– To what extent does the use of unfamiliar situations by the psychologist disturb the trust the anthropologist has established with his usual informants?

In this chapter,[1] I propose a very personal take on the advantages and problems of interdisciplinary fieldwork between an anthropologist and a psychologist, namely Jürg Wassmann and myself. That will give me the option of elaborating on some theoretical and methodological differences between our two disciplines, but without striving for a systematic coverage of the issue, which has been done by Jahoda (1982) with a historical perspective, and in a chapter of which the Indian psychologist Ramesh Mishra, with whom I have mainly been working in the last decade of my career, was the first author (Mishra and Dasen 2007).

Contrary to many other anthropologists, Jürg Wassmann has always had an interest in multi-disciplinary research and has not hesitated to ask colleagues from various fields to join him in fieldwork. As a developmental psychologist, I have worked with him in Papua New Guinea (1992) and twice in Bali (1994 and 2002), each time for two or three months. This has been at the initiative of Jürg himself, and I am very grateful to him. Anthropologists, in my experience, are often quite territorial about «their» location, and do not easily welcome others to join them in the field, which explains why there is hardly any replication of studies in anthropology. Jürg has to be admired for his openness in this respect, even though he has sometimes voiced the difficulties this has created for him (cf. for example in the imaginary dialogue he has invented between the two of us in Wassmann and Keck, 2007: 17-18).

The essential condition for such collaborative work is of course that both members of the team should have a sufficient understanding of one another's discipline. Jürg had a very good background in developmental psychology, and in particular a long standing interest in Piaget's theory (Wassmann 1988), in which I had my own training at the University of Geneva. On my side, while I had no formal training in anthropology, I had come into contact at the University of Nairobi with the research team linked to John and Beatrice Whiting at Harvard, many of which consisted of an anthropologist working with a psychologist (often a married couple). Because of my own previous fieldwork in Australia, the Arctic and West Africa, I had started to realize that it was impossible to carry out meaningful cross-cultural psychological research without a serious grounding in ethnography.

A bit of personal history

But let me first recall briefly the reasons for working together, outlining how this collaboration was beneficial for both of us and led to studies neither of us could have done alone, at least not as well. Among these reasons, there are some practical issues. An anthropologist is allowed or even expected to spend lengthy periods in the field, which is what Jürg was doing. I had done the same as a young researcher, living with my family for two to three years each in Australia, Côte d'Ivoire and Kenya, but by the time I tried to settle down in a teaching position in Switzerland, the reputation of world traveler started to be counterproductive in a faculty of psychology and education. In other words, from then on, I would have to steal time for short periods during university breaks. This would not allow me to set up new field sites, and meant I either had to go back to the locations I already knew well (which I did in Côte d'Ivoire), or I had to work with an anthropologist or with a local colleague.

This is how our first research collaboration with Jürg took place in Papua New Guinea, among the Yupno of the Finisterre Range. Jürg was doing the basic ethnography with his future wife, Verena Keck, who had a special interest in ethnomedicine. He spotted a couple of issues for which working with a psychologist seemed to be productive, classification on the one hand (Wassmann and Dasen 1994a) and the body count number system on the other (Wassmann and Dasen 1994b). The Yupno use a body part number system (meaning that each successive digit is shown on a body part) consisting of the fingers on both hands, both feet, and then symmetric parts on the head and down the torso to the penis (amounting to "one full man" or what we would call 33).

The construction of the concept of number was an important topic in Piagetian developmental psychology, and there had been previous research among the Oksapmin of the PNG highlands by Saxe (1981; summarized and expanded in Saxe 2012) who had found that the Oksapmin children developed the number concept using the local body count system in the same order of sub-stages as described by Piaget, except for an additional difficulty linked to the symmetrical body parts. Saxe, after documenting the traditional number system, had used induced situations (i.e. problems to be solved, followed up by so-called Piagetian clinical interviewing) with both children and adults, which allowed him to specify which cognitive processes were involved. For example, he asked them to perform computations (simple additions and subtractions), which were not normally part of the traditional body part system. Some young adults, particularly those who had set up small shops after having visited the coastal plantations, were able to adapt the system to this novel task; they used the system in an abstract way, even calling some body parts by the names of others. In my view, Saxe's study was the best cross-cultural Piagetian research ever performed, and I was very keen to replicate it among the Yupno with a slightly different body part system.

The second opportunity to join Jürg in the field was when he carried out long-term ethnographic research in a remote location on the North-Eastern coast of Bali. Jürg had spent several years working with the team of cognitive and linguistic anthropologists (CARG) at the Max Planck Institute for Psycholinguistics in Nijmegen, headed by Stephen Levinson (see Levinson 2003 for a summary). This team had found several languages where spatial references are dominated by the so-called "absolute" or "geocentric" frame of reference, meaning that the location of objects, even in small-scale table space and inside a room, is described in terms of far away directions instead of the "relative" or "egocentric" terms of left and right that are familiar in most Indo-European languages and many others including Japanese. The Balinese systematically use such a geocentric system, namely, in Balinese, *kaja* (towards the mountain) and *kelod* (towards the sea) and its orthogonal axis, *kangin* and *kauh* (see below). The Nijmegen group had studied mainly adults, and Jürg asked me to join him in the field to carry out a study on how children learned to deal with this geocentric system. What we found was that even the very young children, aged 4 to 5 years, were using it systematically, with some egocentric references coming in at later ages (Wassmann and Dasen 1996, 1998, 2006). Using mainly non-verbal induced situations developed by the Nijmegen team, which allow to determine which frame of reference the informants use when encoding a spatial situation in memory, we also found that the results depended on which task was used. One of the tasks induced systematically more egocentric responses than the other, suggesting that individuals are not constrained completely by the characteristics of the language they use, as linguistic relativism would have it.

This first study in Bali took us about three months of common fieldwork. Before collecting the psychological data, we were careful to document fully the Balinese orientation system. Since Bali is an island with a central volcanic mountain area, *kaja* indicates North for those living in the Southern part of the island, but South for those living on the North coast. Not only is there this reversal, which had been described before in the literature, but in fact we found that the orientation system rotates as one proceeds along the coast around the island, or around a peninsula such as the one we explored in the North-East of the island. Hence, *kangin* also changes from Sunrise to Sunset, and vice-versa for *kauh*. In other words the system is geocentric, but locally adapted to each particular topography. Jürg had already documented ethnographically how the orientation system was used in daily life (for example when gambling at a cock fight), and how it affected many aspects of Balinese customs (e.g. the orientation of temples and of individual houses, of religious ceremonies and the way adults talk to children), including occasional exceptions.

In other words, what we did was to follow the rules of collaborative fieldwork we had established previously in our research among the Yupno (Wassmann and Dasen 1994a), namely to start with interviewing informants (not only a few main key persons, but as wide a range of people as possible across genders, ages and social groups) and observing daily behavior – following Jürg's previous findings that people do not always do what they say (Wassmann 1993). Only after a wide ethnographic understanding has been established is it acceptable to proceed with so-called induced situations, i.e. tasks or tests which allow the psychologist to assess individual thought processes.

Because a study of child development had not been foreseen in Jürg's initial research project, we did not have access to large numbers of children in the school; our research assistant located them individually in the village, and convinced them to come and «play games» on the terrace of Jürg's house. The sample consisted of 16 children from age 7 to 15 years of age, plus 12 adults. Jürg later on tested a group of 10 children aged 4 to 5 years, using one of the tasks only and in a simplified version. I will come back below to the discussion of whether this can be considered to be a very small or on the contrary quite a large sample, and how this may influence the interpretation of the results.

On the basis of these fieldwork periods in Papua New Guinea and in Bali, I now turn to a series of methodological questions that may arise in such collaborative interdisciplinary work. I will deal with them in a rather personal, informal and even anecdotal way.

Methodological questions.

Do we need a theory to start research?

How important is it to have a theoretical background before starting research? Do we even need a hypothesis to be tested?

Anthropology, and in any case ethnography such as Jürg is doing, seems to proceed without the intention of testing any theory. The emic description of a society and its functioning, both in the symbolic as well as mundane realms, is quite sufficient – and difficult enough. The research is therefore not about hypothesis testing. For me as a cross-cultural psychologist, this is fine, but only as the necessary background to go beyond, particularly into comparing whether a finding in one society holds up in another. Are we dealing with a culture specific process, or is it more general, or even universal? During fieldwork among the Yupno, for example, I seriously hoped to test Saxe's conclusions on the development of the number concept among Oksapmin children – and was therefore very disappointed to find out that Yupno children had no knowledge of the traditional number system (neither did the teachers at the local primary school). Of course, we still managed to do an interesting study with adult males (among the Yupno, "women don't count!" literally; they claim they don't know how to count, but observing them when counting occurs in public, in fact they do).

I experienced a similar disappointment when I wanted to study "parental ethnotheories" among Yupno women, i.e. the ideas the mothers have about how children grow up, what they should be able to do at particular ages, etc. I had previously explored this research topic in East and West Africa, without major problems. Among the Yupno, not only were the women very shy when I tried to interview them (and their children ran away from fear of this bearded white stranger!), but I felt that I could not really get any reliable information because of the complicated sequence of translations. On this project, Verena Keck tried to help me, my hope being that the women would feel more comfortable with a female anthropologist. I would ask my question in English, Verena would translate it into Pidgin, and the local assistant from Pidgin into Yupno; then the answer came back from Yupno to Pidgin to German... by which time I had no confidence at all in really understanding what the mother was supposed to have said. I gave up on this study.

16 The Trouble of Having a Psychologist Sharing Fieldwork 261

Cross-cultural psychologists usually go to the field with a research question in mind, maybe even a theory to test. This is what is called an "imposed etic" (Segall et al. 1999: 41) which needs to be confronted to the local "emic," and has to be validated as being meaningful, i.e. become a "derived etic," before any valid comparison can be attempted. The two anecdotes described above illustrate the fact that this is not always possible, or at least that there can be serious methodological problems. In relation to my second anecdote, it is to be said that cross-cultural psychologists, in contrast to anthropologists, hardly ever take the time to learn the local language.

Early on in the emergence of the field of cross-cultural psychology, we defined the following three goals (Berry and Dasen 1974):
1. Take existing theories to the field to test which aspects are culturally specific and which are shared, or possibly even universal. This, again, starts as an imposed etic.
2. Discover new psychological processes that are unknown in the researcher's original society. This is the emic approach, closer to anthropology, or to what is sometimes called "cultural psychology."
3. Extract the common elements and adapt the theories in order to produce psychological theories that apply to all of humanity (the derived etic).

We later (Segall et al. 1999) added a fourth goal:
4. In research in a single society, variables of interest are sometimes confounded. Quasi-experimental, comparative research (over several field sites) can help to tease out these variables.

For goals 1, 3 and 4, research starts with existing theories; for goal 4, it starts even with hypotheses about confounding variables, and the field sites are selected specifically to tease out these variables. In other words, in proper cross-cultural research, one does not go to a field site because of convenience, but one selects these on the basis of previous (ethnographic) knowledge. Only for goal number 2 might it be possible to go and "explore" with a completely open mind, but even then, how likely is it to find an interesting psychological process just by accident? More likely, one finds it also because of previous ethnographic documentation. Thus, no psychologist had ever studied the geocentric frame of spatial references, because that frame is simply never used, except for large distance travel, in Europe and North America where psychology is enculturated. Neither had any cross-cultural psychologist, and not even a cultural one, discovered it before linguists of the CARG group studied it. I would never have become aware of it had Jürg not been part of that team, and if he had not suggested that we should study it from a developmental psychology perspective.

In summary, hypothesis testing and theory building are important features of psychology, including cross-cultural psychology. The latter, in my opinion, can only be done on the basis of prior cultural knowledge. There is, in this respect, an important difference between the two disciplines.

Sample size

Who are our informants? Is the expert knowledge of one or two key informants enough, or should we have large samples? How do we define "large"? How is a particular knowledge base shared in different population strata?

This is a question to which Jürg has given a lot of thought (e.g. Wassmann 1995), and where he has argued that, in anthropology, the common practice of working with a small number of key informants can be misleading, that knowledge is shared differently in various social segments of a society, and that the anthropologist therefore has to work with all of these, and in particular with "jpfs" ("just plain folks," following Lave 1988).

Yet, when Jürg prepared our common fieldwork among the Yupno, he had asked his main informant, the "big man" of the village, about "the" Yupno number system, assuming quite naturally that if one piece of knowledge had to be standard in a population, it certainly was their number system. It therefore came as a surprise to both of us, when we interviewed several of the older Yupno men, that they came up with several variations of the sequence of body parts. As we mention in the initial publication, we never really figured out whether the phenomenon was real or an artefact. On the one hand, it could have been a traditional feature of a counting system that is always practiced in public, and where the person who counts does so by showing successively (even if sometimes sweepingly) all the body parts up to the final count. The final result of the count is how that particular person has achieved it, and someone else may do it differently. However, when we carried out this study, the full body count system was already on its way out; young men would count only up to two hands and two feet (20), as is done regularly on the coast. Children, as already mentioned, never learned it; in school, they were taught the decimal system. So it could well have been that the various older men actually tried to revive the old counting system mainly to please us, each remembering it somewhat differently. I suppose we would have needed many more observations on the public use of the counting system to solve the quandary, but these were not easy to come by.

Our first fieldwork in Bali provides an example of why large samples are needed for psychological research. Because there are individual differences, small samples may lead to erroneous conclusions precisely because of sampling effects; by accident of probabilities, one may have chosen a few individuals that are not representative of the whole population. In our study, all 10 of the very young children turned out to produce geocentric answers on the one, simplified task Jürg used (the Animals task, described below, with two animals instead of three). This gave us the illusion that child development in Bali started with the construction of geocentric space, and that the egocentric frame of reference came in only later in life. This finding could be interpreted as a sort of reversal of developmental stages, since, according to Piaget and Inhelder (1956), Euclidean space (geocentric) should develop after projective (egocentric) space, or at least the two should be concurrent. A true reversal of stages would have been a scoop in cross-cultural Piagetian research, quite a stroke of luck! However, the increase of egocentric encoding with age could also be attributed to a variety of confounding variables, such as the impact of schooling in Indonesian (a language in which, contrary to Balinese, the egocentric left/right references are preferred), or the impact of increased contact with age with the outside world, with urban areas (in which egocentric references are more functional) or with tourists, or even English. Our sample was too small to be stratified in order to control for any of these variables.

For an anthropologist, a sample of 16 children (and even more, 26 if the very young ones are included) is quite a large one; certainly, collecting data through individual testing takes a lot of time and effort. For a developmental psychologist, such a sample is too small, especially if the age range is quite large, from 4 to 15. We have here a clear example of different traditions and conceptions in the two disciplines. I had the tendency to speak of our "pilot study," which is what psychologists often do, a small study just to make sure that the instrumentation works before collecting data on a "real" sample. In this case, carrying out a larger study in Bali was not feasible immediately; it needed a research permit to have access to schools and some funding. In fact, it took ten years until we were able to return to Bali together to carry out such a larger study.

In the meantime, I had turned to fieldwork in India and Nepal with a local colleague from the Banaras Hindu University, Ramesh Mishra, who had made me aware of the fact that geocentric orientation systems were in common use in those two countries. There it was quite easy to set up a study with large samples, of schooled and unschooled children, boys and girls, in rural and urban areas; in fact, our total sample ended up being 449 children (Mishra et al. 2003; Dasen et al. 2004). Instead of the expected reversal of stages, we found that the geocentric references indeed appeared early in child development but always concurrently with egocentric or intrinsic references, and that the geocentric ones actually increased with age. We did not find any differences between schooled and unschooled children, nor between boys and girls, but a systematic difference between urban and rural areas, with the geocentric references more dominant in the latter.

In 2002, Jürg and I were able to set up a similar study in Bali, with access to schools in the small city of Singaraja and a village, both on the North coast, with a total sample of 170 children aged 4 to 12. We also went back to our original field location in the remote village, and tested 33 children from 4 to 8 years of age. This study allowed us to document the developmental trend with much more confidence (Dasen et al. 2006; Dasen and Wassmann 2008; for an overall summary of the whole research project, see Dasen and Mishra 2010). In the rural, traditional areas, the geocentric frame is indeed present at a very early age, but it still further increases with age; in the urban area, the geocentric system develops more slowly. Furthermore, the study allowed us to measure the impact of speaking Indonesian in addition or in preference to Balinese, which also proved to be a major variable. The fact that, in this second study, we were able to tease out different environmental and socio-cultural variables, those that were confounded in our pilot study, illustrates the advantage of working with large samples.

Statistics

Once the data have been collected, how are they analyzed? What is the use of descriptive statistics? How about some inferential statistics?

Linked to sample size is the possibility of using statistics; on very small samples, this is usually impossible or at least unnecessary. For many studies, qualitative data are quite appropriate, and that would be the case of most ethnographic research. In order to tease out the influence of different variables, as demonstrated above, some statistical treatment is mandatory. This can possibly just be descriptive: we can look at the frequencies (or proportions) of a particular behavior over age between two tasks, or between city and village groups. In the first study, for example, such an inspection of frequencies was sufficient to conclude to task specificity in spatial encoding. But could the difference we see have been obtained by chance, by the sampling effects I mentioned earlier? To answer that question, more powerful, inferential statistics are needed. In our final publication (Dasen and Mishra 2010), we even ended up using correlations, regression analysis and structural equation modeling, which allowed us to show graphically how various variables were linked to geocentric language and encoding.

One statistical technique I find particularly useful is principal component analysis, which allows to combine a number of measures to work out what they have in common, and then use that single measure as a better measure, eliminating a lot of the noise or random variation. For example, we had three different tasks eliciting spatial language, each of them somewhat different, one dealing with the static location of objects, one with movement in space, and one more directly linked to the memory encoding tasks. For some purposes, it is interesting to analyze each of these tasks separately, but to explore the links between spatial language more generally (on the dimension of our main interest, egocentric vs. geocentric) and other variables, it is useful to derive a single summary measure for geocentric spatial language. Being derived from three slightly different tasks, this summary measure can be considered as more valid than the three separate scores, but of course it becomes an abstract scale, losing the immediacy of a frequency count. Structural equation modeling takes several of these scales into account simultaneously, working out the correlations that exist between them, and placing all the variables in a graphic illustration. Such a summary model may even contain so-called "virtual" variables, that are not measured directly in the research but are derived from various measures. In the summary model for Bali (Dasen and Mishra 2010: 160), for example, we included the virtual variable "traditional culture" assessed through the index of speaking Balinese instead of Indonesian, and the knowledge of the Balinese orientation system, a variable strongly linked to rural vs. urban residence.

By using such elaborate analyses, were we just following the fashionable trend in psychology? Or are they really meaningful? Most anthropologists would no doubt either just skip over these analyses if only because they are not familiar with them, or be openly reluctant. When data are fed into factorial or principal component analyses, needing computers to crunch the numbers, one does lose contact with the immediate meaning of the behavior one has observed. This is particularly true if one is unable to handle these tools by oneself, but learning them takes a lot of time and effort, and motivation that is difficult to garner at the end of a career. I try to understand the basics, but always need help with implementing the more complicated calculations. I feel sometimes quite uneasy about this, and I can understand why my anthropologist colleagues might feel even more so....

Observing behavior through induced situations

How important are individual thought processes? Can we study these through observation of daily activities, or do we need to introduce unfamiliar situations that need individual problem solving? If we do use tasks or tests, how do we ensure their ecological validity?

A topic of common interest between Jürg and myself has always been "everyday cognition" (Wassmann and Dasen 1993), i.e. the study of cognitive processes in situations that are culturally meaningful, instead of studying them in a controlled laboratory situation. However, the paradox is that it is usually not possible to observe these behaviors as they occur naturally. One would have to be extremely patient, or very lucky, to wait for appropriate examples, and quite often these would in fact be ambiguous. As a psychologist studying cognitive development, I am interested in individual thought processes, and I therefore want to see informants solve a problem without resorting to previously acquired social knowledge.

For example, counting does not occur very often among the Yupno, it is in fact not a highly valued skill. If an informant demonstrates the counting system, it is still not clear for the psychologist whether this reflects just a shared social knowledge, or indeed an abstract understanding of the number concept. I would therefore want to know, for example, whether that informant can use the system to perform arithmetic, such as an addition. Saxe (1982) was able to carry out some observations in small shops, where a customer may want to buy two or more items, and addition therefore becomes meaningful. There was one such shop in our Yupno field site, but the merchant would only use the body count system up to 20. On local markets, items were sold as heaps which all had the same value, and customers would usually pay for each one separately even if they bought several, thus bypassing the need for addition. Saxe also devised a number of small arithmetic problems, and so did we, in two sets, with or without the presence of objects (such as sticks) to be counted.

I will not go into the details of the results, only to say that asking our informants to solve these problems, individually or in pairs, was for me an absolutely essential element to clarify how they were using the number system and to which limits. Similarly, in Bali, using non-verbal spatial encoding tasks was absolutely essential, since we found repeatedly that the language used (egocentric or geocentric) did not always fit what the individuals did. In fact, in the summary model of our results (Dasen and Mishra 2010: 160), there is no strong correlation between geocentric language and geocentric encoding, each of them being influenced by a number of background variables, but separately. This is an argument against any strong form of linguistic relativism, and hence an important contribution to the theory behind the investigation.

Troublesome psychologists

To what extent does the use of unfamiliar situations by the psychologist disturb the trust the anthropologist has established with his usual informants?

Jürg sometimes said, and I easily believe him, that it would take him weeks to overcome the disturbance produced by the intrusive methods imposed during our collaboration in the field. Anthropologists often take weeks or months to win the confidence of the people they work with, to make them understand why they are there and show that they are willing to participate in daily life, but also that they have to ask questions. Once this trust has been established, it is understandable that anything that comes to disturb this delicate balance is not welcome.

I think there is no real problem when doing research with children (at least with those who do not run away from fear, like some of the Yupno toddlers!). The tasks we were using were always presented as games, and children everywhere like to play games. If need be, we explained that there were no wrong answers, and we spent an enormous amount of time making sure that there were no communication problems. The "games" may seem a bit strange and foreign, but that can actually make them more interesting. If the children have gone to school, even if only briefly for some of them, they have been presented with many out of context questions; schooling is all about learning out of context! But even for the completely unschooled children we were able to include in our study in India and Nepal (Dasen et al. 2004), I never felt that our research was a disturbance.

I am much more uneasy about dealing with adults. Yet, most if not all of the research carried out by the CARG team consists of using so-called "space games" with adults (Senft 2007). Senft (2007: 240) reports that "actually, our consultants enjoyed playing all the games." I personally have some doubts. Most of the tasks and tests I used throughout my career, be it the so-called Piagetian tasks, or the "space games," or even the arithmetic problems we set for the Yupno, I would feel uneasy to use with adults, and indeed, I hardly ever did. They are so simple, "child like," that adults may well think that there must be a hidden difficulty, some trick or another. For example, looking at three or four toy animals set out in line on one table, and then having to set out a second, identical set on a second table (after a 180° rotation) – the so-called Animals task from the CARG set, which we used in all of our spatial frames project – is a case in point. Especially since the instructions ask for five repeat trials. In the few cases when we did ask adult informants to perform this task, I felt silly even though maybe they themselves did not.

The adult-child relationship is always asymmetric. Children ask questions about things they do not know, adults (especially teachers) ask them about things they know very well. With adults, the researchers obviously place the "consultants" into an asymmetrical power relationship, either because they are foreign visitors which one may try to please – despite finding their games and questions ridiculous – or possibly from which one even expects some reward. The classic "participant observation" of the ethnographer may have some aspects of this bizarre and unequal relationship, but certainly fewer than the use of unfamiliar experimental situations.

Unfortunately, using unfamiliar problems is the necessary tool of the psychologist's trade. Even while studying "street mathematics" (e.g. Carraher et al. 1985; Nunes et al. 1993), it will not be enough for the researchers to observe a child vendor in the market being able to add the price of three pineapples. The child may well just remember the total price for a familiar sale, without having to perform any computation. So the researchers will have to buy, say nine pineapples, and also ask the child how he or she worked out the solution. Then, the researchers may even want to simulate a school situation ("A woman goes to the market and buys nine pineapples; each costs 35..." or "How much is 9 times 35?"), and hence come to the interesting discovery that the child is able to solve a particular problem in one situation but not in the other.

It is only by asking to solve an unfamiliar problem that the psychologist can assess which thinking processes are being used; solving a familiar one may be done as a routine, relying on memory and previous social knowledge. Being unfamiliar of course makes it strange, out of context, and possible even disturbing.

So, Jürg, sorry for the disturbance! and thanks for accepting me at your side despite of this. I think the disturbance has been worthwhile, and in any case we had a good time working together. I suspect that you think so too.

Note

1 I wish to thank John Berry, Catherine Dasen, Ramesh Mishra, Rudo Niemeijer and Fabienne Tanon for useful comments on a previous draft.

References

Berry, J. W., and P. R. Dasen (eds.) 1974. *Culture and Cognition. Readings in Cross-cultural Psychology*. London: Methuen.

Carraher, T. N., D. W. Carraher, and A. D. Schliemann. 1985. Mathematics in the Streets and in Schools. *British Journal of Developmental Psychology* 3: 21–29.

Dasen, P. R., R. C. Mishra, and S. Niraula. 2004. The Influence of Schooling on Cognitive Development. Spatial Language, Encoding and Concept Development in India and Nepal. In *Ongoing Themes in Psychology and Culture*, eds. B. N. Setiadi, A. Supratiknya, W. J. Lonner, and Y. H. Poortinga. Yogjakarta: Kanisius, pp. 223–237.

Dasen, P. R., C. R. Mishra, S. Niraula, and J. Wassmann. 2006. Développement du Langage et de la Cognition Spatiale Géocentrique. *Enfance* 58: 146–158.

Dasen, P. R., and J. Wassmann. 2008. A Cross-cultural Comparison of Spatial Language and Encoding in Bali and Geneva. In *Advances in Cognitive Science*, eds. N. Srinivasan, A. K. Gupta, and J. Pandey. New Delhi: Sage, pp. 264–276.

Dasen, P. R., and R. C. Mishra. 2010. *Development of Geocentric Spatial Language and Cognition*. Cambridge: Cambridge University Press.

Jahoda, G. 1982. *Psychology and Anthropology. A Psychological Perspective*. London: AcademicPress.

Lave, J. 1988. *Cognition in Practice. Mind, Mathematics and Culture in Everyday Life*. Cambridge: Cambridge University Press.

Levinson, S. 2003. *Space in Language and Cognition. Explorations in Cognitive Diversity*. Cambridge: Cambridge University Press.

Mishra, R. C., P. R. Dasen, and S. Niraula. 2003. Ecology, Language, and Performance on Spatial Cognitive Tasks. *International Journal of Psychology* 38 (6): 366–383.

Mishra, R. C., and P. R. Dasen. 2007. The Methodological Interface of Psychology and Anthropology. In *Experiencing New Worlds*, eds. J. Wassmann and K. Stockhaus. New York and Oxford: Berghahn, pp. 21–35. (Person, Space and Memory in the Contemporary Pacific, Vol. 1).

Nunes, T., A. S. Schliemann, and D. W. Carraher. 1993. *Street Mathematics and School Mathematics*. Cambridge: Cambridge University Press.

Piaget, J., and B. Inhelder. 1956. *The Child's Conception of Space*. London: Routledge and Kegan Paul. (First published in French, 1948).

Saxe, G. B. 1981. Body Parts as Numerals. A Developmental Analysis of Numeration among Remote Oksapmin Village Populations in Papua New Guinea. *Child Development* 52: 306–316.

— 1982. Developing Forms of Arithmetic Operations among the Oksapmin of Papua New Guinea. *Developmental Psychology* 18 (4): 583–594.

— 2012. *Cultural Development of Mathematical Ideas. Papua New Guinea Studies*. Cambridge: Cambridge University Press.

Segall, M. H., P. R. Dasen, J. W. Berry, and Y. H. Poortinga 1999. *Human Behavior in Global Perspective: An Introduction to Cross-cultural Psychology*. Revised Second Edition. Boston: Allyn and Bacon.

Senft, G. 2007. The Nijmegen Space Games. Studying the Interrelationship between Language,Culture and Cognition. In *Experiencing New Worlds,* eds. J. Wassmann and K. Stockhaus. New York and Oxford: Berghahn, pp. 224–244. (Person, Space and Memory in the Contemporary Pacific, Vol. 1).

Wassmann, J. 1988. Methodische Probleme kulturvergleichender Untersuchungen im Rahmen von Piagets Theorie der kognitiven Entwicklung. Aus der Sicht eines Ethnologen. *Zeitschrift für Ethnologie* 113: 21–66.

— 1993. When Actions Speak Louder Than Words. The Classification of Food among the Yupno of Papua New Guinea. *Quarterly Newsletter of the Laboratory of Comparative Human Cognition* 15 (1): 30–40.
— 1995. The Final Requiem for the Omniscient Informant? An Interdisciplinary Approach to Everyday Cognition. *Culture and Psychology* 1: 167–201.
Wassmann, J., and P. R. Dasen (eds.) 1993. *Alltagswissen / Les Savoirs Quotidiens / Everyday Cognition*. Fribourg: Editions Universitaires.
— 1994a. "Hot" and "Cold." Classification and Sorting among the Yupno of Papua New Guinea. *International Journal of Psychology* 29: 19–38.
— 1994b. Yupno Number System and Counting. *Journal of Cross-Cultural Psychology* 25: 78–94.
— 1996. Comment Ne Pas Perdre le Nord à Bali. Processus Cognitifs – Une Combinaison de Méthodes Ethnographiques et Psychologiques. *Bulletin de l'Académie Suisse des Sciences Humaines et Sociales* (1, 2): 17–26, 13–16.
— 1998. Balinese Spatial Orientation. Some Empirical Evidence for Moderate Linguistic Relativity. *The Journal of the Royal Anthropological Institute*, incorporating *Man* (N.S.) 4: 689–711.
— 2006. How to Orient Yourself in Balinese Space. Combining Ethnographic and Psychological Methods for the Study of Cognitive Processes. In *Pursuit of Meaning. Advances in Cultural and Cross-cultural Psychology*, eds. J. Straub, D. Seidemann, C. Kölbl, and B. Zielke. Bielefeld: transcript, pp. 351–376.
Wassmann, J., and V. Keck 2007. Introduction. In *Experiencing New Worlds*, eds. J. Wassmann and K. Stockhaus. New York and Oxford: Berghahn, pp.1–18. (Person, Space and Memory in the Contemporary Pacific, Vol. 1).

JOACHIM FUNKE

17 "Just Plain Folks". Anthropology Meets Psychology

Near encounter 1973

Back to my earliest memories having to do with Jürg: When I was a young student, I began my studies in psychology and philosophy at Basel University, Switzerland, in the summer of 1973. At that time, I had no clear goal in mind. I was officially enrolled in philosophy as a major and psychology as a minor but the borders were open at that time. I went to lectures in art history, German literature, psychiatry, and sociology. And I also went to the Anthropology Department, located at Münsterplatz, but Meinhard Schuster – head of the Basel Anthropology Department at that time – with his interest in the Sepik region (Papua New Guinea) did not match my interests (at least not in these years). So I was happy with the Philosophy Department (Arnold Künzli, Hans Kunz, Kurt Rossmann, Hansjörg Salmony). During my philosophy studies, I came into contact with a doctoral student named Olga, who was at that time the girl friend of Jürg – unbeknownst to me. I left Basel in 1975 for Trier University to complete my psychology studies. Anthropology was no longer on my intellectual landscape.

So: I *could* have met Jürg during my Basel days but I have no conscious memory of a face-to-face encounter. That happened years later in our Heidelberg faculty when I entered Heidelberg University in 1997. Human memory is not perfectly reliable: I do not remember exactly when I first met Jürg there but it must have been in the context of one of my first faculty meetings shortly after my start at Heidelberg University. Our Heidelberg Faculty of Behavioral and Cultural Studies comprises such heterogeneous departments like Anthropology, Educational Science, Gerontology, Psychology, as well as Sport and Sports Science. Normally, we meet people from other departments only at faculty meetings, because there is little or no overlap in teaching between the mentioned subjects. For some reasons unknown to me, one day I was invited to the Department of Anthropology to drink a glass of wine and eat some finger food together with people from the Department. This type of informal "get-together" was typical at that time for Jürg's style of management.

From these beginnings, my wife Marlene and I became friends with Jürg and his colleague/wife Verena. They introduced the legendary „Zungenschlag" (a local cabaret and entertainment show) to us and during their regularly held „aperos" (informal meetings with colleagues and students at the beginning of a term in their private rooms) I made contact with a lot of interesting friends of Verena and Jürg's. It was a long way from the near-encounter in Basel to the first real encounter in Heidelberg. But from the beginning, it was a mixture of friendship and common research interests in Cognitive Anthropology (see Illustration 17.1).

Illustration 17.1: Jürg Wassmann with the author (July 2013).

Common lectures – common research interests since 1998

Since winter 1998, Jürg and I had repeatedly held cooperative seminars at Heidelberg University. The titles of these seminars were „Research on cognition from the viewpoints of anthropology and psychology" (winter term 1998/99; summer term 2002); "Space and time from the viewpoints of anthropology and psychology" (winter term 1999/2000); "Cognitive anthropology" (winter term 2003/04); "Cognitive psychology meets anthropology" (summer term 2005; summer term 2007). I wrote a short paper about this cooperation in the German anthropological journal "Zeitschrift für Ethnologie" (Funke 2010). Some people from the Anthropology Department in our faculty have since called me the guy who published in "our" journal. That is a consequence of interdisciplinary work.

The battlefield between Psychology and Anthropology was a field of methods, especially the issue of participant observation (a favorite method for anthropology) versus experimental lab research (the ideal method for psychologists). Two different worlds of experience! But the truth is, both have their advantages and their disadvantages (see also the contribution by Dasen, this volume). There is no panacea. Reliance on informants could lead to erroneous conclusions (Margaret Mead could tell a story) – Jürg and his plea for "just plain folks" reads for me like "don't believe in the big man"; ask more than one person (even if this person is the chief).

There was no lecture (and for some time no doctoral examination) without "Animals in a Row": That was a task that Jürg loved very much! Three animals were positioned sequentially on a table on one side of a room, then the participant had to turn 180 degrees and reproduce the sequence on another table. It served to demonstrate egocentric vs. geocentric representations (Wassmann and Dasen 1998, see also Dasen, this volume).

Theory of mind

As a result of our teaching cooperation and with generous support from the "Volkswagen Foundation," five teams of two persons (each team consisting of one psychology student and one anthropology student) went to the Pacific for field studies to test hypotheses about the universality of a unique human "Theory of Mind." The five Pacific societies and the respective research teams (psychologists mentioned first) were Eva Oberle and Jochen Resch on Fais and Yap Islands (Yap State, Federated States of Micronesia), Alexandra Tietz and Svenja Völkel in Tonga, Andreas Mayer and Julius Riese in Samoa, Mirjam Hoelzel and Verena Keck among the Yupno (Papua New Guinea) as well as Bettina Ubl and Anita von Poser with the Bosmun (Papua New Guinea).

Bringing together students from at least two disciplines was necessary to bring experimental research techniques down to earth and to adapt them to local environments. Universality assumptions hold widely in psychological research. The use of objective measurements and the use of (quasi-)experimental methods is standard procedure in normal lab-based research under controlled conditions. But under field conditions, some compromises have to be made: the control of noise factors becomes more problematic, the understanding of instructions has to be proved and test material has to be localized. All in all: not "business as usual" for the psychologists in this enterprise but a lot of challenges that require creative problem solving. The resulting book "Theory of Mind in the Pacific. Reasoning Across Cultures" (Wassmann et al. 2013) shows this in detail. Another point: Psychology is becoming more and more aware of its status as a postcolonial science (see, for instance, Teo 2005). Anthropological insights and knowledge are one of the sources for this process. The fact that most of the psychological experiments were run with WEIRD people (=participants from western, educated, industrialized, rich, and democratic societies), is another relatively recent insight from Henrich, Heine, and Norenzayan (2010). The cooperation with Jürg helped me to overcome these limitations, at least in this case.

Concerning the book from Wassmann et al. (2013), a recent book review from Luhrmann (2015) finishes its critique with the statement: "This is a remarkable book. It represents a quite considerable amount of work and it is a significant achievement. There is nothing like it in the literature. That it leaves you wanting more is a sign of how much it has accomplished." What more could we wish for than such a positive and rewarding evaluation!

The new freedom: Emeritus 2009

Since 2009 Jürg has enjoyed the privileges of an emeritus: Without being disturbed by boring administration, without a teaching load, and without losing time during committee meetings he has focused on the most important issue for a scientist: science! Together with Verena, he has spent a lot of time at their country residence in Feldberg in the Black Forest (see Illustration 17.2), reading and writing books and articles (besides swimming and visiting pubs).

I know of many visitors who have gone to Feldberg to discuss issues in anthropology with Jürg and Verena. Marlene and I have been there repeatedly and were impressed by their hospitality. I hope that the scientific results of this freedom will find their ways into anthropology and also into psychology in the future.

Illustration 17.2: Jürg Wassmann (August 2015) in his Feldberg office, writing his next book.

Final remarks

Nigel Barley, the recalcitrant (and unconventional) anthropologist, author of the famous book "*Adventures in a Mud Hut: An Innocent Anthropologist Abroad*" (in German translation simply labelled: „Traumatische Tropen"), said recently in an interview with the German weekly magazine „Die Zeit":

> „Für mich ist Ethnologie eher eine Form aufgeklärter Subjektivität, Sympathie und Empathie. Deshalb verpacke ich Ethnologie auch gern in Geschichten. Denn Geschichten sind immer vieldeutig und schaffen Freiraum. ... Wenn Sie Ethnologe sind, dann müssen Sie letztlich an die Menschen glauben." (Die Zeit Nr. 31, Juli 2015, Seite 29; translation by JF: "For me, anthropology is preferably a kind of enlightened subjectivity, sympathy and empathy. That's the reason I like to wrap anthropology in stories. Stories are always ambiguous and free up space. ... If you are an anthropologist, eventually you have to believe in people").

Jürg Wassmann would have no problems telling stories about folks. To my knowledge, this is his understanding of anthropology too. I assume that Jürg would also agree with this last statement from Nigel Barley:

> "Collecting and telling stories: that is also part of my own research agenda. It is part of an anthropological research agenda that connects psychology with anthropology: Listening to people and trying to understand them."

Dear Jürg: I will listen to what you say and try to understand you! The funny thing is, the older I become, the better I understand! "Gently bowing" (Wassmann 1993, 2016) is not only a useful metaphor for a person but could also be used for a friendship as well.

References

Funke, J. 2010. Kooperation zwischen Ethnologen und Psychologen. Optionen, Probleme, Visionen. *Zeitschrift für Ethnologie* 135: 249–258.

Henrich, J., S. J. Heine, and A. Norenzayan. 2010. The Weirdest People in the World? *Behavioral and Brain Sciences* 33 (2-3): 61–83; discussion 83–135.

Luhrmann, T. M. 2015. Book Review: Theory of Mind in the Pacific. Reasoning Across Cultures, edited by Jürg Wassmann, Birgit Träuble and Joachim Funke. *Anthropological Forum* 25 (4): 442-444.

Teo, T. 2005. *The Critique of Psychology. From Kant to Postcolonial Theory.* New York: Springer.

Wassmann, J. 1993. *Das Ideal des leicht gebeugten Menschen. Eine ethnokognitive Analyse der Yupno in Papua New Guinea.* Berlin: Reimer.

— 2016. *The Gently Bowing Person. An Ideal among the Yupno in Papua New Guinea.* Heidelberg: Universitätsverlag Winter. (Heidelberg Studies in Pacific Anthropology 4).

Wassmann, J., and P. R. Dasen. 1998. Balinese Spatial Orientation. Some Empirical Evidence of Moderate Linguistic Relativity. *The Journal of the Royal Anthropological Institute* 4 (4): 689–711.

Wassmann, J., B. E. Träuble, and J. Funke (eds.) 2013. *Theory of Mind in the Pacific. Reasoning Across Cultures.* Heidelberg: Universitätsverlag Winter. (Heidelberg Studies in Pacific Anthropology 1).

Notes on Contributors

Raymond Ammann studied ethnomusicology in Basel. After his field research in the Bering Strait area from 1991 to 1992, where he studied Chukchi throat singing as basis for his doctoral thesis, he continued his research in Melanesian countries, New Caledonia, Vanuatu and Papua New Guinea. Fifteen years of field research in these countries allowed him to publish several books, articles, CDs, films. His habilitation thesis in 2001 deals with flutes in Melanesia. Since 2004 Raymond Ammann lives in Switzerland again. He is Professor for Ethnomusicology at the University of Innsbruck and at the Lucerne University of Applied Sciences and Arts (Lucerne School of Music).

Pierre R. Dasen is Professor Emeritus of anthropology of education and cross-cultural psychology at the University of Geneva (Faculty of Psychology and Educational Sciences). He is the co-author (with J. Berry, Y. Poortinga, and M. Segall) of two widely circulated textbooks of cross-cultural psychology. His field of expertise is cross-cultural developmental psychology, and particularly culture and cognition. He has been a research assistant to J. Piaget at the University of Geneva, where he has been teaching for twenty years; he has also been associated with the Australian National University, Université de Montréal, University of Nairobi, and Universities of Nice, Fribourg, Lyon II and EHESS in Paris. He has carried out research in Australia, Canada, Côte d'Ivoire, Kenya and Papua New Guinea, Indonesia, India and Nepal. P. Dasen has been influential in founding the Association pour la Recherche Interculturelle (ARIC), a francophone association for cross-cultural research. His most recent book (together with R. C. Mishra) is *Development of Geocentric Spatial Language and Cognition.* 2010, Cambridge: Cambridge University Press. A CV and list of publications (including papers to be downloaded in pdf format) are available at: http://www.unige.ch/fapse/SSE/teachers/dasen/home/

Antje Denner is Principal Curator, Oceania, Americas and Africa at National Museums Scotland. She specializes in the cultures and material collections of the Pacific, anthropology of art, religion and ritual practices, aesthetics and representation, and socio-cultural change, with a particular interest in further developing cross-disciplinary as well as cross-cultural approaches. She received her PhD from the School of World Art Studies and Museology at the University of East Anglia, Norwich. Denner combines a background in museum anthropology and lecturing, having worked in different capacities in various museums and universities in Switzerland, Germany, Australia and the United Kingdom. Her publications include *The Anir Islands. Religious Beliefs, Ritual Practices, and Aesthetic Expression in the South of New Ireland, Papua New Guinea* (2012) and the edited volume *Visual Encounters – Africa, Oceania, and Modern Art* (2009, together with Oliver Wick). She is presently working on early Pacific collections as well as contemporary Pacific art.

Joachim Funke is since 1997 Full Professor for Theoretical and Cognitive Psychology at the Department of Psychology, Heidelberg University, Germany. His major interests pertain to issues within problem solving and thinking research. He is one of the promoters of the European approach of Complex Problem Solving using computersimulated microworlds. He has been project director of a number of research projects funded by national and international institutions. He published numerous articles for national and international scientific journals, contributed to many book editions, and wrote and edited many books himself.

Edward Gende is an ethnomusicologist at the Institute of Papua New Guinea Studies doing research work on Papua New Guinea music. From 1991 to the present, he has undertaken many recording activities in different parts of the country. He has contributed articles to publications such as *The Garland Encyclopedia of World Music, The New Grove Dictionary of Musical Instruments,* and *Kulele,* and has also made presentations at conferences. He is also a guitarist, performer, and has a repertoire of Papua New Guinea traditional songs which he plays on his classical guitar and in recitals.

Patrick Gesch was born in Townsville in 1944. He joined the Divine Word Missionaries and entered training for the priesthood, which included seven years in the United States. He was posted to Negrie Parish in the Yangoru district of Wewak Catholic diocese in 1973. He did his doctoral studies through Sydney University on the cargo cult-type movement of that area. In 1983, he joined Divine Word University, Madang, and has remained based there ever since, with absences doing editorial work for *Anthropos* journal, and for a stay in Manihiki in the Cook Islands.

Verena Keck received her doctorate in anthropology at Basel University and her habilitation at Goethe University Frankfurt. During the last thirty years, she has carried out repeated field research among the Yupno people in Papua New Guinea, besides research projects in Bali, Indonesia and Guam, Micronesia. She wrote *The Search for a Cause* (Guam 2012*)*, a book on a neurodegenerative disease in Guam, is author of *Social Discord and Bodily Disorders: Healing among the Yupno of Papua New Guinea* (Durham 2005), edited *Common Worlds and Single Lives. Constituting Knowledge in Pacific Societies* (Berg 1998) and published numerous articles in international journals. Her most recent co-edited publication (2015) is *Contradictions and Complexities – Current Perspectives on Pacific Islander Mobilities*, a special issue of *Anthropological Forum* 25 (2).

Angella Meinerzag received her doctorate in anthropology at Heidelberg University. She lectured there several years. She now works as a teacher for languages and cultural integration. Her contribution to this volume emerged out of 14 months of fieldwork in Papua New Guinea in the years 2000/2001 and 2005. Based on this work, she wrote her monograph *Being* Mande*: Person, Land and Names among the Hinihon in the Adelbert Range, Papua New Guinea* (Universitätsverlag Winter 2015).

Hermann Mückler is Professor at the Department for Cultural and Social Anthropology at the University of Vienna. His regional focus is the Pacific Islands as well as Insular South-East Asia. Among his topics are peace and conflict studies, geopolitics, history, political anthropology, forms of colonialism and neo-colonialism, as well as material culture. He is President of the Anthropological Society in

Vienna and Vice-President of the Institute for Comparative Research in Architecture. He published and edited 25 books. www.hermannmueckler.com.

Shahnaz R. Nadjmabadi is a social anthropologist. She has been a Senior Research Fellow of the Crossroads Asia Inter-Disciplinary Area Studies Research Network and a member of the teaching staff at the Department of Ethnology at the Asien-Orient-Institut, Tübingen (Germany) since 2009. In 1973, she received her doctorate in social anthropology (University of Heidelberg), with a thesis on kinship systems among the nomadic populations of Lorestan. After teaching at the University of Zürich (1974-1976), she worked at UNESCO/ Paris (1977-1986), at the Department of Human Settlement and Environment and was a member of the working group "le Monde Iranien Contemporain" of the CNRS/Paris. She has been teaching Anthropology at the University of Heidelberg since 1986, at the University of Maryland and Goethe University, Frankfurt/Main. Her research is focused on transborder mobility (migration, trade and development) in Khorassan, the Eastern Provinces of Iran and the interrelationship between the Iranian coastal population and their neighbors in the Arab Countries of the Persian Gulf.

Don Niles is Acting Director and Senior Ethnomusicologist at the Institute of Papua New Guinea Studies. He has researched and published on many types of music and dance in Papua New Guinea, including traditional, popular, and Christian forms, as well as audiovisual archiving. He edits the Institute's music monograph series (*Apwitihire: Studies in Papua New Guinea Musics*) and journal (*Kulele: Occasional Papers in Pacific Music and Dance*). He is Vice President of the International Council for Traditional Music, former editor of their journal, the *Yearbook for Traditional Music,* and Honorary Associate Professor at the Australian National University.

Alexis Th. von Poser is Curator of the ethnographic collections at the State Museum Hanover. Most recently, he created a large exhibition about colonial traces in anthropological collections and published the exhibition catalogue *Heikles Erbe. Koloniale Spuren bis in die Gegenwart* (Hannover 2016). He received his doctorate from the University of Heidelberg in 2008, and was lecturer at the universities of

Heidelberg, Madang (Divine Word University, Papua New Guinea,) and Free University Berlin. Before joining the State Museum Hanover, he worked as a scientific assistant at the Ethnological Museum in Berlin and was project leader for the digitization of the ethnographic collections of the Hanseatic City of Lübeck. His research, which is based on extensive fieldwork at the North Coast of Papua New Guinea, led to several articles and the monograph *The Accounts of Jong. A Discussion of Time, Space, and Person in Kayan, Papua New Guinea* (Universitätsverlag Winter 2014).

Anita von Poser received her doctorate from Heidelberg University in 2009. As a Doctoral Fellow, she received stipends from the Volkswagen Foundation and the Marsilius Kolleg. As a Postdoctoral Fellow of the Max Planck International Research Network on Aging, she was based at the MPI for Social Anthropology in Halle/Saale. Since 2011, she has been holding a teaching and research position at the Institute of Social and Cultural Anthropology at Free University Berlin. In 2014, she became a Research Fellow of the "Young ZiF" of the Center for Interdisciplinary Research at Bielefeld University. In 2015, she implemented a project on emotion, aging, and migration together with colleagues from psychiatry within the Collaborative Research Center 1171 *Affective Societies*. She has conducted long-term ethnographic fieldwork in Papua New Guinea's Lower Ramu area (*Foodways and Empathy: Relatedness in a Ramu River Society*, Berghahn 2013) and is now focusing her research on Vietnamese lifeworlds in Berlin.

Markus Schindlbeck is the former Curator of the Department of Visual Anthropology and the Collection of Oceania and Australia at the Ethnological Museum, Berlin. He received his doctorate in anthropology from the University of Basel and has done fieldwork among the Sawos people in 1972-74 and Kwanga people in 1979-81 in Papua New Guinea. Further fieldwork and collecting was done in Micronesia in 1986. For the museum in Berlin he assembled contemporary Maori art in 1993. He has taught at the Universities of Basel, Freiburg i. Br., Göttingen as well as at the Free University Berlin. He was Co-editor of the *Zeitschrift für Ethnologie* from 2000 until 2012. His publications comprise books and articles on anthropology, history of collections and photography.

Meinhard Schuster was Professor and Head of the Institute of Anthropology at the University of Basel from 1970 to 2000. He had studied Anthropology, Art History, Classical Archaeology and Prehistory at the University in Frankfurt, where he received his doctorate in 1956. Afterwards, he became scientific assistant at the Frobenius Institute. His first fieldwork was conducted in southern Venezuela. From 1961 on, however, his research focus shifted to Papua New Guinea and to the Sepik River in particular. After 1965, he repeatedly visited the area together with his wife Gisela Schuster. That year, he also moved to Basel, where he worked first as assistant and later as curator for Oceania at the Ethnological Museum. After his habilitation in 1968, he followed Alfred Bühler as full professor at the University of Basel. In the years 1972 to 1974, he led the Basel expedition, during which several of his students conducted fieldwork at the Sepik river and from which a considerable number of monographs and articles arose.

Gunter Senft (1952, PhD 1982) is Senior Investigator at the MPI for Psycholinguistics in Nijmegen and Extraordinary Professor of general linguistics at the University of Cologne. He has been studying the language and the culture of the Trobriand Islanders since 1982 (45 months of fieldwork). His main research interests include Austronesian and Papuan languages, anthropological linguistics, pragmatics, semantics, the interface between language, culture, and cognition, the conceptualization of space, and systems of nominal classification. Gunter Senft is the editor of the series "Culture and Language Use – Studies in Anthropological Linguistics", published by John Benjamins, Amsterdam. http://www.mpi.nl/people/senft-gunter

Svenja Völkel is Associate Professor of Linguistics at the University of Mainz/Germany. Her research interests include ethnolinguistics, language typology, cognitive linguistics, cognitive anthropology and language/culture contact with a regional focus on Oceania, particularly Tonga/Polynesia. Since 2002, she has carried out repeated field research in this area, mostly with an interdisciplinary focus, being fascinated by the interrelation between language, culture and cognition. Her most important publication in this respect is *Social Structure, Space and Possession in Tongan Culture and Language* (John Benjamins, Amsterdam et al. 2010). Since 2014, she has been head of the workgroup for Cognitive and Linguistic Anthropology within the German Anthropological Association (GAA).

Stephanie Walda-Mandel is Assistant Curator in the Oceania department at the Linden-Museum in Stuttgart. She studied Cultural Anthropology with a focus on Oceania at the Ruprecht-Karls-University of Heidelberg and the University of Western Australia in Perth. In 2014, she completed her doctorate on the effects of migration and change on the cultural identity of the Sonsorolese people based on her fieldwork in Palau, Saipan, Guam and the USA mainland. Besides identity building and social transformations, her research interests include Pacific material culture as well as cultural heritage and ethnological museums. She is the author of *"There is no place like home". Migration and Cultural Identity of the Sonsorolese, Micronesia* (Universitätsverlag Winter 2016).

Index

A

Abelam 21-22, 32
Adam, L. 20, 34
Adelbert Range 10, 33, 174, 199
alienation 53
ambivalent feelings 174, 182
Ammann, R. 5, 9, 13, 281
Amit, V. 81-82
Anir 69-73, 75-82, 282
anthropology of landscape 102
anthropology of mining 216
anthropology of villages 108
Antweiler, C. 246, 252
Appadurai, A. 95, 98, 102, 118
archival research 80, 134-136
archive 9, 94, 125, 134, 136-137, 147-150, 162-166, 213
archive culture 136
art 25, 31, 33, 70-71, 77, 80,
Atkinson, R. 134, 137
audio-visual recording 73, 76-77
Australian Broadcasting Commission 151-152

B

Baer, G. 22, 33-34
Bali 5, 255-256, 258-259, 263-267, 283
Barker, J. 113, 118
Barley, N. 53-54, 278
Barth, F. 52, 54
Basel Institute of Anthropology 1
Basel Museum of Ethnology 19, 21-23
"Basel Sepik Expedition" 7-8, 19-33
Basel University 20-21, 24-25, 42, 199, 273, 283, 285-286
Bateson, G. 20, 24, 26, 28, 54
Becker, F. 206-208, 213, 220
Beer, B. 239-240, 243, 252
Beier, U. 148, 167
Bel language 43, 51
Bender, A. 5, 236-237, 246, 252
Bender, B. 102, 110-111, 115, 118
Berg, U.D. 97-98
Berger, P.L. 63, 66
Bergmann, H.F.W. 155, 159, 167
Berlin Museum of Ethnology 20-21, 285
Berlin Phonogramm-Archiv 151
Berry, J.W. 261, 269
biography 134-135
birth ceremonies 53
Bismarck Archipelago 21, 69
Bodenseh, B. 19, 34
body part number system 257
body parts 257-258, 262
Bonnemaison, J. 141, 146
border areas 11, 185-188, 192, 195
border research 186

Bosmun 101-114, 118, 200-201, 276
Bowen, E.S. 173, 182
Broad, C.D. 140, 146
Brown, J.M. 124, 137
Browne, R.C. 104, 109, 118
Bryman, A. 135, 137
Bühler, A. 21-24, 33-34, 286

C

Calderwood, B.R. 104, 118
Camp, C. 44, 54
Candea, M. 90, 98
cargo cult 29, 41, 43, 46-47, 283
carving 11, 28, 132, 163-165, 225-231
Carraher, T.N. 269
Casey, E.S. 102, 118
Catholic Church 72
change (demographic) 8, 58, 60-61
child development 259, 263-264
Chimbu 150, 162-163
Christianity 113, 164-165, 229
Claas, U. 31, 34
Clifford, J. 86, 98
climate change 8, 57-58, 65, 203
cognitive anthropology 5, 12, 66, 235-237, 244, 246-247, 249, 274-275, 286
Cohen, H. 236, 252
Cole, M. 244, 252
collaborative publication 238
Collaer, P. 224, 232

colonial administration 20, 28, 112, 228
colonial history 101
colonial structures 28
Comrie, B. 251-252
Condon, A. 214, 220
contemporary witness 132, 135
contested fields 186
copyright 197, 228
counting system 262-263, 266
Cox, J. 116, 118
creativity 96, 187, 195, 238, 248
critical methodology 187
Cronin, K. 81-82
Crook, T. 198, 220
cross-cultural psychology 236-237, 246, 261-262, 281
cultural anthropology xi, 71, 93, 203, 209, 211, 235-239, 241, 243-245, 251, 285, 287
cultural change 8, 27, 58, 203, 282
cultural difference 43, 89, 205
cultural diversity 147-148, 154, 204, 217, 245, 251
cultural identity 88, 204-205, 220. 287
Cunningham, J. 152-153, 167

D

D'Andrade, R. 244, 252
Daiden 101-116
Dalsgaard, S. 102, 105, 116, 119, 219-220
Danely, J. 2, 13
danger 11, 192, 195
Daniel, E.V. 196

Dasen, P.R. 5, 12-13, 97, 237, 244, 256-259, 261, 264-270, 275, 281
data collection 185, 239
Davies, J. 2, 10, 13, 173-174, 182
Denner, A. 8, 69, 77, 82, 101, 282
desperation 173
dialogic research 72
diaspora 70, 85, 87
digital media 70
discomfort 195
disorientation 174
Divine Word Mission 41, 283
Divine Word University (DWU) 7, 47, 198, 200-202, 205, 209, 214, 218, 220, 283, 285
Douglas, M.A. 104, 109, 119
Duranti, A. 236, 241, 243, 249-252
Dyer, K.W. 109-110, 119

E

Easter Island 123-126, 129-133, 136
Easter Island Expedition 123-126, 129-130, 133, 136
education (schooling) 89, 91, 107, 116, 162, 197, 203, 208, 217, 246
Eichhorn, A. 21
Elkin, A.P. 167
emic approach 43, 110, 187, 239-240, 242, 245-247, 260-261

emotions 10, 77, 173, 179, 245, 249
empiricist tradition 1, 11
endangered areas 185, 187, 195
ethnographic material 195, 197-198
ethnohistorian 124
ethnomusicology 147, 235, 281
etic approach 110, 261
European Society for Oceanists (ESfO) 7, 9, 197
Evans, N. 244, 252
Evans, V. 237, 252
Evans-Pritchard, E.E. 140, 145-146
Evara, R.A. 163, 167
expatriate 43, 107, 109, 132

F

Faubion, J.D. 2, 13, 70, 79-89, 82
fear 195
feelings in the field 174
Feld, S. 102, 119, 223, 227, 232
Ferdon, E.N. 124
Ferguson, J. 70, 81, 85, 94, 97-98
field diary 173-174, 182
fieldwork: risks and dangers 186-187, 192, 195
Finisterre Range 5, 9-10, 32, 141, 198, 257
Fischer, H. 224, 232, 240-242, 250, 252
Fischer, S.R. 124, 130-132, 137
Flitsch, M. 31, 34
Foley, W. 236, 241, 243, 249-252

Forge, A. 22, 33
Fox, J. 108, 111, 119
Frankfurt Museum of Ethnography 23
Frawley, J.W. 112, 119
free-listing 246
Freudenburg, A. 46, 54
Friedman, J. 205, 220
friendship 9, 66, 147, 274, 278
Frodeman, R. 235, 252
fundamentalist Christians 28, 148
Funke, J. 6, 12, 244-246, 249, 275, 278, 282

G

Gallo, E. 96, 98
Gardi, R. 21-22, 242, 232
Garraty, J. 134, 137
Gatewood, J. 246, 252
Geertz, C. 96, 98
Gehrmann, K. 105, 119
Gell, A. 140, 142, 146
gendarmerie 189, 191-193
Gende, E. 10, 147, 154-155, 158, 167, 282,
gender segregation 105
German Academic Exchange Service (DAAD) 201, 232
German Anthropological Association (GAA) 5
Gesch, P.F. 8, 43, 54, 200, 212-213, 220, 283
Gewertz, D. 31, 34
Gibbs, A. 81, 83
Giri 200-201
globalization 4, 70, 81, 85-86, 90, 102, 203-205, 210-211

globalized world 97, 197
Glowczewski, B. 198, 206, 216, 220-221
Gómez, C. 125, 137
Gourlay, K. 225, 232
government officials 189, 195
Graebner, F. 225, 232
Greub, B. see Huber-Greub, B.
group dialogue 72-75, 78-79
group-interview technique 71
Gupta A. 70, 81, 83, 85, 98

H

Haberland, E. 23-24, 34
Hanga Roa 127
Hannerz, U. 88, 98
Hastrup, K. 196
haus tambaran 43, 48-49, 52-53
Hauser-Schäublin, B. 25-27, 29, 31-32, 34, 240, 244, 250, 252
headhunting 104, 229
Healy, J.P. 112, 119
Hediger, H. 21
Heidelberg Institute of Anthropology 5, 10-12, 198, 200-201
Heidelberg University 1, 11-12, 198, 200, 273, 275, 282-283, 285
Heine, S. 245, 249, 252
helplessness (experience of) 195
Henrich, J. 276, 278
Herbst, F. 6, 13, 33, 35, 200, 219-221
Heyerdahl, T. 124, 130, 137-138

Hinderling, P. 21, 35
Hinihon 173-182, 200
Hirsch, E. 102-103, 119
HIV/AIDS 214
holistic approach 238-241, 245-248
Höltker, G. 44, 54, 113, 119
Horst, C. 87, 96-98
hospitality 66, 193, 200, 277
housing (structures) 109-110, 116
Hovland, I. 95, 98
Howell, N. 185, 196
Huber-Greub, B. 31-32, 35
hypothesis (testing) 239-240, 247, 255, 260, 262

I

Iatmul 4, 24-26, 29, 31-32, 145-147, 198
immersion 8, 45, 53, 70, 77-78, 118, 173-174, 177
India 224, 264, 268, 281
indigenous anthropology 205, 209
Indonesia 5, 12, 19, 219, 263-265, 281, 283
informants/ interlocutors 1, 4, 8, 12, 27, 29-30, 47, 63, 71, 75, 78, 80, 91, 103-107, 109-110, 114-115, 117-118, 135, 186, 191-192, 194, 223, 239, 243, 246, 255-256, 258-259, 262, 266-268, 275
Ingold, T. 102, 119
initiation xi, 21, 27-28, 41-54, 86

Institute of Scientific Film/ Göttingen 24
interdisciplinarity 5, 235, 237-239, 243, 248-251
interdisciplinary fieldwork 12, 241, 244, 247-248, 256
Institute of Papua New Guinea Studies (IPNGS) 9, 147-148, 282, 284
interlocutors see informants
intersubjectivity 91, 194
Iran 11, 185-188, 190, 195-196, 284

J

Jaarsma, S.R. 198, 221
Jahoda, G. 256, 270
Jarillo de la Torre, S. 61-66
Jensen, A.E. 30
Johnston, W.J. 113, 119
Jones, T.A. 153, 168
Jong, Blasius 228-231
Josselson, R. 134, 138
"just plain folks" 262, 275

K

Kaeppler, A.L. 153, 168
Kahler, S.P. 113, 119
Kaiserin-Augusta-Fluss Expedition 20-21
kalja 219
Kanak people 142, 144-145
Kaspruś, A. 151, 154, 159, 161-162, 168
kastom 204, 219
Kaufmann, Ch. 19-20, 23-24, 27-28, 31, 33, 35

Kayan 11, 200-201, 223, 225-231
Keesing, R. 241, 253
Keck, V. 4-7, 9-11, 13, 88, 99, 173-174, 179, 183, 197, 199, 204, 221, 237, 252, 256-257, 260, 276, 283
Kenneth, G. 61, 66
key informant 71, 80, 255, 262
Khorramabad 188, 190, 192
kiap 28, 30, 34, 103, 106, 109, 112-113
kinship 30, 45, 88, 110, 178, 188-190, 194, 249-250, 284
Kiriwina (Kiriwila) 60, 62-64, 66
Kirk, M.S. 46, 54
Knoche, W. 123-135, 138
knowledge: anthropological, exchange of 198-199
Korewori 22-23, 27
Korn, F. 45, 54
Krueger, R.A. 81, 83
Kuman 150-151, 154-162, 167
Kunst, J. 225, 232
Kwanga 32, 34, 285

L

Lave, J. 262, 270
Lawrence, P. 41, 54
Leach, J. 224, 226, 232
Leach, J.W. 59, 66
Leenhardt, M. 143-144, 146
Leidecker, C. 225, 232
Letman J. 117, 119
Levinson, S.C. 5, 66, 258, 270
Lewis, M.P. 150, 168
library research 134, 136

life-course perspective 1-3, 12, 118
life history 133-135
linguistic anthropology 217, 235-237, 241, 243, 247, 250-251, 287
linguistics 57, 132, 236-238, 241-244, 246, 249-250, 252, 286
LiPuma, E. 112, 120
long-term fieldwork 8
Lorestan 185, 187-188, 195, 284
Luhrmann, T.M. 276, 279
luluai 228-229
von Luschan, F. 19-21
Lutkehaus, N. 31, 36, 232

M

MacCarthy, M. 60, 62-66
MacClancy, J. 2, 13
Madang 4, 7, 25, 43, 47-53, 103, 116, 154, 174, 176-179, 197-202, 211-213, 215, 219, 283, 285
Maden, M. 214-215, 221
Mahmood, C.K. 196
Malinowski, B. 8, 14, 57, 59, 61, 63, 66, 69-70, 85-87, 97, 99, 211, 214, 241, 253
Malmal 50-51
Marcus, G.E. 2, 80-81, 83, 86-87, 95, 99
Marind-anim 21
material culture 11, 25, 28, 124, 126, 130, 283, 287
Mauksch, S. 82-83

Max Planck Institute for
  Psycholinguistics 5, 8, 57,
  258
McTaggart, J. 140, 146
McLean, M. 225, 232
Mead, M. 24, 275
Media Anthropology 215-216
Meggitt, M.J. 153, 168
Meinerzag, A. 6, 10-11, 14, 33,
  36, 174, 182-183, 200, 221,
  283
Meiser, L. 226, 232
"Melanesian Way" 204, 208
men's house 22, 24, 27-28, 31,
  33, 78, 81, 226
methodology 90, 182, 187, 194,
  196
Meyer, A. 228, 232
micro- vs. macro-history 134
Micronesia 88, 94, 204, 276,
  283, 285
migrants 85, 89, 91, 97, 116
migration 28, 31, 33, 85-95,
  145, 203, 284, 285, 287
military forces 150, 186
Miller, D. 96, 99
Mimica, J. 34, 36
Mines, D.P. 102, 120
mining 203, 214, 216-217
Mishra, R.C. 256, 264-265,
  267, 269-270, 281
modernity 111, 115-116, 216
"mono-culture" 10, 165
Montt, J. 128-129
Monumbo 229
Morauta, L. 206, 221
Morgan, D.L. 81, 83
Morgenthaler, F. 32
Moriguba, B. 150, 168

Mosko, M. 63, 67
mourning ceremonies 53, 63,
  207
Moyle, A.M. 153, 168
Mt Hurun Movement 46-47
Mückler, H. 9, 85, 89, 99, 124,
  138, 283
multidisciplinarity 237
multilocality 8, 72, 80, 97
multi-sited ethnography 9, 70,
  80, 86-97
multivocality 8, 70-71, 81
Münzel, M. 31, 36
Murphy, G. 201
myth, mythological story 26,
  29, 42, 48, 50, 142, 145,
  163, 227
mythology 9, 145

N

Nadai, E. 93, 99
Nadjmabadi, S.R. 10-11, 196,
  284
Narokobi, B. 204, 208
National Cultural Commission
  149
National Research Institute
  (NRI) 10, 66
naven 25, 28, 45
Nditing, Z.Y. 165, 168
Nepal 264, 268, 281
Neuhauss, N. 224, 232
Nevermann, H. 21
New Caledonia 19, 141-142,
  145, 217, 281
New Ireland 21, 69, 76, 81, 151,
  154, 199, 204, 218

Niles, D. 9-10, 66, 147, 150-151, 155, 157, 161, 166, 168-169, 225, 232, 284
nomadic groups 10, 185, 187-193, 284
Nunes, T. 269-270
Nunez, R. 5, 14
Nyaura 26, 29, 198

O

O'Sullivan, J.N. 60, 62-63, 67
Oates, S.B. 134, 138
Obrist van Eeuwijk, B. 32, 36
Oksapmin 257, 260
Orne, J. 2, 14
overpopulation 8, 60-61

P

Palau 88-89, 92, 94, 287
Papua New Guinea 1, 4-5, 7-13, 25, 28, 32-33, 53, 57-59, 66, 69, 101-109, 115-117, 136-137, 141, 147-155, 158, 163-166, 182, 198-219, 223, 225, 227, 229, 255-257, 259, 273, 276, 281-286
Parker, L. 204, 221
participant observation 9, 46, 78, 85-86, 97, 136, 173, 240-241, 243, 245-250, 268
patrol reports 113
Peltier, P. 31, 36
Per, Z. 163, 169
personal aspects of fieldwork 173
personal experience 10, 71, 179
personhood 111
Persson, J. 59, 67
Piaget, J. 256-258, 263, 268, 270, 281
Piagetian developmental psychology 257
place – concept of 101, 103, 115
poetry 157-159
police 186
Pollard, A. 196
Polynesia 12, 132-133, 249, 286
Port Moresby 9, 32, 147, 166, 199, 219
von Poser, A. 2, 6, 9, 14, 33, 36, 70, 104, 109, 111, 114, 116, 120, 174, 200, 213, 219, 221, 276, 285
von Poser, A.Th. 5-6, 11, 14, 33, 36, 200, 213, 220-221, 228, 232, 284
post-colonial history 101
Powdermaker, H. 173, 182-183
Powell, R.A. 71, 83
priesthood 41, 283
psychological anthropology 10
psychological experiments 246, 276
psychology 2-3, 5, 12, 236-238, 246, 256-257, 261-262, 266, 273, 275-278, 281-282

Q

qualitative methods 134
Quanchi, M. 109, 120

R

Ramu River 4, 33, 103-105, 107-109, 112-113, 116-117, 199-200, 214, 216, 225, 231, 285
Ramu River societies 199-200
Rapanui 125, 129-134
reciprocity 11, 198-199, 206
Reck, D. 224, 233
Redfearn, J. 214, 221
Reinhard, K. 167, 169
Reiss-Engelhorn-Museums Mannheim 223, 225
Rempi 50, 53
Renner, E. 31, 36
returning to the field 4, 118, 223
Risimeri, J.B. 62, 67
ritual 25, 28, 32-33, 43-44, 46-48, 50, 53, 63, 70-82, 105, 136, 142, 282
Riwo 50-51
Robben, A.C.G.M. 2, 14, 83
Roberts, R. 134-135, 138
Roesicke, A. 20-22
Roscoe, P.B. 44, 46, 54
Rosi, P. 164, 169
Ross, N. 244-246, 253
Rozier, C. 143, 146

S

Sai, A. 212-213, 220
sample size 262, 265
sanguma 49-50, 53, 214
Sarasin, F. 19
Sarasin, P. 19
Saxe, G. 257-258, 260, 267, 270
Schindlbeck, M. 4, 7-8, 20-22, 25, 27, 31-32, 36-37, 42, 48, 50, 55, 285
Schlaginhaufen, O. 21
Schlehe, J. 219, 221
Schlenker, H. 31
Schmid, J. 26-27, 30, 37-38
Schmidt, W. 21
Schmitz, C.A. 23
Schram, R. 163, 170
Schuster, G. 23, 26, 29
Schuster, M. 1, 4, 7-8, 19-20, 23-24, 26-28, 30, 32-33, 38, 42, 199, 222, 273, 286
second socialization 118
security 185-186, 188-189, 192, 194-196, 203, 219
Segall, M.H. 261, 270
Senft, G. 8, 59-65, 67-68, 236-237, 242-243, 250-251, 253, 268, 270, 286
Sepik 1, 4, 7-8, 10, 19-33, 41-43, 45-52, 151, 154, 198-199, 273, 286
Seyfarth, S. 23
Sharifian, F. 237, 251-253
Sheekey, D.P. 109, 120
Sheridan, R.J. 151-156, 160, 166-167, 170
Shore, B. 244, 253
Silverstein, M. 241, 253
Simet, J. 165, 170
Simpson, C. 152-153, 167
Sinang, C. 79
Skutnabb-Kangas, T. 217, 222
slit drum/ slitgong 11, 28, 49, 223-231
Sluka, J.A. 2, 81

small-scale community 70, 101, 136, 237, 258
social media 70
Sökefeld, M. 196
Solon, M. 200-201, 203, 205, 212-213, 220, 222
Somare, M. 148
Sonsorol 9, 88-95, 287
space (concept of) 4, 9, 32, 103, 106, 139-143, 263
"space games" 268
spatial orientation: egocentric, geocentric 5, 141, 258, 263-267, 275
Speiser, F. 19-21
Spencer, D. 2, 10, 14
spirit drum 229
state 107, 114, 187-188
state authorities 190-191
statistics 247, 255, 264-265
Stanek, M. 26-27, 30-32, 38
Stasch, R. 102-106, 108, 120
Stephenson, N.A. 32, 38
Stevenson, R.L. 57, 68
Stocking, G.W. 81, 83
Streck, B. 33, 38
subjectivity 70. 91, 111, 278
Sullivan, N. 117, 120, 206, 222
surveillance 186, 192, 195
Society of the Divine Word (SVD) 3, 25, 41, 200
Swadling, P. 32, 225, 233

T

Tambiah, S.J. 196
Tedlock, B. 194, 196
Teo, T. 276, 279
tests 246, 255, 259, 266, 268

theory of mind 6, 245, 249, 275-276
Thieberger, N. 242, 244, 251, 253
Tiesler, F. 104, 120
Tietz, A. 235, 245-246, 253, 276
Tilley, C. 102, 120
time (concept of) 4, 9, 32, 103, 139-143, 145, 275
Tok Pisin 46, 49, 69, 72, 81, 104, 106-107, 118, 158, 182, 208, 212, 217, 225
To'Liman-Turalir, J. 150, 170
Tomlinson, K. 93, 99
Tonga 12, 249-250, 276, 286
Tönnies, F. 103, 120
Townsend, P.K. 25, 38-39, 113, 120
transdisciplinary method 133
transnationalism 85, 87
Trobriand Islanders 8, 57-66, 286
Trompf, G. 45
Tuhiwai Smith, L. 206, 222
Tuzin, D.F. 113, 121

U

University of Papua New Guinea (UPNG) 148, 201, 206, 218-219
University partnership program 198, 220
university career 238

V

validity 245, 255, 266
van der Linden, M. 31, 39

Van Heekeren, D. 102, 106, 113, 116, 121
Vanuatu 9, 19-20, 139, 141, 281
village (concept of) 101-118
violence 189, 196, 214
Völkel, S. 12, 97, 235, 242, 245-246, 250-251, 253, 255, 276, 286
Vormann, F. 227, 233

W

Walda-Mandel, S. 6, 9, 14, 33, 39, 80, 88, 99, 287
Wardlow, H. 115, 121
Wassmann, J. ix, 1, 3-9, 14-17, 22, 26-27, 30-33, 39, 41-42, 49, 52, 55, 65, 88, 118, 136, 138, 141, 145-147, 170, 173-174, 178, 183, 198-200, 213, 222, 245-246, 249, 253, 255-259, 262, 264, 266, 270-271, 274-279
Webb, M. 150, 166, 170-171
Webster, E.M. 13, 17
Weichart, G. 125-126
Weiner, A.B. 63, 68
Weiss, F. 26-27, 29-32, 39-40
Welsch, R. 112, 121
Winduo, S. 204, 217-218, 222
Wirz, P. 21-22, 151, 154-161, 171
Wirz, D. 151
working class 116
writing culture 71, 86

Y

Yangoru 42-44, 46-47, 51, 53, 283
Young, M. 57, 68
Yupno 5, 9-10, 32, 141, 147, 198-200, 219, 257-260, 262, 266-268, 276, 283

Z

Z'graggen, J.A. 25, 40
Zemp, H. 224, 233
Zeitgeist 1, 132
Ziegler, S. 151, 171
Zurenuoc, T. 163, 171